Examining the US Capitol Attack
A Review of the Security, Planning, and Response Failures on 6 January 2021

Executive Summary

and

Full Report

From the Committee on Homeland Security and Governmental Affairs

and

Committee on Rules and Administration

Written by the Senate Staff

Editors Note: The black marks on the page edges are to assist the reader in locating the sections of the book corresponding to each title.

edited and arranged by
Brian Greul

On January 6, 2021 protestors stormed the US Capitol. This book is a compilation of the executive summary and the report written by the US Senate. It is being published as an aid to those wishing to read a written version of the report for the purposes of forming their own opinion, research and scholarly activities, or other purposes in the pursuit of the freedom of information. The publisher believes strongly that free information and an educated body politic are critical to a thriving democracy.

Cover image licensed via Creative Commons from Flickr User Tyler Merbler.

Should you have suggestions or feedback on ways to improve this book please send email to Books@OcotilloPress.com

---

Edited 2021 Ocotillo Press
ISBN 978-1-954285-27-9

Printed in the United States of America and other locations.

Ocotillo Press
Houston, TX 77017
Books@OcotilloPress.com

Examining the U.S. Capitol Attack

A Review of the Security, Planning, and Response Failures on January 6

Committee on Homeland Security and Governmental Affairs

U.S. Senator Gary Peters, Chair
U.S. Senator Rob Portman, Ranking Member

Committee on Rules and Administration

U.S. Senator Amy Klobuchar, Chair
U.S. Senator Roy Blunt, Ranking Member

Staff Report

EXAMINING THE U.S. CAPITOL ATTACK: A REVIEW OF THE SECURITY, PLANNING, AND RESPONSE FAILURES ON JANUARY 6

I. EXECUTIVE SUMMARY

On January 6, 2021, the world witnessed a violent and unprecedented attack on the U.S. Capitol, the Vice President, Members of Congress, and the democratic process. Rioters, attempting to disrupt the Joint Session of Congress, broke into the Capitol building, vandalized and stole property, and ransacked offices. They attacked members of law enforcement and threatened the safety and lives of our nation's elected leaders. Tragically, seven individuals, including three law enforcement officers, ultimately lost their lives.

Rioters were intent on disrupting the Joint Session, during which Members of Congress were scheduled to perform their constitutional obligation to count the electoral votes for President and Vice President of the United States and announce the official results of the 2020 election. Due to the heroism of United States Capitol Police ("USCP") officers, along with their federal, state, and local law enforcement partners, the rioters failed to prevent Congress from fulfilling its constitutional duty. In the early hours of January 7, the President of the Senate, Vice President Pence, announced Joseph Biden and Kamala Harris as the President-elect and Vice President-elect of the United States.

This report addresses the security, planning, and response failures of the entities directly responsible for Capitol security—USCP and the Capitol Police Board, which is comprised of the House and Senate Sergeants at Arms and the Architect of the Capitol as voting members, and the USCP Chief as a non-voting member—along with critical breakdowns involving several federal agencies, particularly the Federal Bureau of Investigation ("FBI"), Department of Homeland Security ("DHS"), and Department of Defense ("DOD"). The Committees also made a series of recommendations for the Capitol Police Board, USCP, federal intelligence agencies, DOD, and other Capital region law enforcement agencies to address the intelligence and security failures.

* * * * *

The Committees' investigation uncovered a number of intelligence and security failures leading up to and on January 6 that allowed for the breach of the Capitol. These breakdowns ranged from federal intelligence agencies failing to warn of a potential for violence to a lack of planning and preparation by USCP and law enforcement leadership.

The federal Intelligence Community—led by FBI and DHS—did not issue a threat assessment warning of potential violence targeting the Capitol on January 6. Law enforcement entities, including USCP, largely rely on FBI and DHS to assess and communicate homeland security threats. Throughout 2020, the FBI and DHS disseminated written documents detailing the potential for increased violent extremist activity at lawful protests and targeting of law enforcement and government facilities and personnel. Despite online calls for violence at the Capitol, neither the FBI nor DHS issued a threat assessment or intelligence bulletin warning law enforcement entities in the National Capital Region of the potential for violence. FBI and DHS officials stressed the difficulty in discerning constitutionally protected free speech versus actionable, credible threats of violence. In testimony before the Committees, officials from both

FBI and DHS acknowledged that the Intelligence Community needs to improve its handling and dissemination of threat information from social media and online message boards.

USCP's intelligence components failed to convey the full scope of threat information they possessed. Although USCP mainly relies on the FBI and DHS for intelligence and threat information, USCP has three components responsible for intelligence-related activities. These components, and the materials they produce, are supposed to inform USCP's security and operational planning. This, however, was not the case for January 6.

USCP's lead intelligence component—the Intelligence and Interagency Coordination Division ("IICD")—was aware of the potential for violence in the days and weeks ahead of January 6. It received information from a variety of sources about threats of violence focused on the Joint Session and the Capitol Complex and the large crowds expected to gather in Washington, D.C. on January 6. Yet, IICD failed to fully incorporate this information into all of its internal assessments about January 6 and the Joint Session. As a result, critical information regarding threats of violence was not shared with USCP's own officers and other law enforcement partners.

USCP's preparations for the Joint Session also suffered because of the decentralized nature of its intelligence components. On January 5, an employee in a separate USCP intelligence-related component received information from the FBI's Norfolk Field Office regarding online discussions of violence directed at Congress, including that protestors were coming to Congress "prepared for war." This report, similar to other information received by IICD, was never distributed to IICD or USCP leadership before January 6.

USCP was not adequately prepared to prevent or respond to the January 6 security threats, which contributed to the breach of the Capitol. Steven Sund, the USCP Chief on January 6, and Yogananda Pittman, who was designated as Acting Chief after Steven Sund announced his resignation on January 7, both attributed the breach of the Capitol to intelligence failures across the federal government. USCP leadership, however, also failed to prepare a department-wide operational plan for the Joint Session. Similarly, USCP leadership did not develop a comprehensive staffing plan for the Joint Session detailing, among other things, where officers would be located. USCP could not provide the Committees any documents showing where officers were located at the start of the attack and how that changed throughout the attack.

USCP leadership also failed to provide front-line officers with effective protective equipment or training. Although USCP activated seven specialty Civil Disturbance Unit ("CDU") platoons in advance of the Joint Session, only four of those platoons were outfitted with special protective equipment, including helmets, hardened plastic armor, and shields. The many other USCP officers who fought to defend the Capitol were left to do so in their daily uniforms. Many of those front-line officers had not received training in basic civil disturbance tactics since their initial Recruit Officer Class training. While some CDU officers were issued special protective equipment, the platoons were not authorized to wear the equipment at the beginning of their shifts. Instead, USCP staged equipment on buses near the Capitol. In at least one instance, when the platoon attempted to retrieve the equipment, the bus was locked, leaving the platoon without access to this critical equipment. USCP also failed to provide equipment training to support the CDU platoons and did not authorize CDU platoons to use all available less-than-lethal munitions, which could have enhanced officers' ability to push back rioters.

These operational failures were exacerbated by leadership's failure to clearly communicate during the attack. USCP leadership gathered in a command center, blocks away from the Capitol building. Two incident commanders identified as responsible for relaying information to front-line officers were forced to engage with rioters during the attack, making it difficult for them to relay information. As a result, communications were chaotic, sporadic, and, according to many front-line officers, non-existent.

Opaque processes and a lack of emergency authority delayed requests for National Guard assistance. The USCP Chief has no unilateral authority to request assistance from the National Guard; the USCP Chief must submit a request for assistance to the Capitol Police Board for approval. Steven Sund never submitted a formal request to the Capitol Police Board for National Guard support in advance of January 6. Instead, Steven Sund had informal conversations with the House Sergeant at Arms, Paul Irving, and the Senate Sergeant at Arms, Michael Stenger, regarding the potential need for National Guard support. No one ever discussed the possibility of National Guard support with the Architect of the Capitol, the third voting member of the Capitol Police Board.

The members of the Capitol Police Board who were in charge on January 6 did not appear to be fully familiar with the statutory and regulatory requirements for requesting National Guard support, which contributed to the delay in deploying the National Guard to the Capitol. In their testimony before the Committees, Paul Irving and Steven Sund offered different accounts of when Steven Sund first requested National Guard assistance during the attack. Phone records reveal a number of conversations between Steven Sund and Paul Irving on January 6. However, because there is no transcription of the conversations, there is no way for the Committees to determine when the request was made. National Guard assistance was delayed while Steven Sund attempted to contact the Capitol Police Board members and obtain the required approvals. Regardless of what time the request was made, the need to await Capitol Police Board approval during an emergency hindered the ability to request District of Columbia National Guard ("DCNG") assistance quickly.

The intelligence failures, coupled with the Capitol Police Board's failure to request National Guard assistance prior to January 6, meant DCNG was not activated, staged, and prepared to quickly respond to an attack on the Capitol. As the attack unfolded, DOD required time to approve the request and gather, equip, and instruct its personnel on the mission, which resulted in additional delays. Prior to January 6, USCP informed DOD officials on two separate occasions that it was not seeking DCNG assistance for the Joint Session of Congress. The D.C. government, by contrast, did request unarmed troops for traffic support, and on January 6, 154 unarmed DCNG personnel were staged at traffic control points throughout the city. As the attack unfolded, USCP and the Metropolitan Police Department of the District of Columbia ("MPD") both pleaded with DOD officials for immediate assistance. DOD officials claimed they received a "workable" request for assistance from USCP at approximately 2:30 p.m. The request was presented to the Acting Secretary of Defense and approved at approximately 3:00 p.m. For the next ninety minutes, DOD officials ordered DCNG personnel to return to the Armory, obtain necessary gear, and prepare for deployment as leaders quickly prepared a mission plan. Miscommunication and confusion during response preparations, demonstrated by conflicting records about who authorized deployment and at what time, contributed to the delayed deployment. DCNG began arriving at the Capitol Complex at 5:20 p.m.—nearly three hours after DOD received USCP's request for assistance and more than four hours after the barriers at the Capitol were first breached.

The Committees' Recommendations

Based on the findings of the investigation, the Committees identified a number of recommendations to address the intelligence and security failures leading up to and on January 6. Recommendations specific to the Capitol Complex include empowering the USCP Chief to request assistance from the DCNG in emergency situations and passing legislation to clarify the statutes governing requests for assistance from executive agencies and departments in non-emergency situations. To address the preparedness of the USCP, the Committees recommend improvements to training, equipment, intelligence collection, and operational planning.

The Committees further recommend intelligence agencies review and evaluate criteria for issuing and communicating intelligence assessments and the establishment of standing "concept of operation" scenarios and contingency plans to improve DOD and DCNG response to civil disturbance and terrorism incidents. These scenarios and plans should detail what level of DOD or DCNG assistance may be required, what equipment would be needed for responding personnel, and the plan for command-and-control during the response.

The Committees' Investigation

Two days after the January 6 attack, the Senate Committee on Rules and Administration and Senate Homeland Security and Governmental Affairs Committee announced a joint bipartisan oversight investigation to examine the intelligence and security failures that led to the attack. On February 23, 2021, the Committees held the first public oversight hearing on the attack. The hearing, entitled *Examining the January 6 Attack on the U.S. Capitol*, featured testimony from the USCP Chief, House Sergeant at Arms, and Senate Sergeant at Arms in charge on January 6. The Committees also heard testimony from the Acting Chief of MPD. One week later, on March 3, 2021, the Committees held a second oversight hearing, which included witnesses from DOD, DCNG, FBI, and DHS.

As part of their investigation, the Committees reviewed thousands of documents. The Committees also received written statements from more than 50 USCP officers about their experiences. In addition, the Committees interviewed numerous current and former officials from USCP, Senate Sergeant at Arms, House Sergeant at Arms, Architect of the Capitol, FBI, DHS, MPD, DOD, and DCNG. Most entities cooperated with the Committees' requests. There were notable exceptions, however: the Department of Justice and DHS have yet to fully comply with the Committees' requests for information, the Office of the House of Representatives Sergeant at Arms did not comply with the Committees' information requests, and a USCP Deputy Chief of Police declined to be interviewed by the Committees. The Committees will continue to pursue responses from those who have failed to fully comply. The oversight of events related to January 6, including intelligence and security failures, will continue.

II. FINDINGS OF FACT AND RECOMMENDATIONS

Findings of Fact

(1) **Neither the Department of Homeland Security ("DHS") nor the Federal Bureau of Investigation ("FBI") issued formal intelligence bulletins about the potential for violence at the Capitol on January 6, which hindered law enforcement's preparations for the Joint Session of Congress.** The DHS Office of Intelligence and Analysis ("I&A") issued no intelligence products specific to January 6. Rather, it issued 15 intelligence products in 2020 related to domestic violent extremism, the last of which was issued on December 30 without any mention of the Joint Session of Congress or the Capitol. The FBI similarly did not issue any formal intelligence assessment specific to January 6; however, late on January 5, the FBI's Norfolk Field Office circulated a Situational Information Report, which is used by field offices "to share locally-derived information that is typically operational in nature" and does not meet the same criteria as intelligence assessments. That report warned of individuals traveling to Washington, D.C. for "war" at the Capitol on January 6. In the five months since the attack, neither agency has fully complied with the Committees' request for information on the events of January 6.

(2) **Neither the FBI nor DHS deemed online posts calling for violence at the Capitol as credible.** In testimony before the Committees, representatives from both agencies noted that much of the rhetoric online prior to January 6 was "First Amendment protected speech" of limited credibility and acknowledged areas for improvement in the handling and dissemination of threat information from social media and online message boards to enhance law enforcement and intelligence agencies' abilities to counter that threat.

(3) **The United States Capitol Police's ("USCP") Intelligence and Interagency Coordination Division ("IICD") possessed information about the potential for violence at the Capitol on January 6 but did not convey the full scope of information, which affected its preparations.** Internal records and USCP officials' testimony confirm that USCP began gathering information about events planned for January 6 in mid-December 2020. Through open source collection, tips from the public, and other sources, USCP IICD knew about social media posts calling for violence at the Capitol on January 6, including a plot to breach the Capitol, the online sharing of maps of the Capitol Complex's tunnel systems, and other specific threats of violence. Yet, IICD did not convey the full scope of known information to USCP leadership, rank-and-file officers, or law enforcement partners.

(4) **Important intelligence information received by internal USCP components was not appropriately shared among USCP's distinct intelligence-related components.** USCP has three units responsible for intelligence-related activities—IICD, the Threat Assessment Section ("TAS"), and the Intelligence Operations Section ("IOS")—all of which are organized within USCP's Protective Services Bureau ("PSB"). Although the three components support one another, they have different responsibilities. The decentralized nature of intelligence resources led to

vital intelligence information not being shared with senior USCP intelligence officials or USCP leadership.

(5) **IICD issued multiple intelligence reports prior to January 6 that reflected inconsistent assessments of the risk of violence at the Capitol.** IICD issued intelligence products related to expected activities on January 6, but the products were contradictory as to the threat level. For example, although a January 3 Special Event Assessment warned of the Capitol being a target of armed violence on January 6, IICD's daily intelligence reports rated the likelihood of civil disturbance on January 6 as "remote" to "improbable."

(6) **USCP did not prepare a department-wide operational plan or staffing plan for the Joint Session.** In advance of January 6, Steven Sund, USCP Chief of Police on January 6, believed USCP would need support to secure the Capitol perimeter in light of the large number of expected protestors at the Capitol, but he did not order the creation of a department-wide operational plan. Although the Uniformed Services Bureau and the Civil Disturbance Unit prepared component-specific plans, neither was sufficiently detailed to inform officers of their responsibilities or authorities nor did they reference warnings contained in IICD's January 3Special Event Assessment.

(7) **USCP's Civil Disturbance Unit operates on an "ad hoc" basis, without sufficient training or equipment.** Of USCP's 1,840 sworn officers, only approximately 160 are trained in advanced civil disturbance tactics and use of "hard" protective equipment. Fewer than ten are trained to use USCP's full suite of less-than-lethal munitions. On January 6, some of the "hard" protective equipment was defective or not staged in close proximity to the officers.

(8) **USCP's rank-and-file officers were not provided periodic training in basic civil disturbance tactics or basic protective equipment.** All officers receive basic civil disturbance training during initial Recruit Officer Class training, but there is no further training requirement after graduation. As a result, some who responded to the Capitol attack had not received training in civil disturbance tactics in years. Officers were also not uniformly provided helmets, shields, gas masks, or other crowd control equipment prior to January 6, which would have aided their response.

(9) **USCP's Incident Command System broke down during the attack, leaving front-line officers without key information or instructions as events unfolded.** USCP did not formally designate incident commanders in advance of January 6 through a department-wide operational plan. Senior officers were directly engaged with rioters during the attack, and USCP leadership never took control of the radio system to communicate orders to front-line officers.

(10) **Capitol Police Board members in charge on January 6 did not fully understand the statutory or regulatory requirements for requesting assistance from Executive agencies and departments or declaring emergencies.** Capitol Police Board members also disagreed as to whether unanimity was required to approve a

request from USCP for assistance from the District of Columbia National Guard ("DCNG").

(11) **Steven Sund never submitted a formal request to the Capitol Police Board for an emergency declaration and DCNG assistance before January 6.** Steven Sund had informal conversations with the House and Senate Sergeants at Arms, but no request was ever provided to the full Board. In fact, no one ever informed the Architect of the Capitol, the third voting member of the Board, of a potential request for DCNG assistance.

(12) **As the attack unfolded, Steven Sund lacked the authority to request National Guard assistance unilaterally.** Under the existing statute, the USCP Chief may obtain support from law enforcement and uniformed services only after the Capitol Police Board declares an emergency. This process constrained Steven Sund's ability to act quickly during the attack and contributed to the delay in the provision of assistance.

(13) **The Department of Defense ("DOD") confirmed with USCP on two separate occasions before January 6 that USCP was not requesting assistance from DCNG.** According to DOD records, USCP confirmed on January 3 and January 4 that it did not need DCNG assistance. Meanwhile, DOD continued to communicate with the D.C. Mayor's office regarding its request for unarmed DCNG personnel support.

(14) **DOD's response to January 6 was informed by criticism it received about its response to the civil unrest after the murder of George Floyd during the summer of 2020.** DOD was criticized for its heavy-handed response, particularly flying military helicopters over the protests in summer 2020. DOD officials cited lessons learned from the summer 2020 as guiding its decision-making for January 6. DOD officials believed it needed "control measures" and "rigor" before deploying DCNG personnel, including a clear deployment plan to avoid the appearance of over-militarization.

(15) **DOD imposed control measures on DCNG deployment, including requiring the Army Secretary's approval before deploying a Quick Reaction Force ("QRF") and doing so "only as a last resort."** DOD set forth requirements in a pair of memoranda issued on January 4 and January 5 that allowed William Walker, DCNG Commanding General, to deploy a QRF only as a last resort and upon the express approval of a concept of operations for any use of the QRF by the Secretary of the Army, Ryan McCarthy. General William Walker testified that, absent these requirements, he would have been able to immediately deploy the QRF to support USCP. DOD officials disputed that characterization and asserted that the memoranda simply memorialized longstanding policy. Christopher Miller, the Acting Secretary of Defense on January 6, was not aware that General William Walker wanted to deploy the QRF on January 6.

(16) **As the attack unfolded, DOD officials claimed they did not have a clear request for DCNG assistance until approximately 2:30 p.m.** Ryan McCarthy indicated that Muriel Bowser, the Mayor of Washington, D.C., called him around 1:34 p.m. but did not request assistance at that time. Rather, she asked whether DOD had received requests from USCP because the crowd was "getting out of control." Steven Sund called DCNG Commanding General William Walker at 1:49 p.m. to request assistance. According to Army officials, however, the requests were not specific and clarity on the scope of the request was needed.

(17) **Inaccurate media reports stating that DOD had denied a request for DCNG support slowed DOD's mission analysis efforts.** At 2:55 p.m., a reporter tweeted that DOD "had just denied a request by D.C. officials to deploy the National Guard to the US Capitol," despite the fact that no denial had been ordered and senior DOD officials were still analyzing the request. Christopher Miller approved DCNG mobilization at 3:04 p.m., understanding that DOD officials would then conduct "mission analysis." Ryan McCarthy, however, spent at least half an hour fielding calls and reassuring Congressional and local leaders that DOD "was indeed coming."

(18) **DOD spent hours "mission planning."** Christopher Miller indicated that he gave all necessary approvals for deployment at 3:04 p.m. with the understanding that Ryan McCarthy would conduct mission analysis with General William Walker. Ryan McCarthy, by contrast, felt he needed to brief and receive Christopher Miller's approval before DCNG personnel could leave the Armory. Ryan McCarthy co-located with D.C. officials and developed a concept of operations for DCNG personnel. The plan was approved and DCNG authorized to deploy by 4:35 p.m. All DOD officials who spoke with the Committees described the time spent on mission analysis as vital to DCNG's effectiveness. By contrast, General William Walker believed DCNG was fully equipped and ready to respond to the Capitol much earlier.

(19) **DOD officials denied mentioning or discussing the "optics" of sending DCNG personnel to the Capitol and disagreed with purported statements by an Army official that deploying DCNG to the Capitol would not be "best military advice."** As Christopher Miller told the Committees, "[t]heir best military advice is theirs. The best military advice that I take is from the Chairman of the Joint Chiefs of Staff, statutorily. So the best military advice that I received was, 'Let's go. Agree.'"

(20) **DOD and DCNG have conflicting records of when orders and authorizations were given, and no one could explain why DCNG did not deploy until after 5:00 p.m.** One current DOD official acknowledged that DOD and DCNG could have "tightened up" their response time between 4:35 p.m., when DCNG was authorized to deploy, and 5:02 p.m., when Army documents reflect DCNG's deployment. Officials attributed the delay to confusion and noted that it takes time to get personnel staged for deployment once the order is given. Concerning the conflicting records and accounts as to who needed to approve deployment orders, DOD officials cited confusion, the lack of a lead federal agency with an integrated security plan, and breakdowns in communication as to when those orders were given, and when those orders were executed.

(21) **According to DOD, the Department of Justice ("DOJ") was designated as the lead federal agency in charge of security preparations and response on January 6, but DOJ did not conduct interagency rehearsals or establish an integrated security plan.** DOD officials understood DOJ was designated prior to January 6. According to Ryan McCarthy, DOJ never established a point of contact and did not effectively coordinate a response during the attack. As noted above, DOJ has not fully complied with the Committees' requests for information.

Recommendations

CAPITOL POLICE BOARD

(1) **Empower the Chief of USCP to request assistance from the D.C. National Guard in emergency situations.** Congress should pass legislation to clarify the statutes governing requests for assistance from executive agencies and departments in non-emergency situations. Under existing statute, the Chief of USCP may request support from law enforcement and uniformed services only after the Capitol Police Board declares an emergency. This process can constrain USCP's ability to act quickly in an emergency and delay the provision of assistance.

(2) **Document and streamline Board policies and procedures for submitting, reviewing, and approving requests from USCP to ensure coordination among all members of the Board.** Board policies and procedures should include a requirement that Board members regularly review the policies and procedures to acknowledge their understanding and ensure adherence to the processes outlined therein.

(3) **Ensure the Board is appropriately balancing the need to share information with officials with the need to protect sensitive and classified information.**

(4) **Appoint a new Chief of USCP with appropriate input from USCP officers, congressional leadership, and the committees of jurisdiction.** In addition, the new Chief should evaluate the leadership team and ensure that promotions for leadership positions in USCP are handled in a transparent manner and based on merit.

U.S. CAPITOL POLICE

(1) **Ensure USCP has sufficient civilian and sworn personnel, with appropriate training and equipment, in the roles necessary to fulfill its mission.** This includes providing all officers annual training on basic civil disturbance tactics and equipping them with ballistic helmets, gloves, and gas masks—the same equipment that the District of Columbia Metropolitan Police Department ("MPD") provides to its officers. USCP should maintain an inventory of all issued equipment and ensure that the equipment is periodically replaced. Congress should authorize sufficient funding to support the additional training and equipment requirements, as well as adequate staffing levels.

(2) **Require a department-wide operational plan for special events.** These procedures should include a bureau-specific security plan, which informs the USCP-wide operational plan. The plans should detail, at a minimum: the threat assessment for the event, staffing, deployment strategy, mission objectives, incident command system, authorized use of force, and relevant contingencies in the event of an emergency. USCP should ensure that the operational plans are informed by available intelligence and threat assessments.

(3) **Establish the Civil Disturbance Unit ("CDU") as a formal, permanent component of USCP and ensure that its dedicated officers are properly trained and equipped at all times.** USCP should ensure that all members of the CDU are equipped with "hard" gear and receive annual training in advanced civil disturbance tactics and less-than-lethal munitions. USCP should also ensure that all "hard" protective equipment is properly maintained and regularly replaced.

(4) **Consolidate and elevate all USCP intelligence units into an Intelligence Bureau, led by a civilian Director of Intelligence reporting to the Assistant Chief of Police for Protective and Intelligence Operations; ensure the Bureau is adequately staffed and all agents and analysts are properly trained to receive and analyze intelligence information; and develop policies to disseminate intelligence information to leadership and rank-and-file officers effectively.** Currently, USCP has three separate intelligence-related entities within the Protective Services Bureau. Elevating these entities into a Bureau will increase focus on USCP's intelligence capabilities, improve the timely sharing of relevant intelligence up the chain of command, and decrease lack of coordination within the agency and with law enforcement partners. USCP should ensure that all training given to agents and analysts is consistent with best practices of the Intelligence Community and law enforcement partners, including the determination of credibility and overall threat assessment. USCP should enhance its relationships with Intelligence Community partners, and increase the number of liaisons USCP has integrated in National Capital Region task forces, including those with the FBI and D.C. Fusion Center.

(5) **Update its Incident Command System Directive to address how Incident Commanders are to communicate priorities, strategies, tactics, and threat assessment to front-line officers prior to and during an incident and ensure that the Directive is followed.** USCP should also formalize the process for designating incident commanders for large events and account for contingencies should incident commanders be unable to communicate to officers, including requiring senior leaders to take over communication responsibilities.

HOUSE AND SENATE SERGEANTS AT ARMS

Develop protocols for communicating with Members of Congress, staff, and other employees during emergencies.

INTELLIGENCE AGENCIES

(1) **Review and evaluate handling of open-source information, such as social media, containing threats of violence.**

(2) **Review and evaluate criteria for issuing and communicating intelligence assessments, bulletins, and other products to consumer agencies, such as USCP.**

(3) **Fully comply with statutory reporting requirements to Congress on domestic terrorism data, including on the threat level and the resources dedicated to countering the threat.**

DEPARTMENT OF DEFENSE/D.C. NATIONAL GUARD

(1) **Develop standing "concept of operation" scenarios and contingency plans for responding quickly to civil disturbance and terrorism incidents.** These scenarios and plans should detail what level of DOD or DCNG assistance may be required, what equipment would be needed for responding personnel, and the plan for command-and-control during the response. These scenarios and plans can help reduce confusion or the necessary planning time to allow DOD to respond more quickly to unfolding emergencies. DOD and DCNG should perform tabletop and joint training exercises concerning responding to an attack on the Capitol, which includes coordinating with local law enforcement and neighboring states.

(2) **Enhance communications prior to and during an event between DOD and DCNG strategic, operational, and tactical decision-makers and commanding generals.** These communications should include regular updates prior to an event concerning operations and strategy, as well as regular updates on the day of an event through direct communications between the decision-makers and commanding generals, including by co-locating leaders where practicable.

(3) **Practice the mobilization of National Guard members from neighboring jurisdictions to provide immediate assistance and report to command and control in the event of an emergency.** Those Guard members should be trained and equipped to respond to emergencies.

(4) **For special events in which a Quick Reaction Force ("QRF") is approved, consider proximity and response time, among other factors, when deciding where to stage the QRF to ensure the ability to quickly respond to incidents at the Capitol.**

(5) **Clarify the approval processes and chain of command within DOD to prevent delays in the deployment of DCNG when authorized.**

LAW ENFORCEMENT AND UNIFORMED SERVICES IN THE NATIONAL CAPITAL REGION

(1) **Ensure that Mutual Aid Agreements among federal, state, and local law enforcement agencies include all partners in the National Capital Region and that those agreements are regularly reviewed and updated.**

(2) **Conduct joint training exercises to ensure coordination across federal, state, and local governments concerning security threats in the Washington, D.C. area for requesting, receiving, and utilizing emergency assistance.** Training exercises should cover command-and-control processes during an emergency to ensure the prompt response and timely integration of personnel.

Additional USCP Inspector General Recommendations

After January 6, a number of Inspectors General announced investigations into their agencies' preparation and response to the attack on the Capitol. The Committees support these oversight efforts. To date, the USCP Office of Inspector General has released a number of recommendations for USCP, which are summarized at Appendix A.

Examining the U.S. Capitol Attack

A Review of the Security, Planning, and Response Failures on January 6

nmittee on Homeland Security and Governmental Affairs

U.S. Senator Gary Peters, Chair
Senator Rob Portman, Ranking Member

Committee on Rules and Administration

U.S. Senator Amy Klobuchar, Chair
U.S. Senator Roy Blunt, Ranking Member

Staff Report

EXAMINING THE U.S. CAPITOL ATTACK: A REVIEW OF THE SECURITY, PLANNING, AND RESPONSE FAILURES ON JANUARY 6

TABLE OF CONTENTS

EXAMINING THE U.S. CAPITOL ATTACK: A REVIEW OF THE SECURITY, PLANNING, AND RESPONSE FAILURES ON JANUARY 6

I. EXECUTIVE SUMMARY

On January 6, 2021, the world witnessed a violent and unprecedented attack on the U.S. Capitol, the Vice President, Members of Congress, and the democratic process. Rioters, attempting to disrupt the Joint Session of Congress, broke into the Capitol building, vandalized and stole property, and ransacked offices. They attacked members of law enforcement and threatened the safety and lives of our nation's elected leaders. Tragically, seven individuals, including three law enforcement officers, ultimately lost their lives.

Rioters were intent on disrupting the Joint Session, during which Members of Congress were scheduled to perform their constitutional obligation to count the electoral votes for President and Vice President of the United States and announce the official results of the 2020 election. Due to the heroism of United States Capitol Police ("USCP") officers, along with their federal, state, and local law enforcement partners, the rioters failed to prevent Congress from fulfilling its constitutional duty. In the early hours of January 7, the President of the Senate, Vice President Pence, announced Joseph Biden and Kamala Harris as the President-elect and Vice President-elect of the United States.

This report addresses the security, planning, and response failures of the entities directly responsible for Capitol security—USCP and the Capitol Police Board, which is comprised of the House and Senate Sergeants at Arms and the Architect of the Capitol as voting members, and the USCP Chief as a non-voting member—along with critical breakdowns involving several federal agencies, particularly the Federal Bureau of Investigation ("FBI"), Department of Homeland Security ("DHS"), and Department of Defense ("DOD"). The Committees also made a series of recommendations for the Capitol Police Board, USCP, federal intelligence agencies, DOD, and other Capital region law enforcement agencies to address the intelligence and security failures.

* * * * *

The Committees' investigation uncovered a number of intelligence and security failures leading up to and on January 6 that allowed for the breach of the Capitol. These breakdowns ranged from federal intelligence agencies failing to warn of a potential for violence to a lack of planning and preparation by USCP and law enforcement leadership.

The federal Intelligence Community—led by FBI and DHS—did not issue a threat assessment warning of potential violence targeting the Capitol on January 6. Law enforcement entities, including USCP, largely rely on FBI and DHS to assess and communicate homeland security threats. Throughout 2020, the FBI and DHS disseminated written documents detailing the potential for increased violent extremist activity at lawful protests and targeting of law enforcement and government facilities and personnel. Despite online calls for violence at the Capitol, neither the FBI nor DHS issued a threat assessment or intelligence bulletin warning law enforcement entities in the National Capital Region of the potential for violence. FBI and DHS officials stressed the difficulty in discerning constitutionally protected free speech versus actionable, credible threats of violence. In testimony before the Committees, officials from both

FBI and DHS acknowledged that the Intelligence Community needs to improve its handling and dissemination of threat information from social media and online message boards.

USCP's intelligence components failed to convey the full scope of threat information they possessed. Although USCP mainly relies on the FBI and DHS for intelligence and threat information, USCP has three components responsible for intelligence-related activities. These components, and the materials they produce, are supposed to inform USCP's security and operational planning. This, however, was not the case for January 6.

USCP's lead intelligence component—the Intelligence and Interagency Coordination Division ("IICD")—was aware of the potential for violence in the days and weeks ahead of January 6. It received information from a variety of sources about threats of violence focused on the Joint Session and the Capitol Complex and the large crowds expected to gather in Washington, D.C. on January 6. Yet, IICD failed to fully incorporate this information into all of its internal assessments about January 6 and the Joint Session. As a result, critical information regarding threats of violence was not shared with USCP's own officers and other law enforcement partners.

USCP's preparations for the Joint Session also suffered because of the decentralized nature of its intelligence components. On January 5, an employee in a separate USCP intelligence-related component received information from the FBI's Norfolk Field Office regarding online discussions of violence directed at Congress, including that protestors were coming to Congress "prepared for war." This report, similar to other information received by IICD, was never distributed to IICD or USCP leadership before January 6.

USCP was not adequately prepared to prevent or respond to the January 6 security threats, which contributed to the breach of the Capitol. Steven Sund, the USCP Chief on January 6, and Yogananda Pittman, who was designated as Acting Chief after Steven Sund announced his resignation on January 7, both attributed the breach of the Capitol to intelligence failures across the federal government. USCP leadership, however, also failed to prepare a department-wide operational plan for the Joint Session. Similarly, USCP leadership did not develop a comprehensive staffing plan for the Joint Session detailing, among other things, where officers would be located. USCP could not provide the Committees any documents showing where officers were located at the start of the attack and how that changed throughout the attack.

USCP leadership also failed to provide front-line officers with effective protective equipment or training. Although USCP activated seven specialty Civil Disturbance Unit ("CDU") platoons in advance of the Joint Session, only four of those platoons were outfitted with special protective equipment, including helmets, hardened plastic armor, and shields. The many other USCP officers who fought to defend the Capitol were left to do so in their daily uniforms. Many of those front-line officers had not received training in basic civil disturbance tactics since their initial Recruit Officer Class training. While some CDU officers were issued special protective equipment, the platoons were not authorized to wear the equipment at the beginning of their shifts. Instead, USCP staged equipment on buses near the Capitol. In at least one instance, when the platoon attempted to retrieve the equipment, the bus was locked, leaving the platoon without access to this critical equipment. USCP also failed to provide equipment training to support the CDU platoons and did not authorize CDU platoons to use all available less-than-lethal munitions, which could have enhanced officers' ability to push back rioters.

These operational failures were exacerbated by leadership's failure to clearly communicate during the attack. USCP leadership gathered in a command center, blocks away from the Capitol building. Two incident commanders identified as responsible for relaying information to front-line officers were forced to engage with rioters during the attack, making it difficult for them to relay information. As a result, communications were chaotic, sporadic, and, according to many front-line officers, non-existent.

Opaque processes and a lack of emergency authority delayed requests for National Guard assistance. The USCP Chief has no unilateral authority to request assistance from the National Guard; the USCP Chief must submit a request for assistance to the Capitol Police Board for approval. Steven Sund never submitted a formal request to the Capitol Police Board for National Guard support in advance of January 6. Instead, Steven Sund had informal conversations with the House Sergeant at Arms, Paul Irving, and the Senate Sergeant at Arms, Michael Stenger, regarding the potential need for National Guard support. No one ever discussed the possibility of National Guard support with the Architect of the Capitol, the third voting member of the Capitol Police Board.

The members of the Capitol Police Board who were in charge on January 6 did not appear to be fully familiar with the statutory and regulatory requirements for requesting National Guard support, which contributed to the delay in deploying the National Guard to the Capitol. In their testimony before the Committees, Paul Irving and Steven Sund offered different accounts of when Steven Sund first requested National Guard assistance during the attack. Phone records reveal a number of conversations between Steven Sund and Paul Irving on January 6. However, because there is no transcription of the conversations, there is no way for the Committees to determine when the request was made. National Guard assistance was delayed while Steven Sund attempted to contact the Capitol Police Board members and obtain the required approvals. Regardless of what time the request was made, the need to await Capitol Police Board approval during an emergency hindered the ability to request District of Columbia National Guard ("DCNG") assistance quickly.

The intelligence failures, coupled with the Capitol Police Board's failure to request National Guard assistance prior to January 6, meant DCNG was not activated, staged, and prepared to quickly respond to an attack on the Capitol. As the attack unfolded, DOD required time to approve the request and gather, equip, and instruct its personnel on the mission, which resulted in additional delays. Prior to January 6, USCP informed DOD officials on two separate occasions that it was not seeking DCNG assistance for the Joint Session of Congress. The D.C. government, by contrast, did request unarmed troops for traffic support, and on January 6, 154 unarmed DCNG personnel were staged at traffic control points throughout the city. As the attack unfolded, USCP and the Metropolitan Police Department of the District of Columbia ("MPD") both pleaded with DOD officials for immediate assistance. DOD officials claimed they received a "workable" request for assistance from USCP at approximately 2:30 p.m. The request was presented to the Acting Secretary of Defense and approved at approximately 3:00 p.m. For the next ninety minutes, DOD officials ordered DCNG personnel to return to the Armory, obtain necessary gear, and prepare for deployment as leaders quickly prepared a mission plan. Miscommunication and confusion during response preparations, demonstrated by conflicting records about who authorized deployment and at what time, contributed to the delayed deployment. DCNG began arriving at the Capitol Complex at 5:20 p.m.—nearly three hours after DOD received USCP's request for assistance and more than four hours after the barriers at the Capitol were first breached.

The Committees' Recommendations

Based on the findings of the investigation, the Committees identified a number of recommendations to address the intelligence and security failures leading up to and on January 6. Recommendations specific to the Capitol Complex include empowering the USCP Chief to request assistance from the DCNG in emergency situations and passing legislation to clarify the statutes governing requests for assistance from executive agencies and departments in non-emergency situations. To address the preparedness of the USCP, the Committees recommend improvements to training, equipment, intelligence collection, and operational planning.

The Committees further recommend intelligence agencies review and evaluate criteria for issuing and communicating intelligence assessments and the establishment of standing "concept of operation" scenarios and contingency plans to improve DOD and DCNG response to civil disturbance and terrorism incidents. These scenarios and plans should detail what level of DOD or DCNG assistance may be required, what equipment would be needed for responding personnel, and the plan for command-and-control during the response.

The Committees' Investigation

Two days after the January 6 attack, the Senate Committee on Rules and Administration and Senate Homeland Security and Governmental Affairs Committee announced a joint bipartisan oversight investigation to examine the intelligence and security failures that led to the attack. On February 23, 2021, the Committees held the first public oversight hearing on the attack. The hearing, entitled *Examining the January 6 Attack on the U.S. Capitol*, featured testimony from the USCP Chief, House Sergeant at Arms, and Senate Sergeant at Arms in charge on January 6. The Committees also heard testimony from the Acting Chief of MPD. One week later, on March 3, 2021, the Committees held a second oversight hearing, which included witnesses from DOD, DCNG, FBI, and DHS.

As part of their investigation, the Committees reviewed thousands of documents. The Committees also received written statements from more than 50 USCP officers about their experiences. In addition, the Committees interviewed numerous current and former officials from USCP, Senate Sergeant at Arms, House Sergeant at Arms, Architect of the Capitol, FBI, DHS, MPD, DOD, and DCNG. Most entities cooperated with the Committees' requests. There were notable exceptions, however: the Department of Justice and DHS have yet to fully comply with the Committees' requests for information, the Office of the House of Representatives Sergeant at Arms did not comply with the Committees' information requests, and a USCP Deputy Chief of Police declined to be interviewed by the Committees. The Committees will continue to pursue responses from those who have failed to fully comply. The oversight of events related to January 6, including intelligence and security failures, will continue.

II. FINDINGS OF FACT AND RECOMMENDATIONS

Findings of Fact

(1) **Neither the Department of Homeland Security ("DHS") nor the Federal Bureau of Investigation ("FBI") issued formal intelligence bulletins about the potential for violence at the Capitol on January 6, which hindered law enforcement's preparations for the Joint Session of Congress.** The DHS Office of Intelligence and Analysis ("I&A") issued no intelligence products specific to January 6. Rather, it issued 15 intelligence products in 2020 related to domestic violent extremism, the last of which was issued on December 30 without any mention of the Joint Session of Congress or the Capitol. The FBI similarly did not issue any formal intelligence assessment specific to January 6; however, late on January 5, the FBI's Norfolk Field Office circulated a Situational Information Report, which is used by field offices "to share locally-derived information that is typically operational in nature" and does not meet the same criteria as intelligence assessments. That report warned of individuals traveling to Washington, D.C. for "war" at the Capitol on January 6. In the five months since the attack, neither agency has fully complied with the Committees' request for information on the events of January 6.

(2) **Neither the FBI nor DHS deemed online posts calling for violence at the Capitol as credible.** In testimony before the Committees, representatives from both agencies noted that much of the rhetoric online prior to January 6 was "First Amendment protected speech" of limited credibility and acknowledged areas for improvement in the handling and dissemination of threat information from social media and online message boards to enhance law enforcement and intelligence agencies' abilities to counter that threat.

(3) **The United States Capitol Police's ("USCP") Intelligence and Interagency Coordination Division ("IICD") possessed information about the potential for violence at the Capitol on January 6 but did not convey the full scope of information, which affected its preparations.** Internal records and USCP officials' testimony confirm that USCP began gathering information about events planned for January 6 in mid-December 2020. Through open source collection, tips from the public, and other sources, USCP IICD knew about social media posts calling for violence at the Capitol on January 6, including a plot to breach the Capitol, the online sharing of maps of the Capitol Complex's tunnel systems, and other specific threats of violence. Yet, IICD did not convey the full scope of known information to USCP leadership, rank-and-file officers, or law enforcement partners.

(4) **Important intelligence information received by internal USCP components was not appropriately shared among USCP's distinct intelligence-related components.** USCP has three units responsible for intelligence-related activities—IICD, the Threat Assessment Section ("TAS"), and the Intelligence Operations Section ("IOS")—all of which are organized within USCP's Protective Services Bureau ("PSB"). Although the three components support one another, they have different responsibilities. The decentralized nature of intelligence resources led to

vital intelligence information not being shared with senior USCP intelligence officials or USCP leadership.

(5) **IICD issued multiple intelligence reports prior to January 6 that reflected inconsistent assessments of the risk of violence at the Capitol.** IICD issued intelligence products related to expected activities on January 6, but the products were contradictory as to the threat level. For example, although a January 3 Special Event Assessment warned of the Capitol being a target of armed violence on January 6, IICD's daily intelligence reports rated the likelihood of civil disturbance on January 6 as "remote" to "improbable."

(6) **USCP did not prepare a department-wide operational plan or staffing plan for the Joint Session.** In advance of January 6, Steven Sund, USCP Chief of Police on January 6, believed USCP would need support to secure the Capitol perimeter in light of the large number of expected protestors at the Capitol, but he did not order the creation of a department-wide operational plan. Although the Uniformed Services Bureau and the Civil Disturbance Unit prepared component-specific plans, neither was sufficiently detailed to inform officers of their responsibilities or authorities nor did they reference warnings contained in IICD's January 3Special Event Assessment.

(7) **USCP's Civil Disturbance Unit operates on an "ad hoc" basis, without sufficient training or equipment.** Of USCP's 1,840 sworn officers, only approximately 160 are trained in advanced civil disturbance tactics and use of "hard" protective equipment. Fewer than ten are trained to use USCP's full suite of less-than-lethal munitions. On January 6, some of the "hard" protective equipment was defective or not staged in close proximity to the officers.

(8) **USCP's rank-and-file officers were not provided periodic training in basic civil disturbance tactics or basic protective equipment.** All officers receive basic civil disturbance training during initial Recruit Officer Class training, but there is no further training requirement after graduation. As a result, some who responded to the Capitol attack had not received training in civil disturbance tactics in years. Officers were also not uniformly provided helmets, shields, gas masks, or other crowd control equipment prior to January 6, which would have aided their response.

(9) **USCP's Incident Command System broke down during the attack, leaving front-line officers without key information or instructions as events unfolded.** USCP did not formally designate incident commanders in advance of January 6 through a department-wide operational plan. Senior officers were directly engaged with rioters during the attack, and USCP leadership never took control of the radio system to communicate orders to front-line officers.

(10) **Capitol Police Board members in charge on January 6 did not fully understand the statutory or regulatory requirements for requesting assistance from Executive agencies and departments or declaring emergencies.** Capitol Police Board members also disagreed as to whether unanimity was required to approve a

request from USCP for assistance from the District of Columbia National Guard ("DCNG").

(11) **Steven Sund never submitted a formal request to the Capitol Police Board for an emergency declaration and DCNG assistance before January 6.** Steven Sund had informal conversations with the House and Senate Sergeants at Arms, but no request was ever provided to the full Board. In fact, no one ever informed the Architect of the Capitol, the third voting member of the Board, of a potential request for DCNG assistance.

(12) **As the attack unfolded, Steven Sund lacked the authority to request National Guard assistance unilaterally.** Under the existing statute, the USCP Chief may obtain support from law enforcement and uniformed services only after the Capitol Police Board declares an emergency. This process constrained Steven Sund's ability to act quickly during the attack and contributed to the delay in the provision of assistance.

(13) **The Department of Defense ("DOD") confirmed with USCP on two separate occasions before January 6 that USCP was not requesting assistance from DCNG.** According to DOD records, USCP confirmed on January 3 and January 4 that it did not need DCNG assistance. Meanwhile, DOD continued to communicate with the D.C. Mayor's office regarding its request for unarmed DCNG personnel support.

(14) **DOD's response to January 6 was informed by criticism it received about its response to the civil unrest after the murder of George Floyd during the summer of 2020.** DOD was criticized for its heavy-handed response, particularly flying military helicopters over the protests in summer 2020. DOD officials cited lessons learned from the summer 2020 as guiding its decision-making for January 6. DOD officials believed it needed "control measures" and "rigor" before deploying DCNG personnel, including a clear deployment plan to avoid the appearance of over-militarization.

(15) **DOD imposed control measures on DCNG deployment, including requiring the Army Secretary's approval before deploying a Quick Reaction Force ("QRF") and doing so "only as a last resort."** DOD set forth requirements in a pair of memoranda issued on January 4 and January 5 that allowed William Walker, DCNG Commanding General, to deploy a QRF only as a last resort and upon the express approval of a concept of operations for any use of the QRF by the Secretary of the Army, Ryan McCarthy. General William Walker testified that, absent these requirements, he would have been able to immediately deploy the QRF to support USCP. DOD officials disputed that characterization and asserted that the memoranda simply memorialized longstanding policy. Christopher Miller, the Acting Secretary of Defense on January 6, was not aware that General William Walker wanted to deploy the QRF on January 6.

(16) **As the attack unfolded, DOD officials claimed they did not have a clear request for DCNG assistance until approximately 2:30 p.m.** Ryan McCarthy indicated that Muriel Bowser, the Mayor of Washington, D.C., called him around 1:34 p.m. but did not request assistance at that time. Rather, she asked whether DOD had received requests from USCP because the crowd was "getting out of control." Steven Sund called DCNG Commanding General William Walker at 1:49 p.m. to request assistance. According to Army officials, however, the requests were not specific and clarity on the scope of the request was needed.

(17) **Inaccurate media reports stating that DOD had denied a request for DCNG support slowed DOD's mission analysis efforts.** At 2:55 p.m., a reporter tweeted that DOD "had just denied a request by D.C. officials to deploy the National Guard to the US Capitol," despite the fact that no denial had been ordered and senior DOD officials were still analyzing the request. Christopher Miller approved DCNG mobilization at 3:04 p.m., understanding that DOD officials would then conduct "mission analysis." Ryan McCarthy, however, spent at least half an hour fielding calls and reassuring Congressional and local leaders that DOD "was indeed coming."

(18) **DOD spent hours "mission planning."** Christopher Miller indicated that he gave all necessary approvals for deployment at 3:04 p.m. with the understanding that Ryan McCarthy would conduct mission analysis with General William Walker. Ryan McCarthy, by contrast, felt he needed to brief and receive Christopher Miller's approval before DCNG personnel could leave the Armory. Ryan McCarthy co-located with D.C. officials and developed a concept of operations for DCNG personnel. The plan was approved and DCNG authorized to deploy by 4:35 p.m. All DOD officials who spoke with the Committees described the time spent on mission analysis as vital to DCNG's effectiveness. By contrast, General William Walker believed DCNG was fully equipped and ready to respond to the Capitol much earlier.

(19) **DOD officials denied mentioning or discussing the "optics" of sending DCNG personnel to the Capitol and disagreed with purported statements by an Army official that deploying DCNG to the Capitol would not be "best military advice."** As Christopher Miller told the Committees, "[t]heir best military advice is theirs. The best military advice that I take is from the Chairman of the Joint Chiefs of Staff, statutorily. So the best military advice that I received was, 'Let's go. Agree.'"

(20) **DOD and DCNG have conflicting records of when orders and authorizations were given, and no one could explain why DCNG did not deploy until after 5:00 p.m.** One current DOD official acknowledged that DOD and DCNG could have "tightened up" their response time between 4:35 p.m., when DCNG was authorized to deploy, and 5:02 p.m., when Army documents reflect DCNG's deployment. Officials attributed the delay to confusion and noted that it takes time to get personnel staged for deployment once the order is given. Concerning the conflicting records and accounts as to who needed to approve deployment orders, DOD officials cited confusion, the lack of a lead federal agency with an integrated security plan, and breakdowns in communication as to when those orders were given, and when those orders were executed.

(21) **According to DOD, the Department of Justice ("DOJ") was designated as the lead federal agency in charge of security preparations and response on January 6, but DOJ did not conduct interagency rehearsals or establish an integrated security plan.** DOD officials understood DOJ was designated prior to January 6. According to Ryan McCarthy, DOJ never established a point of contact and did not effectively coordinate a response during the attack. As noted above, DOJ has not fully complied with the Committees' requests for information.

Recommendations

CAPITOL POLICE BOARD

(1) **Empower the Chief of USCP to request assistance from the D.C. National Guard in emergency situations.** Congress should pass legislation to clarify the statutes governing requests for assistance from executive agencies and departments in non-emergency situations. Under existing statute, the Chief of USCP may request support from law enforcement and uniformed services only after the Capitol Police Board declares an emergency. This process can constrain USCP's ability to act quickly in an emergency and delay the provision of assistance.

(2) **Document and streamline Board policies and procedures for submitting, reviewing, and approving requests from USCP to ensure coordination among all members of the Board.** Board policies and procedures should include a requirement that Board members regularly review the policies and procedures to acknowledge their understanding and ensure adherence to the processes outlined therein.

(3) **Ensure the Board is appropriately balancing the need to share information with officials with the need to protect sensitive and classified information.**

(4) **Appoint a new Chief of USCP with appropriate input from USCP officers, congressional leadership, and the committees of jurisdiction.** In addition, the new Chief should evaluate the leadership team and ensure that promotions for leadership positions in USCP are handled in a transparent manner and based on merit.

U.S. CAPITOL POLICE

(1) **Ensure USCP has sufficient civilian and sworn personnel, with appropriate training and equipment, in the roles necessary to fulfill its mission.** This includes providing all officers annual training on basic civil disturbance tactics and equipping them with ballistic helmets, gloves, and gas masks—the same equipment that the District of Columbia Metropolitan Police Department ("MPD") provides to its officers. USCP should maintain an inventory of all issued equipment and ensure that the equipment is periodically replaced. Congress should authorize sufficient funding to support the additional training and equipment requirements, as well as adequate staffing levels.

(2) **Require a department-wide operational plan for special events.** These procedures should include a bureau-specific security plan, which informs the USCP-wide operational plan. The plans should detail, at a minimum: the threat assessment for the event, staffing, deployment strategy, mission objectives, incident command system, authorized use of force, and relevant contingencies in the event of an emergency. USCP should ensure that the operational plans are informed by available intelligence and threat assessments.

(3) **Establish the Civil Disturbance Unit ("CDU") as a formal, permanent component of USCP and ensure that its dedicated officers are properly trained and equipped at all times.** USCP should ensure that all members of the CDU are equipped with "hard" gear and receive annual training in advanced civil disturbance tactics and less-than-lethal munitions. USCP should also ensure that all "hard" protective equipment is properly maintained and regularly replaced.

(4) **Consolidate and elevate all USCP intelligence units into an Intelligence Bureau, led by a civilian Director of Intelligence reporting to the Assistant Chief of Police for Protective and Intelligence Operations; ensure the Bureau is adequately staffed and all agents and analysts are properly trained to receive and analyze intelligence information; and develop policies to disseminate intelligence information to leadership and rank-and-file officers effectively.** Currently, USCP has three separate intelligence-related entities within the Protective Services Bureau. Elevating these entities into a Bureau will increase focus on USCP's intelligence capabilities, improve the timely sharing of relevant intelligence up the chain of command, and decrease lack of coordination within the agency and with law enforcement partners. USCP should ensure that all training given to agents and analysts is consistent with best practices of the Intelligence Community and law enforcement partners, including the determination of credibility and overall threat assessment. USCP should enhance its relationships with Intelligence Community partners, and increase the number of liaisons USCP has integrated in National Capital Region task forces, including those with the FBI and D.C. Fusion Center.

(5) **Update its Incident Command System Directive to address how Incident Commanders are to communicate priorities, strategies, tactics, and threat assessment to front-line officers prior to and during an incident and ensure that the Directive is followed.** USCP should also formalize the process for designating incident commanders for large events and account for contingencies should incident commanders be unable to communicate to officers, including requiring senior leaders to take over communication responsibilities.

HOUSE AND SENATE SERGEANTS AT ARMS

Develop protocols for communicating with Members of Congress, staff, and other employees during emergencies.

INTELLIGENCE AGENCIES

(1) **Review and evaluate handling of open-source information, such as social media, containing threats of violence.**

(2) **Review and evaluate criteria for issuing and communicating intelligence assessments, bulletins, and other products to consumer agencies, such as USCP.**

(3) **Fully comply with statutory reporting requirements to Congress on domestic terrorism data, including on the threat level and the resources dedicated to countering the threat.**

DEPARTMENT OF DEFENSE/D.C. NATIONAL GUARD

(1) **Develop standing "concept of operation" scenarios and contingency plans for responding quickly to civil disturbance and terrorism incidents.** These scenarios and plans should detail what level of DOD or DCNG assistance may be required, what equipment would be needed for responding personnel, and the plan for command-and-control during the response. These scenarios and plans can help reduce confusion or the necessary planning time to allow DOD to respond more quickly to unfolding emergencies. DOD and DCNG should perform tabletop and joint training exercises concerning responding to an attack on the Capitol, which includes coordinating with local law enforcement and neighboring states.

(2) **Enhance communications prior to and during an event between DOD and DCNG strategic, operational, and tactical decision-makers and commanding generals.** These communications should include regular updates prior to an event concerning operations and strategy, as well as regular updates on the day of an event through direct communications between the decision-makers and commanding generals, including by co-locating leaders where practicable.

(3) **Practice the mobilization of National Guard members from neighboring jurisdictions to provide immediate assistance and report to command and control in the event of an emergency.** Those Guard members should be trained and equipped to respond to emergencies.

(4) **For special events in which a Quick Reaction Force ("QRF") is approved, consider proximity and response time, among other factors, when deciding where to stage the QRF to ensure the ability to quickly respond to incidents at the Capitol.**

(5) **Clarify the approval processes and chain of command within DOD to prevent delays in the deployment of DCNG when authorized.**

LAW ENFORCEMENT AND UNIFORMED SERVICES IN THE NATIONAL CAPITAL REGION

(1) **Ensure that Mutual Aid Agreements among federal, state, and local law enforcement agencies include all partners in the National Capital Region and that those agreements are regularly reviewed and updated.**

(2) **Conduct joint training exercises to ensure coordination across federal, state, and local governments concerning security threats in the Washington, D.C. area for requesting, receiving, and utilizing emergency assistance.** Training exercises should cover command-and-control processes during an emergency to ensure the prompt response and timely integration of personnel.

Additional USCP Inspector General Recommendations

After January 6, a number of Inspectors General announced investigations into their agencies' preparation and response to the attack on the Capitol. The Committees support these oversight efforts. To date, the USCP Office of Inspector General has released a number of recommendations for USCP, which are summarized at Appendix A.

III. BACKGROUND

A. Agencies Responsible for Protecting the U.S. Capitol Complex

The U.S. Capitol Complex consists of approximately twenty buildings spread across roughly two square miles in Washington, D.C.[1] It includes the office buildings of the House of Representatives and Senate, the Library of Congress, and the U.S. Supreme Court.[2]It also includes various parks, the U.S. Botanic Garden, and the Capitol Reflecting Pool.[3] The Capitol Building—the citadel of democracy—is the centerpiece of the Capitol Complex. Maintaining, protecting, and securing the Capitol Complex, including those who work in and visit the Capitol Complex, is divided among four entities: (1) the United States Capitol Police; (2) the Senate Sergeant at Arms and Doorkeeper; (3) the House of Representatives Sergeant at Arms; and (4) the Architect of the Capitol. This section details the role and mission of each of these entities.

1. The United States Capitol Police

a) Mission and Organization

The United States Capitol Police ("USCP") is the sole federal law enforcement agency with jurisdiction over the Capitol Complex. Although its origins trace back to 1800, Congress formally established USCP in 1828.[4]It is responsible for protecting not only the Capitol Complex's buildings, but also Members of Congress, staff, and the millions of individuals who visit the Capitol Complex annually.[5] The emphasis on protection is outlined in USCP's mission: to "[p]rotect the Congress – its Members, employees, visitors, and facilities – so it can fulfill its constitutional and legislative responsibilities in a safe, secure and open environment."[6]Steven Sund, USCP Chief on January 6, further emphasized this when testifying before Congress in 2019:

> The type of policing [USCP does] is unlike any other police department. It is highly specialized to focus on the unique requirements of protecting [the] legislative process and the First Amendment rights of our citizens, maintaining an open and accessible campus, and preventing crime and terrorism. Our daily reality is that the U.S. Capitol remains a desired target for assailants both domestic and foreign. Therefore, [USCP] continually assess[es] the risk and adjust[s] [its] strategies for addressing any threats.[7]

[1]ARCHITECT OF THE CAPITOL, *Who We Are*, https://www.aoc.gov/about-us/who-we-are.
[2]*Id.*
[3]*Id.*
[4]An Act Making Appropriations for the Public Buildings, and For Other Purposes, 2 U.S.C. § 1901; U.S. CAPITOL POLICE, *Our History*, https://www.uscp.gov/the-department/our-history.
[5]*See, e.g.*, *Oversight of the United States Capitol Police: Hearing before the H. Comm. on Admin.*, 116th Cong. 2 (2019) (statement of Rep. Zoe Lofgren, Chairperson, H. Comm. on Admin.).
[6]U.S. CAPITOL POLICE, *Our Mission*, https://www.uscp.gov/the-department/our-mission.
[7]*Oversight of the United States Capitol Police: Hearing before the H. Comm. on Admin.*, 116th Cong. (2019). USCP's duties extend beyond the Capitol Complex. It also provides protection for Members of Congress, officers of Congress, and their immediate family members where necessary. *See* 2 U.S.C. § 1966.

To fulfill its mission, USCP employs approximately 1,840 sworn officers and 400 civilian employees.[8] Its budget has grown in recent years and currently exceeds $500 million, more than many large metropolitan cities, including Detroit, Michigan; Minneapolis, Minnesota; St. Louis, Missouri; and Columbus, Ohio.[9]

	FY14	FY15	FY16	FY17	FY18	FY19	FY20	FY21
Appropriations (in thousands of dollars)	$338,459	$347,959	$375,000	$393,300	$426,500	$456,308	$464,341	$515,541

[10]

USCP's budget is similar to that of the Metropolitan Police Department of the District of Columbia ("MPD"), which has primary law enforcement jurisdiction over the 61 square miles of land in the District of Columbia.[11] MPD's FY2020 budget was approximately $559 million—roughly 17 percent more than USCP's FY2020 budget.[12] Yet, MPD employed nearly 3,800 sworn officers, more than double the number of USCP officers.[13]

A Chief of Police leads USCP.[14] The Chief is appointed by and serves at the pleasure of the Capitol Police Board.[15] The Chief is supported by an Executive Team comprised of an Assistant Chief of Police for Uniformed Operations, an Assistant Chief of Police for Protective and Intelligence Operations, and a Chief Administrative Officer.[16] The Executive Team manages eleven bureaus, offices, and divisions that cover a range of police services, including patrol officers, detectives and analysts, dignitary protection, K9 units, and other special response teams.

[8]Joint Committee Interview of Yogananda Pittman, Acting Chief, U.S. Capitol Police, 17:16–23 (Apr. 20, 2021) [hereinafter Pittman Interview (Apr. 20, 2021)]; U.S. CAPITOL POLICE, SWORN STAFFING – JANUARY 6, 2021 INSURRECTION (on file with the Committees). As noted *supra* note 7, USCP's responsibilities extend outside of the Capitol Complex. The current staffing levels are approximately the same as on January 6. Pittman Interview (Apr. 20, 2021), *supra*, at 51:21–52:8.

[9]V ERA, WHAT POLICING COSTS: A LOOK AT SPENDING IN AMERICA'S BIGGEST CITIES, https://www.vera.org/publications/what-policing-costs-in-americas-biggest-cities.

[10]I DA A. BRUDNICK, CONG. RESEARCH SERV., IN11570, THE U.S. CAPITOL POLICE: BRIEF BACKGROUND 2 (2021).

[11]D.C. Code § 5-101.02 (declaring MPD's jurisdiction to be "coextensive with the District of Columbia"); U.S. CENSUS BUREAU, *Quick Facts – District of Columbia*, https://www.census.gov/quickfacts/DC.

[12]M ETRO. POLICE DEP'T OF THE DIST. OF COLUMBIA, FY 2020 APPROVED GROSS FUNDS OPERATING BUDGET (2020).

[13]Letter from Metro. Police Dep't of the Dist. of Columbia to Hon. Charles Allen, Chair, Dist. of Columbia Comm. on the Judiciary (Mar. 2, 2020), https://dccouncil.us/wp-content/uploads/2020/03/JPS-Performance-Oversight-Responses-2020-MPD.pdf.

[14]2 U.S.C. § 1901 ("The Capitol Police shall be headed by a Chief who shall be appointed by the Capitol Police Board and shall serve at the pleasure of the Board.").

[15]*See id.*

[16]U.S. CAPITOL POLICE, *Executive Team*, https://www.uscp.gov/the-department/executive-team.

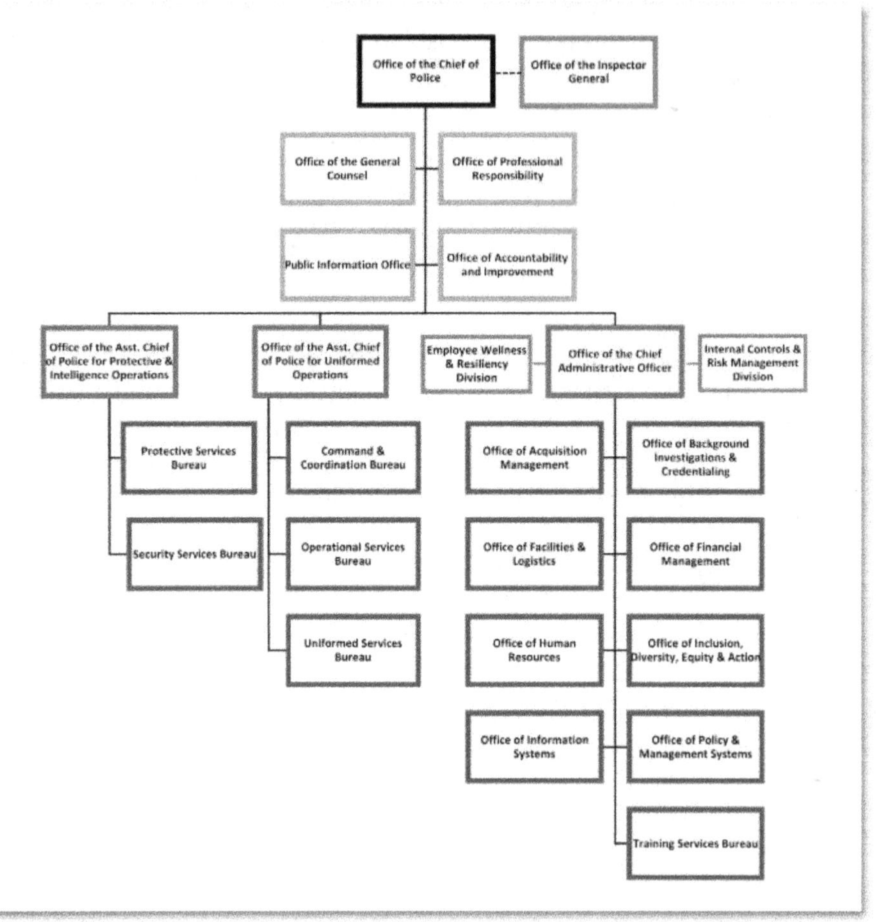

[17]

The majority of USCP's uniformed officers fall under the Office of the Assistant Chief of Police for Uniformed Operations.[18] These are the "primary officers" seen around the Capitol Complex and other officers assigned to entities commonly found in traditional police departments, including hazardous devices response teams, SWAT teams, and K9 teams.[19] The Office of the Assistant Chief of Police for Protective and Intelligence operations is responsible for USCP's intelligence analysis and physical security infrastructure.[20]

As of June 2019 and on January 6, Steven Sund served as USCP Chief. Yogananda Pittman served as the Assistant Chief of Police for Protective and Intelligence Operations and Chad Thomas served as the Assistant Chief of Police for Uniformed Operations.[21] Mr. Sund submitted a letter of resignation on January 7.[22] Ms. Pittman was named Acting Chief, and Sean

[17]U.S. Capitol Police, Department Strategic Plan 9 (2021–2025).
[18]Pittman Interview (Apr. 20, 2021), *supra* note 8, at 18:1–10.
[19]*Id.* at 18:18–22.
[20]Joint Committee Interview of Yogananda Pittman, Acting Chief, U.S. Capitol Police, 46:17–47:15 (Apr. 22, 2021) [hereinafter Pittman Interview (Apr. 22, 2021)]. USCP also works closely with other law enforcement and intelligence entities within the National Capital Region. Pittman Interview (Apr. 20, 2021), *supra* note 8, at 34:2–6.
[21]U.S. Capitol Police, Command Staff on January 6, 2021 (on file with the Committees).
[22]Memorandum from Steven Sund, Chief, U.S. Capitol Police, to Members of the Capitol Police Bd. (Jan. 7, 2021) (submitting a letter of resignation effective Sunday, January 16); Email from Jennifer Hemingway, Acting Sergeant

Gallagher, who was Deputy Chief for the Protective Services Bureau on January 6, was promoted to Acting Assistant Chief for Protective and Intelligence Operations.[23]

b) Oversight by the Capitol Police Board

The Capitol Police Board ("the Board") is charged with overseeing USCP.[24] It is comprised of the House and Senate Sergeants at Arms and the Architect of the Capitol.[25] A Chairman presides over the Board, a position that alternates annually between the House and Senate Sergeants at Arms.[26] The USCP Chief serves as an *ex officio*, non-voting member.[27]

The Board's stated aim is to "direct, oversee and support the Capitol Police in its mission, as well as to advance coordination between Congress, the Capitol Police, the Sergeants at Arms of the House and the Senate and the Architect of the Capitol" by establishing "general goals and objectives covering its major functions and operations to improve the efficiency and effectiveness of its operations."[28] The scope of the Board's authority, however, is broader, covering certain personnel and operational security matters.[29] For example, the Board appoints the USCP Chief and Inspector General; establishes and maintains unified schedules of rates of pay; selects and regulates USCP uniforms; and must approve the termination of USCP employees.[30] The Board can also regulate USCP's law enforcement authority.[31] In terms of security matters, the Board is responsible for the design, installation, and maintenance of security systems for the Capitol Complex, as well as the regulation and movement of all traffic and

at Arms, U.S. Senate, to Senate Sergeant at Arms Official et al. (Jan. 8, 2021, 12:36 PM) (confirming Mr. Sund's resignation effective immediately) (on file with the Committees).

[23] U.S. CAPITOL POLICE, *Executive Team*, https://www.uscp.gov/the-department/executive-team. *See also* Pittman Interview (Apr. 20, 2021), *supra* note 8, at 16:13–16, 55:4–5.

[24] Pub. L. No. 108-7, § 1014(a)(1), 117 Stat. 11, 361 (2003) (codified as amended 2 U.S.C. § 1901 note); CAPITOL POLICE BD., MANUAL OF PROCEDURES § 1.1 (June 17, 2013) [hereinafter CAPITOL POLICE BD. MANUAL]. *See also* U.S. GOV'T ACCOUNTABILITY OFFICE, GAO-17-112, CAPITOL POLICE BOARD: FULLY INCORPORATING LEADING GOVERNANCE PRACTICES WOULD HELP ENHANCE ACCOUNTABILITY, TRANSPARENCY, AND EXTERNAL COMMUNICATION 5 (2017).

[25] Pub. L. No. 108-7, § 1014(a)(2), 117 Stat. 11, 361 (2003) (codified as amended 2 U.S.C. § 1901 note); CAPITOL POLICE BD. MANUAL, *supra* note 24, at § 1.2; U.S. CAPITOL POLICE, *Capitol Police Board*, https://www.uscp.gov/the-department/oversight/capitol-police-board.

[26] CAPITOL POLICE BD. MANUAL, *supra* note 24, at § 1.4; U.S. CAPITOL POLICE, *Capitol Police Board*, https://www.uscp.gov/the-department/oversight/capitol-police-board; *see also* U.S. GOV'T ACCOUNTABILITY OFFICE, *supra* note 24, at 6 n.14 ("The House Sergeant-at-Arms serves as the chairman in even-numbered calendar years and the Senate Sergeant-at-Arms in odd-number[ed] ones.").

[27] Pub. L. No. 108-7, § 1014(a)(2), 117 Stat. 11, 361 (2003) (codified as amended 2 U.S.C. § 1901 note); CAPITOL POLICE BD. MANUAL, *supra* note 24, at § 1.2; *see also* U.S. CAPITOL POLICE, *Capitol Police Board*, https://www.uscp.gov/the-department/oversight/capitol-police-board.

[28] CAPITOL POLICE BD. MANUAL, *supra* note 24, at § 1.1 (internal references omitted); Pub. L. No. 108-7, § 1014(a)(1), 117 Stat. 11, 361 (2003) (codified as amended 2 U.S.C. § 1901 note); *see also* U.S. CAPITOL POLICE, *Capitol Police Board*, https://www.uscp.gov/the-department/oversight/capitol-police-board.

[29] U.S. GOV'T ACCOUNTABILITY OFFICE, *supra* note 24, at 10.

[30] 2 U.S.C. §§ 1901, 1907, 1909, 1923, 1941. The Board is deemed to have approved the termination of an employee if the termination is not disapproved within 30 days of receiving notice of the proposed termination. *Id.* at § 1907(e)(1)(B).

[31] 2 U.S.C. § 1967; CAPITOL POLICE BD. MANUAL, *supra* note 24, at § 4.1.

parking within the Capitol Complex.[32] The following diagram details the roles and responsibilities of the Board and USCP:

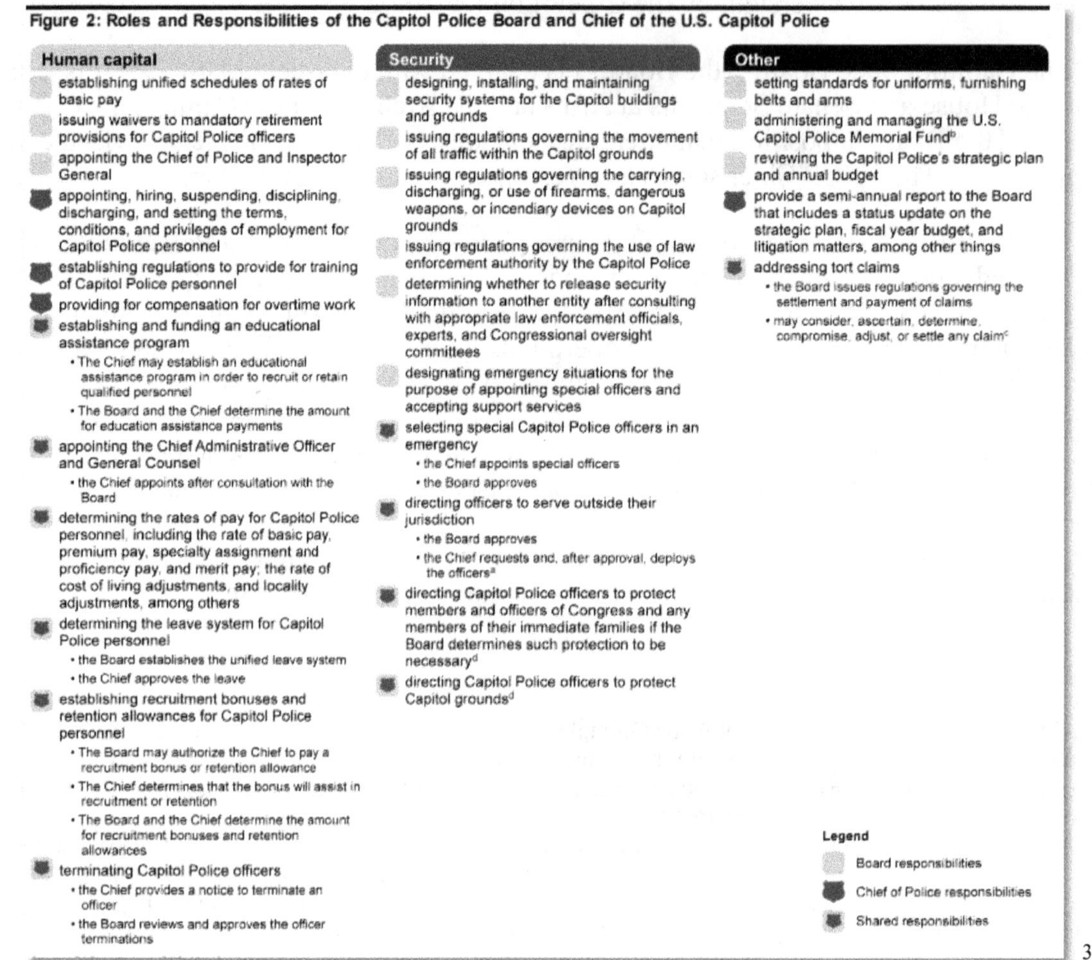

Figure 2: Roles and Responsibilities of the Capitol Police Board and Chief of the U.S. Capitol Police
Human capital
establishing unified schedules of rates of basic pay
issuing waivers to mandatory retirement provisions for Capitol Police officers
appointing the Chief of Police and Inspector General
appointing, hiring, suspending, disciplining, discharging, and setting the terms, conditions, and privileges of employment for Capitol Police personnel
establishing regulations to provide for training of Capitol Police personnel
providing for compensation for overtime work
establishing and funding an educational assistance program
• The Chief may establish an educational assistance program in order to recruit or retain qualified personnel
• The Board and the Chief determine the amount for education assistance payments
appointing the Chief Administrative Officer and General Counsel
• the Chief appoints after consultation with the Board
determining the rates of pay for Capitol Police personnel, including the rate of basic pay, premium pay, specialty assignment and proficiency pay, and merit pay; the rate of cost of living adjustments, and locality adjustments, among others
determining the leave system for Capitol Police personnel
• the Board establishes the unified leave system
• the Chief approves the leave
establishing recruitment bonuses and retention allowances for Capitol Police personnel
• The Board may authorize the Chief to pay a recruitment bonus or retention allowance
• The Chief determines that the bonus will assist in recruitment or retention
• The Board and the Chief determine the amount for recruitment bonuses and retention allowances
terminating Capitol Police officers
• the Chief provides a notice to terminate an officer
• the Board reviews and approves the officer terminations
Security
designing, installing, and maintaining security systems for the Capitol buildings and grounds
issuing regulations governing the movement of all traffic within the Capitol grounds
issuing regulations governing the carrying, discharging, or use of firearms, dangerous weapons, or incendiary devices on Capitol grounds
issuing regulations governing the use of law enforcement authority by the Capitol Police
determining whether to release security information to another entity after consulting with appropriate law enforcement officials, experts, and Congressional oversight committees
designating emergency situations for the purpose of appointing special officers and accepting support services
selecting special Capitol Police officers in an emergency
• the Chief appoints special officers
• the Board approves
directing officers to serve outside their jurisdiction
• the Board approves
• the Chief requests and, after approval, deploys the officers[a]
directing Capitol Police officers to protect members and officers of Congress and any members of their immediate families if the Board determines such protection to be necessary[d]
directing Capitol Police officers to protect Capitol grounds[d]
Other
setting standards for uniforms, furnishing belts and arms
administering and managing the U.S. Capitol Police Memorial Fund[b]
reviewing the Capitol Police's strategic plan and annual budget
provide a semi-annual report to the Board that includes a status update on the strategic plan, fiscal year budget, and litigation matters, among other things
addressing tort claims
• the Board issues regulations governing the settlement and payment of claims
• may consider, ascertain, determine, compromise, adjust, or settle any claim[c]
Legend
Board responsibilities
Chief of Police responsibilities
Shared responsibilities

[33]

2. The Senate and House Sergeants at Arms

The Senate and House Sergeants at Arms ("SAAs") are officers of the Senate and House, respectively.[34] They are nominated by the Senate Majority Leader and Speaker of the House, respectively, and elected by their respective chambers.[35] The SAAs serve as the chief law

[32] 2 U.S.C. §§ 1964, 1969.
[33] U.S. GOV'T ACCOUNTABILITY OFFICE, *supra* note 24, at 13.
[34] U.S. SENATE, *Sergeant at Arms*, https://www.senate.gov/artandhistory/history/common/briefing/sergeant_at_arms.htm; HISTORY, ART & ARCHIVES OF THE U.S. HOUSE OF REPRESENTATIVES, *Sergeants at Arms*, https://history.house.gov/People/Office/Sergeants-at-Arms/.
[35] U.S. SENATE, *Sergeant at Arms*, https://www.senate.gov/artandhistory/history/common/briefing/sergeant_at_arms.htm; HISTORY, ART & ARCHIVES OF THE U.S. HOUSE OF REPRESENTATIVES, *Sergeants at Arms*, https://history.house.gov/People/Office/Sergeants-at-Arms/.

enforcement, protocol, and executive officers for their respective chambers.[36] The Senate SAA is responsible for maintaining security in the Capitol and all Senate buildings, protecting Members, coordinating official events and visits, and enforcing all rules of the Senate.[37] The House SAA has similar responsibilities.[38]

On January 6, Michael Stenger was the Senate Sergeant at Arms; Paul Irving was the House Sergeant at Arms.[39]Following Mr. Stenger's resignation on January 7, Deputy Senate Sergeant at Arms Jennifer Hemingway became Acting Senate Sergeant at Arms; retired Army Lieutenant General Karen H. Gibson became Senate Sergeant at Arms on March 22.[40] Following Mr. Irving's resignation, Deputy House Sergeant at Arms Timothy Blodgett became Acting House Sergeant at Arms on January 11; Major General William J. Walker, who served as Commanding General of the District of Columbia National Guard ("DCNG") on January 6, became House Sergeant at Arms on April 26.[41]

3. The Architect of the Capitol

The Architect of the Capitol is the "builder and steward of the landmark buildings and grounds of Capitol Hill."[42] Appointed by the President with the advice and consent of the Senate,[43]the Architect manages " the operations and care of more than 18.4 million square feet of facilities, 570 acres of grounds and thousands of works of art."[44]This includes operating the Capitol Visitor Center and the U.S. Botanic Garden, maintaining facilities and grounds for the Congress and the U.S. Supreme Court, and managing construction and renovation across the Capitol Complex.[45] The current Architect of the Capitol, J. Brett Blanton, has served in the role since January 2020.[46]

Among the offices under the Architect is the Office of the Chief Security Officer, which "coordinates interagency emergency preparedness and supports [USCP] in protecting, policing

[36]U.S. SENATE, *Sergeant at Arms*, https://www.senate.gov/artandhistory/history/common/briefing/sergeant_at_arms.htm.
[37]*Id.*
[38]U.S. HOUSE OF REPRESENTATIVES, *Sergeant at Arms*, https://www.house.gov/the-house-explained/officers-and-organizations/sergeant-at-arms.
[39]*Examining the U.S. Capitol Attack: Joint Hearing Before the S. Comm. on Homeland Sec. & Governmental Affairs and the S. Comm. on Rules & Admin.*, 117th Cong. (2021) (written testimonies of Steven Sund, Former Chief, U.S. Capitol Police; Paul Irving, Former Sergeant at Arms, U.S. House of Representatives; and Michael Stenger, Former Sergeant at Arms, U.S. Senate).
[40]U.S. SENATE, *Sergeant at Arms*, https://www.senate.gov/artandhistory/history/common/briefing/sergeant_at_arms.htm.
[41]OFFICE OF THE HISTORIAN, U.S. HOUSE OF REPRESENTATIVES, *Sergeants at Arms*, https://history.house.gov/People/Office/Sergeants-at-Arms/.
[42]ARCHITECT OF THE CAPITOL, *About Us – Who We Are*, https://www.aoc.gov/about-us/who-we-are.
[43]2 U.S.C. § 1801.
[44]ARCHITECT OF THE CAPITOL, *About Us – Who We Are*, https://www.aoc.gov/about-us/who-we-are.
[45]ARCHITECT OF THE CAPITOL, STRATEGIC PLAN 2017–2021 5 (2017).
[46]ARCHITECT OF THE CAPITOL, *J. Brett Blanton – Twelfth Architect of the Capitol*, https://www.aoc.gov/about-us/history/architects-of-the-capitol/j-brett-blanton.

and providing security for the congressional community and its visitors."[47]The office of twenty -four employees is led by Valerie Hasberry, the Chief Security Officer.[48]

B. Role of Federal Intelligence Agencies

The Federal Bureau of Investigation ("FBI") is the primary investigative arm of the Department of Justice ("DOJ") and a member of the U.S. Intelligence Community, with both intelligence and law enforcement responsibilities and the broadest investigative authority of all federal law enforcement agencies.[49] Countering terrorism is the FBI's top investigative priority, and its intelligence responsibilities focus on specific terrorist plots, both international and domestic.[50] The FBI works with other law enforcement agencies through partnerships and information sharing.[51] The FBI is the U.S. Government's lead domestic counterterrorism entity.[52]

The Department of Homeland Security's ("DHS") Office of Intelligence and Analysis ("I&A") is also a member of the Intelligence Community. Its mission is "to equip the Department with the intelligence and information it needs to keep the Homeland safe, secure, and resilient."[53] I&A does this by accessing, receiving, and analyzing law enforcement information and intelligence and facilitating multi-directional transfers of intelligence between DHS, the Intelligence Community, state, local, tribal, and territorial governments, and the private sector.[54]According to I&A, the intelligence activities its personnel perform support DHS 's mission by identifying threats and other acts that could potentially affect homeland security, including relating to domestic terrorism.[55]

The FBI and DHS I&A participate in information sharing and partnerships with federal and local law enforcement, including USCP and MPD. Intelligence is usually conveyed via written analytical products, including (1) threat assessments, (2) bulletins, and (3) information reports.[56]As the DOJ Inspector General has previously described:

[47]*See* ARCHITECT OF THE CAPITOL, OFFICE OF THE ARCHITECT – ORGANIZATIONAL CHART (on file with the Committees); *see also* ARCHITECT OF THE CAPITOL, *Capitol Police Buildings, Grounds, and Security*, https://www.aoc.gov/about-us/organizational-directory/capitol-police-buildings-grounds-security-jurisdiction.

[48]*See* ARCHITECT OF THE CAPITOL, *Capitol Police Buildings, Grounds, and Security*, https://www.aoc.gov/about-us/organizational-directory/capitol-police-buildings-grounds-security-jurisdiction; *see also* Joint Committee Interview of J. Brett Blanton, Architect of the Capitol, 109:24–110:2 (Apr. 23, 2021) [hereinafter Blanton Interview].

[49] *See* DEP'T OF JUSTICE, *Organization, Mission and Function Manual: Federal Bureau of Investigation*, https://www.justice.gov/jmd/organization-mission-and-functions-manual-federal-bureau-investigation.

[50]*See id.*

[51]*See* FED. BUREAU OF INVESTIGATION, *Partnerships*, https://www.fbi.gov/about/partnerships.

[52]*See* FED. BUREAU OF INVESTIGATION, *About*, https://www.fbi.gov/about.

[53]OFFICE OF INTELLIGENCE & ANALYSIS, U.S. DEP'T OF HOMELAND SEC., STRATEGIC PLAN FY2020-2024 (Feb. 6, 2020) [hereinafter OFFICE OF INTELLIGENCE & ANALYSIS, STRATEGIC PLAN].

[54]U.S. DEP'T OF HOMELAND SEC., *Office of Intelligence and Analysis*, https://www.dhs.gov/office-intelligence-and-analysis.

[55]OFFICE OF INTELLIGENCE & ANALYSIS, STRATEGIC PLAN, *supra* note 53.

[56]*See, e.g.*, OFFICE OF INSPECTOR GEN., DEP'T OF JUSTICE, FOLLOW-UP AUDIT OF THE FEDERAL BUREAU OF INVESTIGATION'S EFFORTS TO HIRE, TRAIN, AND RETAIN INTELLIGENCE ANALYSTS – AUDIT REP. 07-30 (2007);

> Assessments may be either strategic or tactical. Strategic assessments support [department]-wide programs, plans, and strategies or provide information to policy-makers. Tactical assessments support . . . cases or operations, or cover specific threats. [Information reports] contain single-source intelligence that . . . has not deeply evaluated. Bulletins are unclassified descriptions of significant developments or trends that are shared broadly within the law enforcement community.[57]

FBI and DHS frequently provide threat assessments in advance of high profile events designated as National Special Security Events or Special Event Assessment Ratings, such as inaugurations and Super Bowls.[58] They also issue bulletins to highlight an actual or emerging threat or significant threat-related development.[59]

C. The Attack

January 6, 2021 marked the most significant breach of the Capitol in over 200 years.[60] Seven hours elapsed between when the security perimeter was first breached and when USCP declared the building secure.[61] On that day, officers faced violent physical and verbal assaults; three officers, and four other individuals, ultimately lost their lives. The following section provides a high-level overview of the attack on the Capitol and some of the efforts of the brave men and women who worked to repel the attack.

1. Events of January 6

On November 7, with some states still counting votes, the major news networks projected that Joe Biden had secured enough electoral votes to win the 2020 Presidential election. In response, President Trump issued a statement that he planned to pursue legal challenges to election results in certain states.[62]Nearly all cases were ultimately dismissed or withdrawn. By December 14, all 50 states and the District of Columbia had certified their respective election results, which totaled 306 electoral votes for Biden and 232 for Trump.

MARK A. RANDOL, CONG. RESEARCH SERV., R40602, THE DEPARTMENT OF HOMELAND SECURITY INTELLIGENCE ENTERPRISE: OPERATIONAL OVERVIEW AND OVERSIGHT CHALLENGES FOR CONGRESS 9 (2010).

[57]*See* OFFICE OF INSPECTOR GEN., DEP'T OF JUSTICE, *supra* note 56. *See also* RANDOL, *supra* note 56.

[58]*See, e.g.*, Email from DHS to Committee Staff (June 3, 2021); FED. BUREAU OF INVESTIGATION ET AL., JOINT THREAT ASSESSMENT – 59TH PRESIDENTIAL INAUGURATION, WASHINGTON D.C. (Jan. 14, 2021), https://publicintelligence.net/dhs-fbi-usss-inauguration-threats-2021/; DEP'T OF HOMELAND SEC. ET AL., JOINT THREAT ASSESSMENT – SUPER BOWL XLV (Jan. 11, 2011), https://publicintelligence.net/ufouo-dhs-fbi-northcom-super-bowl-2011-joint-special-event-threat-assessment/.

[59]*See* Email from DHS to Committee Staff (June 3, 2021).

[60]*See* Amy Sherman, *A History of Breaches and Violence at the US Capitol*, POLITIFACT (Jan. 6, 2021), https://www.politifact.com/article/2021/jan/07/history-breaches-and-violence-us-capitol/.

[61]*See* U.S. CAPITOL POLICE, TIMELINE OF EVENTS FOR JANUARY 6, 2021 ATTACK 8 (2021) (on file with the Committees) (putting the first breach before 1:00 p.m. and securing of the building around 8:00 p.m.) [hereinafter U.S. CAPITOL POLICE, TIMELINE OF EVENTS].

[62]The Trump campaign and its allies filed and lost dozens of legal challenges to the election. Alexa Corse, *Election Fraud Claims: A State-by-State Guide*, WALL ST. J. (Jan. 6, 2021).

Following the states' certification, President Trump continued to assert that the election was stolen from him. His statements focused on the January 6 counting of the Electoral College votes during a joint session of Congress. The process in Congress on January 6 is based on a federal law that allows Congress to consider objections to a state's certification of its electors. If both a member of the House and a member of the Senate object to a state's certification of electors, it requires a Congressional vote on whether to reject that state's electors. Congress has only voted on objections twice in the 133 years since enacting this statute, prior to 2020. Pro-Trump groups planned rallies for January 6 that President Trump promoted, and on January 5 President Trump announced that he would speak during the "Save America" rally at the White House Ellipse.

On the morning of January 6, thousands of people began gathering across Washington, D.C. Law enforcement agencies, including USCP and MPD, were monitoring the demonstrators as early as 6:00 a.m. and releasing demonstration updates throughout the day.[63] Most demonstrators headed to the Ellipse, near the White House, for the "Save America" rally, where then-President Trump would speak. By 10:30 a.m., a USCP demonstration update indicated that somewhere between 25,000 and 30,000 people were at the Ellipse; the 10:30 a.m. USCP update also noted that organizers of the rally planned to march to the Capitol after the President's speech.[64]

In addition to those demonstrators at the Ellipse, other demonstrators headed directly to the Capitol Complex. By 11:00 a.m., USCP was aware of "large crowd[s]" around the Capitol building, including a group of approximately 200 Proud Boys.[65] Throughout the city, law enforcement agencies were aware of and responding to reports of suspicious packages and individuals with firearms.[66]

President Trump began his address just before noon.[67] During the next 75 minutes, the President continued his claims of election fraud and encouraged his supporters to go to the Capitol. President Trump's speech is included in its entirety in Appendix B.

Before the President finished his address, crowds began leaving the Ellipse for the Capitol. USCP received reports of "a very large group . . . heading to the U.S. Capitol from eastbound on Pennsylvania Avenue . . . ."[68] By 12:45 p.m. "what look[ed] like a wall of people suddenly arriv[ed] about a block west of the Capitol."[69] At the same time, USCP received a report of a pipe bomb at the Republican National Committee headquarters.[70] Law enforcement

[63] *See* U.S. CAPITOL POLICE, TIMELINE OF EVENTS, *supra* note 61.
[64] *See id.* at 9.
[65] *See id.*; *see also* Martha Mendoza & Juliet Linderman, *Officers Maced, Trampled: Docs Expose Depth of Jan. 6 Chaos*, AP NEWS (Mar. 10, 2021) (referencing a group of approximately 300 Proud Boys having gathered at the Capitol before noon on January 6).
[66] *See* U.S. CAPITOL POLICE, TIMELINE OF EVENTS, *supra* note 61, at 9–10.
[67] *See id.* at 10.
[68] *See id.*
[69] *See id.*
[70] *See id.*; *Examining the U.S. Capitol Attack: Joint Hearing Before the S. Comm. on Homeland Sec. & Governmental Affairs and the S. Comm. on Rules & Admin.*, 117th Cong. (2021) (written testimony of Robert Contee III, Acting Chief, Metro. Police Dep't of the Dist. of Columbia).

officials would discover a similar pipe bomb at the Democratic National Committee headquarters shortly after 1:00 p.m.[71] While responding to these explosive devices, USCP officers discovered a vehicle containing a firearm and eleven Molotov cocktails.[72]

At the Capitol, a large group amassed near the Capitol Reflecting Pool. At approximately 12:53 p.m., individuals within that group picked up one of the metal bike racks that demarcated USCP's security perimeter and shoved it into the USCP officers standing guard.[73] This marked the initial breach of USCP's outer security perimeter; crowds began to flow onto the Capitol's West Front grounds.[74] "All available USCP units" were ordered to respond to the West Front.[75] Five minutes after the initial breach, Mr. Sund called MPD Acting Chief Robert Contee to request immediate assistance.[76] Nearby MPD officers began to arrive at the West Front of the Capitol within minutes, where MPD bicycle patrol officers temporarily reestablished a perimeter.[77]At approximately 1:00 p.m., a USCP Inspector ordered a lockdown of the Capitol Building.[78] At 1:01 p.m., Mr. Sund also requested assistance from the United States Secret Service.[79] Mr. Sund has stated that he also sought approval from the House and Senate SAAs to request National Guard support.[80] As the situation outside continued to deteriorate, inside the Capitol building, Congress was convening in a Joint Session to certify results of the Electoral College vote. Vice President Pence, who presided over the Joint Session, gaveled in at 1:03

[71]*See* U.S. CAPITOL POLICE, TIMELINE OF EVENTS, *supra* note 61, at 12. As a precaution, USCP cleared residences and businesses near the Republican and Democratic National Committee headquarters. USCP also ordered the evacuation of two office buildings nearest to the location of the explosive devices: the Cannon House Office Building and the James Madison Memorial Building of the Library of Congress. *Id.* at 12–13.
[72]*See id.* at 12.
[73]*See id.* at 11.
[74]*See id.*
[75]*See id.*
[76]*See id.*; GOV'T OF THE DIST. OF COLUMBIA, TIMELINE OF PREPARATIONS FOR, AND THE RESPONSE TO, THE LARGE-SCALE DEMONSTRATIONS IN WASHINGTON, D.C. ON JANUARY 5–6, 2021 4 (on file with the Committees) [hereinafter GOV'T OF THE DIST. OF COLUMBIA TIMELINE]; *Examining the U.S. Capitol Attack: Joint Hearing Before the S. Comm. on Homeland Sec. & Governmental Affairs and the S. Comm. on Rules & Admin.*, 117th Cong. (2021) (written testimony of Robert Contee III, Acting Chief, Metro. Police Dep't of the Dist. of Columbia). In his own testimony before the Committees, Mr. Sund did not indicate when he called Acting Chief Contee. He did, however, state that by 12:50 p.m., he understood the situation to be "deteriorating rapidly" and at 12:53 p.m. called an MPD Assistant Chief to request assistance. *Examining the U.S. Capitol Attack: Joint Hearing Before the S. Comm. on Homeland Sec. & Governmental Affairs and the S. Comm. on Rules & Admin.*, 117th Cong. (2021) (written testimony of Steven Sund, Former Chief, U.S. Capitol Police); Steven A. Sund, Responses to Questions for the Record (Apr. 6, 2021) (on file with the Committees).
[77]GOV'T OF THE DIST. OF COLUMBIA TIMELINE, *supra* note 76 (arriving at 1:03 p.m., five minutes after the initial request); *Examining the U.S. Capitol Attack: Joint Hearing Before the S. Comm. on Homeland Sec. & Governmental Affairs and the S. Comm. on Rules & Admin.*, 117th Cong. (2021) (written testimony of Robert Contee III, Acting Chief, Metro. Police Dep't of the Dist. of Columbia); Joint Committee Interview with USCP Inspector (May 27, 2021).
[78]Joint Committee Interview with USCP Inspector (May 27, 2021); Media Release, U.S. Capitol Police Labor Comm., Capitol Police Officers "Leadership Betrayed Our Mission," (Jan 27, 2021), https://www.scribd.com/document/492350885/Read-U-S-Capitol-Police-Labor-Committee-statement [hereinafter USCP Labor Comm. Media Release].
[79]*See* U.S. CAPITOL POLICE, TIMELINE OF EVENTS, *supra* note 61, at 12.
[80]*Examining the U.S. Capitol Attack: Joint Hearing Before the S. Comm. on Homeland Sec. & Governmental Affairs and the S. Comm. on Rules & Admin.*, 117th Cong. (2021) (written testimony of Steven Sund, Former Chief, U.S. Capitol Police).

p.m.[81]President Trump concluded his speech at 1:10 p.m .[82] At 1:12 p.m., the two chambers separated and began to debate objections to the certification of Arizona's Electoral College votes.[83]

After overrunning USCP's security perimeter on the West Front of the building, rioters pressed towards the Capitol building—climbing the inaugural platform and scaling walls.[84] The only remaining security perimeter consisted of the USCP officers positioned around the grounds, who were overwhelmed and outnumbered. USCP officers attempted to hold back the rioters with chemical munitions, such as oleoresin capsicum ("OC") spray, more commonly known as "pepper spray."[85] Muriel Bowser, Mayor of Washington, D.C., called the Secretary of the Army, Ryan McCarthy, at approximately 1:34 p.m. to seek National Guard support.[86] By 1:49 p.m., rioters had breached the Upper West Terrace.[87] At 1:49 p.m., Mr. Sund called William Walker, DCNG Commanding General, to request immediate assistance.[88] At the same time, MPD declared a riot at the Capitol.[89] Two minutes later, at 1:51 p.m., Mr. Sund activated USCP's mutual aid agreement with National Capital Region law enforcement entities.[90] At 2:00 p.m., then-Assistant Chief Pittman also ordered a lockdown of the Capitol Building.[91]

Rioters continued to push toward the Capitol building, reaching the Rotunda steps by 2:06 p.m. and the House Plaza by 2:08 p.m.[92]Ms. Pittman then expanded the lockdown to cover the entire Capitol Complex.[93] At 2:10 p.m., rioters breached the final barricade on the West Front and northwest side of the Capitol, quickly approaching an entrance near the Senate chamber.[94]A lso at 2:10 p.m., House SAA Irving and Senate SAA Stenger issued an emergency declaration on behalf of the Capitol Police Board and formally approved requesting National Guard assistance.[95]A minute later, rioters sm ashed through first-floor windows on the Capitol's south side, making a hole big enough to climb through; a stream of protesters entered, with two

[81]William M. Arkin, *Exclusive: How Officials' Fear of Donald Trump Paralyzed Intelligence Agencies, Led to Capitol Riot*, NEWSWEEK (Jan. 21, 2021).
[82]*See* U.S. CAPITOL POLICE, TIMELINE OF EVENTS, *supra* note 61, at 13.
[83]U.S. SENATE SERGEANT AT ARMS, TIMELINE OF EVENTS FOR JANUARY 6, 2021 ATTACK REGARDING SAA DOORKEEPERS OPERATIONS 2 (2021) (on file with the Committees).
[84]*Cf.* U.S. CAPITOL POLICE, TIMELINE OF EVENTS, *supra* note 61, at 11–12, 14.
[85]*See id.* at 12.
[86]OFFICE OF THE SEC'Y OF DEF., DEP'T OF DEF., TIMELINE FOR DECEMBER 31, 2020 – JANUARY 6, 2021 3 (2021) [hereinafter DEP'T OF DEF. TIMELINE]. According to the Department of Defense, Mayor Bowser's call came at 1:34 p.m. The Office of the Mayor indicated to the Committees that Mayor Bowser did not speak to Secretary McCarthy until after 1:49 p.m. *See* GOV'T OF THE DIST. OF COLUMBIA TIMELINE, *supra* note 76, at 4.
[87]*See* U.S. CAPITOL POLICE, TIMELINE OF EVENTS, *supra* note 61, at 14.
[88]*Id.*
[89]GOV'T OF THE DIST. OF COLUMBIA TIMELINE, *supra* note 76, at 4.
[90]*See* U.S. CAPITOL POLICE, TIMELINE OF EVENTS, *supra* note 61, at 14.
[91]*See id.* at 15.
[92]*See id.*
[93]*See id.* at 16.
[94]Lauren Leatherby & Anjali Singhvi, *How Trump's Call to G.O.P. Lawmakers Fit in the Timeline of the Capitol Riot*, N.Y. TIMES (Feb. 13, 2021).
[95]U.S. CAPITOL POLICE, TIMELINE OF EVENTS, *supra* note 61, at 16.

individuals kicking open a nearby door to let others into the Capitol.[96] According to reports, officers attempted to disperse the group with pepper balls and smoke bombs.[97]

At 2:13 p.m., two minutes after rioters breached the building, the Senate went into recess.[98] At 2:14 p.m., USCP Officer Eugene Goodman redirected rioters away from the Senate chamber.[99] Vice President Pence and congressional leaders were evacuated to secure locations.[100] An order to lock down the House and Senate c hambers was issued at 2:15 p.m.[101] The House declared a brief recess at 2:18 p.m.[102] All active USCP Civil Disturbance Unit ("CDU") platoons were deployed to either the House side of the Capitol or the Rotunda.[103]

After receiving the Board's 2:10 p.m. authorization, Mr. Sund urgently requested National Guard support. During a teleconference around 2:30 p.m. with Pentagon officials and D.C. government officials, including Mayor Bowser, Director of the D.C. Homeland Security and Emergency Management Agency Dr. Christopher Rodriguez, and Acting MPD Chief Contee, Mr. Sund pleaded for immediate backup.[104] According to the testimony of Mr. Sund, Acting MPD Chief Contee, and Commanding General Walker, officials from the Department of the Army at DOD headquarters—particularly Lieutenant Generals Walter Piatt and Charles Flynn—responded that it was not their best military advice to support the request because they did not "like the optics of the National Guard standing a line at the Capitol."[105]

At 2:43 p.m., rioters broke the glass of a door to the Speaker's Lobby, a hallway that would have given the rioters direct access to the House chamber.[106] When the rioters tried to lift Ashli Babbitt through the opening, a USCP officer fatally shot her.[107] Less than ten minutes

[96] Marc Fisher et al., *The Four-Hour Insurrection*, WASH. POST (Jan. 7, 2021).
[97] *Id.*
[98] Dalton Bennett et al., *41 Minutes of Fear: A Video Timeline from Inside the Capitol Siege*, WASH. POST (Jan. 16, 2021).
[99] *Id.*
[100] Ashley Parker et al., *How the Rioters Who Stormed the Capitol Came Dangerously Close to Pence*, WASH. POST (Jan. 15, 2021).
[101] *See* U.S. CAPITOL POLICE, TIMELINE OF EVENTS, *supra* note 61, at 16.
[102] Dalton Bennett et al., *supra* note 98.
[103] *See* U.S. CAPITOL POLICE, TIMELINE OF EVENTS, *supra* note 61, at 17.
[104] *See id.*
[105] *Id. See also Examining the U.S. Capitol Attack: Joint Hearing Before the S. Comm. on Homeland Sec. & Governmental Affairs and the S. Comm. on Rules & Admin.*, 117th Cong. (2021) (written testimonies of Steven Sund, Former Chief, U.S. Capitol Police, and Robert Contee III, Acting Chief, Metro. Police Dep't of the Dist. of Columbia); *Examining the U.S. Capitol Attack – Part II: Joint Hearing Before the S. Comm. on Homeland Sec. & Governmental Affairs and the S. Comm. on Rules & Admin.*, 117th Cong. (2021) (testimony of William Walker, Commanding Gen., Dist. of Columbia Nat'l Guard) ("So the Army senior leaders did not think that it looked good, it would be a good optic. They further stated that it could incite the crowd."). The Army official alleged to have made the comment has denied doing so. *See Examining the U.S. Capitol Attack – Part II: Joint Hearing Before the S. Comm. on Homeland Sec. & Governmental Affairs and the S. Comm. on Rules & Admin.*, 117th Cong. 57 (2021) (testimony of Robert Salesses, Senior Official Performing the Duties of the Ass't Sec'y for Homeland Def. & Global Sec., Dep't of Def.) ("General Piatt told me yesterday that he did not say anything about optics.").
[106] *See* U.S. CAPITOL POLICE, TIMELINE OF EVENTS, *supra* note 61, at 18.
[107] *See id.* at 17. On April 14, DOJ announced that it had closed its investigation into Ms. Babbitt's death, citing insufficient evidence to support a criminal prosecution of the USCP officer. Press Release, U.S. Attorney's Office

later, rioters breached the Senate chamber.[108]In the House chamber, USCP officers barricaded the door with furniture and drew their weapons to hold off rioters.[109] The last Members were evacuated from the House chamber by 2:57 p.m.[110]

After 3:00 p.m., additional reinforcements from federal agencies began to arrive, and USCP turned to extracting and securing congressional staff.[111] A number of agencies and entities provided assistance, including DHS; the FBI; the Bureau of Alcohol, Tobacco, Firearms and Explosives; the Montgomery County Police Department; the Arlington County Police Department; the Fairfax Police Department; and Virginia State Troopers.[112] With this help, USCP secured the Senate and House chambers, along with the basement, subways, first floor, and crypts by 4:28 p.m.[113] DCNG personnel began arriving at the Capitol at approximately 5:20 p.m.[114] By 6:14 p.m., USCP, DCNG, and MPD successfully established a security perimeter on the west side of the Capitol building.[115]

At 8:00 p.m., after completing a sweep of the Capitol grounds with partner law enforcement agencies, USCP declared the Capitol secure, and the Senate reconvened to resume consideration of the objection to Arizona's electoral votes.[116] Shortly afterwards, at approximately 9:00 p.m., the House reconvened.[117]After rejecting objections to the counting of electoral votes from Arizona and Pennsylvania, the Joint Session of Congress officially affirmed the results of the Electoral College at 3:42 a.m. on January 7, formally declaring Joseph Biden and Kamala Harris as winners of the 2020 Presidential Election.[118]

2. Communication with Capitol Staff

Both USCP and the Sergeants at Arms alert employees working at the Capitol Complex about ongoing security threats through the use of automated email alerts, but primary responsibility for security notifications to Senators and Senate staff resides with the Senate SAA. In the days leading up to and around 11:39 a.m. on January 6, the Senate SAA issued a reminder

for the Dist. of Columbia, Department of Justice Closes Investigation into the Death of Ashli Babbitt (Apr. 14, 2021), https://www.justice.gov/usao-dc/pr/department-justice-closes-investigation-death-ashli-babbitt.

[108]*See* U.S. CAPITOL POLICE, TIMELINE OF EVENTS, *supra* note 61, at 18.

[109]*See id.*

[110]*See id.*

[111]*See id.* at 18–20; Joint Committee Interview with USCP Inspector (May 27, 2021).

[112]*See* U.S. CAPITOL POLICE, TIMELINE OF EVENTS, *supra* note 61, at 18–20.

[113]*See id.* at 20.

[114]OFFICE OF THE SEC'Y OF DEF., DEP'T OF DEF., MEMORANDUM FOR THE RECORD – RECORD OF EVENTS AND ACTIVITIES OF THE OFFICE OF THE SECRETARY OF DEFENSE AND ACTING SECRETARY MILLER RELATED TO THE CIVIL DISTURBANCE AND EFFORTS TO SUPPORT LOCAL LAW ENFORCEMENT RESPONSE ON 06 AND 07 JANUARY 2021 7 (2021) [hereinafter OFFICE OF THE SEC'Y OF DEF. MEMORANDUM FOR THE RECORD]; *Examining the U.S. Capitol Attack – Part II: Joint Hearing Before the S. Comm. on Homeland Sec. & Governmental Affairs and the S. Comm. on Rules & Admin.*, 117th Cong. (2021) (written testimony of Maj. Gen. William Walker, Commanding Gen., Dist. of Columbia Nat'l Guard).

[115]DEP'T OF DEF. TIMELINE, *supra* note 86, at 3.

[116]*Id.*

[117]Shelly Tan et al., *How One of America's Ugliest Days Unraveled Inside and Outside the Capitol*, WASH. POST (Jan. 9, 2021).

[118]*Id.*

to staff of "several First Amendment activities" scheduled to take place "throughout the District of Columbia." The alert reassured employees that USCP and the SAA were "aware of these First Amendment activities and [monitoring] impacts to Congressional activities[, and] [t]o support the safety and security of Senators and staff, [USCP had] additional personnel throughout Capitol Grounds."[119] Although USCP issued several email alerts on January 6, the Senate SAA did not issue any Senate-wide email alerts during the attack.[120]

USCP issued nineteen email alerts between 11:15 a.m. and 7:24 p.m. on January 6— more than half of which were sent before the Capitol Building was breached. Still, those alerts contained little information or context for employees. They simply noted that USCP was investigating suspicious packages, informed employees of road closures, and ordered staff to relocate from the Cannon House Office Building.[121] Although Ms. Pittman ordered a lockdown of the Capitol Building at 2:00 p.m., Capitol employees were not made aware of this until 2:10 p.m. The alert informed staff that no entry or exit was permitted but that staff were still able to "move throughout the buildings."[122] At 2:18 p.m., USCP circulated an updated warning:

> Capitol Staff: Due to a security threat inside the building, immediately: move inside your office or the nearest office. Take emergency equipment and visitors. Close, lock, and stay away from external doors and windows. If you are in a public space, find a place to hide or seek cover. Remain quiet and silence electronics. Once you are in a safe location, immediately check in with your [Office Emergency Contact]. No one will be permitted to enter or exit the building until directed by USCP.[123]

USCP re-sent the same message three additional times on January 6—at 3:41 p.m., 4:09 p.m., and 6:44 p.m.[124] No further context, information, or direction was provided via these automated emergency alert systems. Staff were not informed until 7:24 p.m. that "if anyone must leave," they could do so via certain doors.[125]

3. Experience of Law Enforcement Officers

Throughout the seven hours of the riot on the Capitol grounds, law enforcement officers faced verbal and "absolutely brutal," violent physical abuse.[126] One officer described an interaction with a group of protestors during the evacuation of the Senate: "[W]e stopped several

[119] *See, e.g.*, Email from "Notice (SAA)" to Capitol Hill employees (Jan. 6, 2021, 11:39 AM) (on file with the Committees).
[120] Senate SAA sent alerts to emergency coordinators for individual Senate offices. *See, e.g.,* Email from "Senate Alerts (SAA)" to Senate Office Emergency Coordinators (Jan. 6, 2021, 2:24 PM) (on file with the Committees).
[121] *See generally* U.S. CAPITOL POLICE, TIMELINE OF EVENTS, *supra* note 61.
[122] *See id.* at 15–16.
[123] *See id.* at 16–17.
[124] *See id.* at 19, 20, 22.
[125] *See id.* at 23. According to press accounts, these vague and sparse communications left many Congressional employees who were working on January 6 feeling helpless and fearful. One congressional staffer described how his colleagues were forced to evacuate and shelter in the halls of Longworth for hours, not fully aware of everything that was happening above ground. Katherine Tully-McNamus, ROLL CALL, *Insurrection aftermath: Staffers struggle with trauma, guilt and fear* (Jan. 28, 2021).

[126] Joint Committee Interview with USCP Inspector (May 27, 2021).

men in full tactical gear and they stated 'You better get out of our way boy or we'll go through you to get [the Senators].'"[127] Recounting initial encounters with the crowd along the metal bike racks, another officer recalled:

> [We] did what we could against impossible odds and a volatile crowd which many times threatened us with phrases like "We're gonna kill you!", "We're gonna murder you and then them!", "You guys are traitors and should be killed!" . . . I felt at this time a tangible fear that maybe I or some of my colleagues might not make it home alive.[128]

Other officers have publicly described instances of racial abuse from the crowd. Many were called "traitors" and "nazis."[129] An officer described being "called a pawn of China" and seeing "someone give a Nazi salute to the Capitol behind me."[130] Officer Harry Dunn told *ABC News*, "I got called a [N-word] a couple dozen times today protecting th[e Capitol] building."[131] He also described Black officers feeling targeted because of their race, saying "we fought against not just people that hated what we represented, but they hate our skin color also."[132]

Officers responding to the attack suffered a range of injuries in the line of duty. Many officers have recounted repeated attacks with chemical irritants from the crowd, including bear spray and insecticide. One officer stated that he was "sprayed in the eyes with some kind of chemical irritant that was far stronger than any pepper spray I have ever had used against me in training."[133] Other officers reported burns, breathing and lung complications, and their eyes sealing shut from irritation due to repeated exposure to the chemical irritants.[134] Captain Carneysha Mendoza testified to the Committees that she received chemical burns to her face, which had not healed nearly two months after the attack.[135]

Officers were also physically assaulted with a range of objects thrown from the crowds, pinned against surfaces, and beaten with flag poles and other weapons carried or found by rioters, including frozen water bottles.[136] For example, rioters disassembled a fence in front of the inaugural platform and used the pieces to assault officers.[137] One officer described the fear experienced that day, stating, "[a]t one point, I was pushed so hard and crushed in between

[127] Officer Statement #35 provided to the Committees (on file with the Committees).
[128] Officer Statement #51 provided to the Committees (on file with the Committees).
[129] *See, e.g.*, Celine Castronuovo, *Videos Shows Rioters Calling Capitol Police 'Traitors'*, THE HILL (Feb. 11, 2021).
[130] Officer Statement #56 provided to the Committees (on file with the Committees).
[131] Pierre Thomas et al., *Capitol Police Officer Recounts Jan. 6 Attack: Exclusive*, ABC NEWS (Feb. 22, 2021).
[132] Caroline Kelly, *Black US Capitol Police Officer Recounts January 6: 'They Showed That They Hated Us and They Hated Our Skin Color*," CNN (Mar. 17, 2021).
[133] Officer Statement #46 provided to the Committees (on file with the Committees).
[134] Officer Statements #48, 46, 52, 53 provided to the Committees (on file with the Committees); Joint Committee Interview with USCP Inspector (May 27, 2021).
[135] *Examining the U.S. Capitol Attack: Joint Hearing Before the S. Comm. on Homeland Sec. & Governmental Affairs and the S. Comm. on Rules & Admin.*, 117th Cong. (2021) (written testimony of Captain Carneysha Mendoza, Field Commander, Special Operations Div., U.S. Capitol Police).
[136] Joint Committee Interview with USCP Inspector (May 27, 2021); Michael S. Schmidt & Luke Broadwater, *Officers' Injuries, Including Concussions, Show Scope of Violence at Capitol Riot*, N.Y. TIMES (updated May 7, 2021).
[137] Joint Committee Interview with USCP Inspector (May 27, 2021).

people that I could not breathe. This was a frightening situation."[138]Another officer recounted the various types of weapons used by the crowd:

> The objects thrown at us varied in size, shape and consistency, some were frozen cans and bottles, rebar from the construction, bricks, liquids, pepper spray, bear spray, sticks of various widths, pipes, bats, some were armed with guns and some had tasers or something similar. I specifically remember being sprayed with bear spray at least 6-8 times while tussling with rioters who were trying to use the bike racks against us as weapons.[139]

Approximately 140 law enforcement officers reported injuries suffered during the attack.[140]The Capitol Police Labor Committee released a statement recounting some of the more serious injuries: "I have officers who were not issued helmets prior to the attack who have sustained brain injuries. One officer has two cracked ribs and two smashed spinal discs. One officer is going to lose his eye, and another was stabbed with a metal fence stake."[141]Patrick Burke, executive director of the Washington, D.C. Police Foundation, reported that one officer suffered a heart attack after being attacked several times with a stun gun.[142]

Three officers lost their lives following the attack. USCP Officer Brian Sicknick, a 13-year veteran and member of the First Responder Unit, was stationed on the West Front of the Capitol, where rioters attacked him with bear spray.[143]Officer Sicknick passed away at 9:30 p.m. on January 7.[144]Officer Howard Liebengood, a 16-year veteran of USCP, died on January 9.[145]Officer Jeffrey Smith, a 12 -year veteran of MPD, died on January 15.[146]

Despite the hardships they faced, officers engaged in countless acts of bravery and heroism. One officer noted that, "[t]he officers inside all behaved admirably and heroically and, even outnumbered, went on the offensive and took the Capitol back."[147]Another officer described a situation where an officer went above and beyond to help out however possible:

[138]Officer Statement #23 provided to the Committees (on file with the Committees).
[139]Officer Statement #51 provided to the Committees (on file with the Committees).
[140]USCP reported 73 injured officers, and MPD reported 65 injured officers. Schmidt & Broadwater, *supra* note 136. "Many more sustained injuries from the assault – scratches, bruises, eyes burning from bear mace – that they did not even bother to report." *Examining the U.S. Capitol Attack: Joint Hearing Before the S. Comm. on Homeland Sec. & Governmental Affairs and the S. Comm. on Rules & Admin.*, 117th Cong. (2021) (written testimony of Robert Contee III, Acting Chief, Metro. Police Dep't of the Dist. of Columbia).
[141]USCP Labor Comm. Media Release, *supra* note 78.
[142]Schmidt & Broadwater, *supra* note 136.
[143]Evan Hill et al., *Officer Brian Sicknick Died After the Capitol Riot. New Videos Show How He Was Attacked*, N.Y. TIMES (Mar. 24, 2021).
[144]Spencer S. Hsu et al., *Two Arrested in Assault on Police Officer Brian D. Sicknick, Who Died after Jan. 6 Capitol Riot*, WASH. POST (Mar. 15, 2021).
[145]Allison Klein & Rebecca Tan, *Capitol Police Officer Who Was on Duty During the Riot Has Died by Suicide, His Family Says*, WASH. POST (Jan. 11, 2021).
[146]Peter Hermann, *Two Officers Who Helped Fight the Capitol Mob Died by Suicide. Many More are Hurting*, WASH. POST (Feb. 12, 2021).
[147]Officer Statement #21 provided to the Committees (on file with the Committees).

> A light duty officer in a suit from the Capitol Division . . . came up to me at the Triage site on the [Capitol Visitor Center] landing and asked how he could help. I told him that we needed bottles of water in a bad way for rinsing eyes out. I figured he would go back to the detail where there was a pile, but he instead went to the Senate Carry-out and returned with a few cases of water, being carried by him and the Senate Carry-out cook, still wearing his white apron and paper hat. They brought us [Smartwater], seriously expensive stuff.[148]

Another officer stated that he "saw officers responding to save members and staff in offices," "saw many officers get sprayed [with] irritants," and "saw officers standing in the way of the blood thirsty [mob, to prevent them] from achieving their goals."[149]Describing the aftermath of that day, another officer recounted:

> I wandered around the building for a little bit, looking at the wreckage and trying to take everything in before people cleaned up. Doors and windows were broken, and had been barricaded with furniture and display cases. There was broken glass, trash, banners and signs. I went down to the [Lower West Terrace] through the tunnel and it was just trashed. Knives, baseball bats, flag poles, banners, CDU shields, body armor, pants, socks, shoes, hats, uniform items, jackets, wallets, cash, phones, flags and signs littered the ground. Everything was covered in white from the tear gas and I could still smell the pepper spray.[150]

IV. FEDERAL INTELLIGENCE AGENCIES DID NOT ISSUE A THREAT ASSESSMENT OR BULLETIN FOR THE JOINT SESSION OF CONGRESS

Neither DHS nor FBI issued a threat assessment or joint intelligence bulletin specific to the January 6 Joint Session of Congress.[151]Mr. Sund attributed the security failures of January 6, in part, to not having better intelligence from federal partners.[152]He has stated that in a January 5 meeting with USCP leadership, members of the Capitol Police Board, and officials from the FBI, U.S. Secret Service, and DCNG, no entity "provided any intelligence indicating that there would be a coordinated violent attack on the United States Capitol by thousands of well-equipped armed insurrectionists."[153]

[148]Officer Statement #13 provided to the Committees (on file with the Committees).

[149]Officer Statement #35 provided to the Committees (on file with the Committees).

[150]Officer Statement #12 provided to the Committees (on file with the Committees).

[151]*See, e.g.*, *Examining the U.S. Capitol Attack – Part II: Joint Hearing Before the S. Comm. on Homeland Sec. & Governmental Affairs and the S. Comm. on Rules & Admin.*, 117th Cong. (2021) (testimonies of Jill Sanborn, Ass't Dir., Counterterrorism Div., Fed. Bureau of Investigation, and Melissa Smislova, Acting Under Secretary, Office of Intelligence & Analysis, Dep't of Homeland Sec.).

[152]*Examining the U.S. Capitol Attack: Joint Hearing Before the S. Comm. on Homeland Sec. & Governmental Affairs and the S. Comm. on Rules & Admin.*, 117th Cong. (2021) (written testimony of Steven Sund, former Chief, U.S. Capitol Police).

[153]Letter from Steven Sund, Former Chief, U.S. Capitol Police, to Nancy Pelosi, Speaker of the House of Representatives (Feb. 1, 2021).

A. FBI Released a Situational Information Report on January 5 by Email

According to reports, shortly following the attack the director of the FBI's Washington Field Office, Steven D'Antuono, told reporters that, prior to January 6, there was no indication of anything other than First Amendment activity.[154] Thus, the FBI did not issue a threat assessment or intelligence bulletin specific to the Joint Session or January 6.[155] Although not a formal intelligence bulletin, the FBI did disseminate at least one report warning of violence at the Capitol. On January 5, the FBI's Norfolk Field Office disseminated a Situational Information Report ("SIR") that warned of online discussions of potential violence on January 6.[156]A SIR is a mechanism used by field offices "to share locally derived information" that "is typically operational in nature and actionable by or relevant to only a limited audience in specific domains" and does not meet the same criteria as an intelligence assessment.[157] A SIR's specific purpose is "to disseminate potential threat information to relevant partners."[158]

The Norfolk SIR highlighted a particular online thread stating, "Be Ready to Fight. Congress needs to hear glass breaking, doors being kicked in, and blood from their BLM and Pantifa slave soldiers being spilled. Get violent . . . stop calling this a march, or rally, or a protest. Go there ready for war . . . ."[159] Jill Sanborn, then-Assistant Director of the FBI's Counterterrorism Division, characterized the Norfolk SIR as "information off the Internet, unattributable to a specific person."[160] However, she acknowledged that it was "concerning enough" that the Washington Field Office disseminated the report to law enforcement partners via email, briefed it verbally during an interagency Command Post meeting, and uploaded the report to the FBI's "LEEP portal," which is available to all state and local partners.[161]

Documents provided to the Committees show that an FBI Norfolk Field Office analyst emailed the SIR, which was described as relating to "potential criminal activities in the Washington DC area planned for tomorrow (01/06)," to the FBI Washington Field Office at 6:52 p.m. on January 5.[162] At 7:37 p.m., an intelligence analyst with FBI's Washington Field Office

[154]Ken Dilanian & Julia Ainsley, *Worried About Free Speech, FBI Never Issued Intelligence Bulletin about Possible Capitol Violence*, NBC NEWS (Jan. 12, 2021); Julian Baron, *Reports: Officials Were Aware of Threat to U.S. Capitol during Electoral College Vote*, FOXNEWS5 BALTIMORE (Feb. 10, 2021).
[155]*See Examining the U.S. Capitol Attack – Part II: Joint Hearing Before the S. Comm. on Homeland Sec. & Governmental Affairs and the S. Comm. on Rules & Admin.*, 117th Cong. (2021) (testimony of Jill Sanborn, Ass't Dir., Counterterrorism Div., Fed. Bureau of Investigation).
[156]*See id.*
[157]FED. BUREAU OF INVESTIGATION, FBI INFORMATION SHARING REPORT 39 (2011).
[158]*See* Email from FBI to Committee Staff (June 3, 2021).
[159]FBI_SIR_000001–2. *See also* Devlin Barrett & Matt Zapotosky, *FBI Report Warned of 'War' at Capitol, Contradicting Claims There Was No Indication of Looming Violence*, WASH. POST (Jan. 12, 2021).
[160]*Examining the U.S. Capitol Attack – Part II: Joint Hearing Before the S. Comm. on Homeland Sec. & Governmental Affairs and the S. Comm. on Rules & Admin.*, 117th Cong. (2021) (testimony of Jill Sanborn, FBI Assistant Director, Counterterrorism).
[161]*Id.* FBI informed the Committees that the interagency command post briefings occurred in person and included representatives from USCP, MPD, and US Park Police. Email from FBI to Committee staff (June 3, 2021).
[162]Email from FBI Norfolk JTTF Intelligence Analyst to FBI Washington Field Office Intelligence Analyst (Jan. 5, 2021, 6:52 PM) (on file with the Committees). FBI informed the Committees that the FBI Norfolk Field Office drafted, approved, and placed the SIR on an FBI internal case management system at 6:43 p.m. Email from FBI to Committee staff (June 3, 2021).

sent the SIR to law enforcement partners in the National Capital Region, including USCP, MPD, U.S. Park Police, and others, writing only, "[p]lease see the attached SIR released this evening by Norfolk for awareness."[163] As noted above, FBI Washington Field Office officials also briefed the contents of the SIR during an interagency Command Post meeting, which included USCP, MPD, and US Park Police, at 8:00 PM.[164]

Acting MPD Chief Contee criticized the FBI's reliance on email, testifying that the FBI failed to ensure the intelligence was escalated appropriately and arguing that "something of this magnitude" should prompt phone calls immediately.[165] Acting MPD Chief Contee testified, "If there was information about . . . a federal building being overrun . . . I assure you that I would be on the phone directly with the officials that are responsible for the law enforcement response."[166] He added that officials should not "rely[] on technology in the form of an email" and "hope [the information] makes it to where it needs to be."[167]

B. DHS Did Not Produce Any Intelligence Product Specific to January 6

DHS I&A never produced an intelligence product, bulletin, or warning specific to the January 6 Joint Session of Congress.[168] One I&A official informed the Committees that he was "not aware of any known direct threat to the Capitol before January 6," despite many online posts mentioning violence.[169] In briefings with the Committees, I&A officials highlighted the difficulty in discerning credible threats from online bravado and constitutionally protected speech, which limits its collection capabilities.[170] They a sserted, however, that I&A produced

[163] Email from FBI Washington Field Office Intelligence Analyst to Incident Listserv (Jan. 5, 2021, 7:37 PM) (on file with the Committees). *See also Examining the U.S. Capitol Attack – Part II: Joint Hearing Before the S. Comm. on Homeland Sec. & Governmental Affairs and the S. Comm. on Rules & Admin.*, 117th Cong. (2021) (testimony of Jill Sanborn, Ass't Dir., Counterterrorism Div., Fed. Bureau of Investigation) (indicating that the Washington Field Office disseminated the SIR within an hour of receiving it).

[164] *Examining the U.S. Capitol Attack – Part II: Joint Hearing Before the S. Comm. on Homeland Sec. & Governmental Affairs and the S. Comm. on Rules & Admin.*, 117th Cong. (2021) (testimony of Jill Sanborn, FBI Assistant Director, Counterterrorism); Email from FBI to Committee Staff (June 3, 2021).

[165] *Examining the U.S. Capitol Attack: Joint Hearing Before the S. Comm. on Homeland Sec. & Governmental Affairs and the S. Comm. on Rules & Admin.*, 117th Cong. (2021) (testimony of Robert Contee III, Acting Chief, Metro. Police Dep't of the Dist. of Columbia).

[166] *Id.*

[167] *Id.* Ms. Smislova told the Committees that DHS I&A also uses e-mail and online portals to distribute intelligence products. According to her, intelligence agencies are charged with disseminating intelligence, but it is not the agencies' role to ensure anyone acts on the information. DHS Briefing to the Committees (Mar. 31, 2021).

[168] *Examining the U.S. Capitol Attack – Part II: Joint Hearing Before the S. Comm. on Homeland Sec. & Governmental Affairs and the S. Comm. on Rules & Admin.*, 117th Cong. (2021) (testimony of Melissa Smislova, Acting Under Secretary, Office of Intelligence and Analysis, Dep't of Homeland Sec.); *see also* DHS Briefing to the Committees (Mar. 1, 2021).

[169] DHS Briefing to the Committees (Mar. 1, 2021); DHS Briefing to the Committees (Mar. 31, 2021). According to DHS, I&A personnel report on social media posts or other open source activities when (1) it is specific enough to meet a validated intelligence reporting or warning threshold; (2) the analyst reasonably believes it constitutes a "true threats," or would incite violence against, individuals or property; or (3) it would provide analytically significant insights concerning individuals already reasonably believed to pose such a threat to homeland security. DHS officials again stressed the need for analysts to distinguish between credible threats and "mere statements of violence, however hyperbolic, controversial, or coarse." Email from DHS to Committee Staff (June 3, 2021).

[170] *See* DHS Briefing to the Committees (Mar. 1, 2021).

approximately 15 "broad strategic warnings" and assessments relating to domestic violent extremism, including the potential for violence and threats against government officials, buildings, and events related to the 2020 Presidential and general elections and transition period.[171]

The majority of I&A's products were specific to domestic violent extremists' particular methods or targets, such as the targeting of "open-air, publicly accessible" locations or national icons and the use of vehicle ramming.[172] Other reports were broad assessments of key threats to the homeland or the different types of domestic violent extremism. For example, in October 2020, DHS issued the Homeland Threat Assessment; I&A released a related summary of key threats.[173] Domestic terrorism, along with cyber threats, malign influence, threats to U.S. economic security, and exploitation of U.S. academic and research institutions, was among the threats discussed in that document[174] A week before the January 6 attack, I&A released an "Intelligence In Depth" report on the "diverse domestic violent extremist landscape."[175] That report referenced potential violence associated with political grievances and highlighted a number of other domestic violent extremist threats from across the ideological spectrum.[176]

Certain reports did warn of the potential for violent extremists to "quickly mobilize" to commit violence, but those reports did not reveal any intelligence indicators or warnings specific enough to have prompted a stronger security posture by USCP or MPD.[177] The only report containing actionable recommendations was the October 2020 report on vehicle-ramming, which recommended law enforcement consider restricting vehicle access to protest sites.[178] As discussed below, this was among the steps taken by USCP prior to January 6.

While I&A issued reports prior to January 6 that identified government facilities, personnel, and events related to the 2020 general election and political transition period as likely targets of domestic violent extremists, no report specifically identified the Joint Session of Congress or the Capitol.[179]Nevertheless, M elissa Smislova, Acting Under Secretary of I&A,

[171]*See Examining the U.S. Capitol Attack – Part II: Joint Hearing Before the S. Comm. on Homeland Sec. & Governmental Affairs and the S. Comm. on Rules & Admin.*, 117th Cong. (2021) (testimony of Melissa Smislova, Acting Under Secretary, Office of Intelligence and Analysis, Dep't of Homeland Sec.); DHS Briefing to the Committees (Mar. 1, 2021).
[172]*See* IIF – Physical Threats to the 2020 Election Season (Aug. 17, 2020) (on file with the Committees); Substantive Revision IIB – National Icons and Public Statutes (Sept. 29, 2020) (on file with the Committees); IIF – Vehicle Ramming Use at Lawful Protests (Oct. 22, 2020) (on file with the Committees).
[173]*See* U.S. DEP'T OF HOMELAND SEC., HOMELAND THREAT ASSESSMENT (Oct. 6, 2020); IID – Key Threats to the Homeland Through 2021 (Oct. 1, 2020).
[174]*See* U.S. DEP'T OF HOMELAND SEC., *supra* note 173; IID – Key Threats to the Homeland Through 2021 (Oct. 1, 2020).
[175]IID – Diverse DVE Landscape Probably Will Persist (Dec. 30, 2020) (on file with the Committees).
[176]*Id.*
[177]*See, e.g., id.;* IIF – Physical Threats to the 2020 Election Season (Aug. 17, 2020) (on file with the Committees); IIF – Vehicle Ramming Use at Lawful Protests (Oct. 22, 2020) (on file with the Committees).
[178]IIF – Vehicle Ramming Use at Lawful Protests (Oct. 22, 2020) (on file with the Committees).
[179]*See, e.g.*, IID – Diverse DVE Landscape Probably Will Persist (Dec. 30, 2020) (on file with the Committees); IIF – Physical Threats to the 2020 Election Season (Aug. 17, 2020) (on file with the Committees); IIF – Vehicle Ramming Use at Lawful Protests (Oct. 22, 2020) (on file with the Committees).

testified that I&A's reports were sufficiently specific to warn law enforcement partners of the *type of violence* that occurred on January 6:

> I actually in preparation for this hearing did review all of those reports and was impressed with how well the team did. They were very well written and very specific. The point, Senator, is that we thought we had provided that warning. We did not have anything specific about an attack on the Capitol to occur on January 6, so we did not issue a separate report. In hindsight, we probably should have, but we had just issued a report on December 30 with our colleagues at FBI and the National Counterterrorism Center where we had thought . . . that that was sufficient.[180]

She added that it was unclear to her why consumers of I&A's intelligence products "were not better prepared" for the attack.[181] Still, Ms. Smislova pledged to provide better information and intelligence to I&A's partners going forward to allow for strong security preparations.[182]

C. FBI and DHS Did Not Deem Credible Online Posts Calling for Violence at the Capitol

Of the intelligence products DHS and DOJ provided to the Committees, almost all referenced violent extremists' use of online message boards, social media, memes, or hashtags. The majority of these referenced particular threats of violence posted on social media or posts encouraging others to commit violent acts.[183] For example, DHS's October 2020 Homeland Threat Assessment noted that "violent extremist media almost certainly will spread violent extremist ideologies, especially via social media, that encourage violence and influence action within the United States."[184] Further, I&A's December 30, 2020 report on the "diverse domestic violence extremism landscape" stated that "the use of social media to make threats of violence upon which [domestic violent extremists] often do not act" is a limitation on DHS's ability to detect and disrupt domestic violent extremist plots.[185]

When asked how I&A did not identify any of the social media posts calling for attacking the Capitol prior to January 6, one DHS I&A official cautioned that social media is "nuanced" and that it can be difficult to distinguish between mere rhetoric and overt threats.[186] Ms.

[180] *Examining the U.S. Capitol Attack – Part II: Joint Hearing Before the S. Comm. on Homeland Sec. & Governmental Affairs and the S. Comm. on Rules & Admin.*, 117th Cong. (2021) (testimony of Melissa Smislova, Acting Under Secretary, Office of Intelligence and Analysis, Dep't of Homeland Sec.).

[181] *Id. See also* DHS Briefing to the Committees (Mar. 1, 2021) (suggesting that January 6 would certainly be the type of event discussed in I&A's products).

[182] *Examining the U.S. Capitol Attack – Part II: Joint Hearing Before the S. Comm. on Homeland Sec. & Governmental Affairs and the S. Comm. on Rules & Admin.*, 117th Cong. (2021) (testimony of Melissa Smislova, Acting Under Secretary, Office of Intelligence and Analysis, Dep't of Homeland Sec.).

[183] IIF – Physical Threats to the 2020 Election Season 2 (Aug. 17, 2020) (on file with the Committees); Substantive Revision IIB – National Icons and Public Statutes (Sept. 29, 2020) (on file with the Committees).

[184] U.S. DEP'T OF HOMELAND SEC., *supra* note 173, at 17; IID – Key Threats to the Homeland Through 2021 (Oct. 1, 2020).

[185] IID – Diverse DVE Landscape Probably Will Persist 3 (Dec. 30, 2020) (on file with the Committees).

[186] DHS Briefing to the Committees (Mar. 1, 2021).

Smislova also acknowledged shortcomings with the Intelligence Community's current approach to domestic violent extremism, particularly online. She testified to the Committees:

> A lesson learned from the events of January 6th is that distinguishing between those engaged in constitutionally-protected activities from those involved in destructive, violent, and threat-related behavior is a complex challenge. For example, domestic violent extremists may filter or disguise online communications with vague in[n]uendo to protect operational security, avoid violating social media platforms' terms of service, and appeal to a broader pool of potential recruits. Under the guise of the First Amendment, domestic violent extremists recruit supporters, and incite and engage in violence. Further complicating the challenge, these groups migrate to private or closed social media platforms, and encrypted channels to obfuscate their activity. We must develop the tools to overcome this challenge if we are to effectively address the rising levels of violence perpetrated by those who are inspired by domestic extremist ideological beliefs.[187]

Ms. Smislova acknowledged that DHS needs to better understand the domestic violent extremism threat and improve its abilities to counter it:

> We are also working much more focused on applying more resources to better understanding this particular threat. We also are looking at how we can better understand social media to get those tips and maybe get better insight into what this adversary is doing. This is a very difficult threat for us and the Intelligence Community to understand. It will require more partnerships with nontraditional partners and with our standard State and local partners. And you will see that we will reinforce our already good partnership with the FBI. We will do better.[188]

When asked if the FBI was aware of specific conversations on social media calling for violence in the lead up to January 6, Ms. Sanborn testified:

> To my knowledge, no, . . . and I would just sort of articulate why that is. So under our authorities, because being mindful of the First Amendment and our dual-headed mission to uphold the Constitution, we cannot collect First Amendment-protected activities without sort of the next step, which is the intent. And so we would have to have an already predicated investigation that allowed us access to those comms and/or a lead or a tip or a report from a community citizen or a fellow law enforcement partner for us to gather that information.[189]

[187] *Examining the U.S. Capitol Attack – Part II: Joint Hearing Before the S. Comm. on Homeland Sec. & Governmental Affairs and the S. Comm. on Rules & Admin.*, 117th Cong. (2021) (written testimony of Melissa Smislova, Acting Under Secretary, Office of Intelligence and Analysis, Dep't of Homeland Sec.). DHS officials noted that I&A may have identified social media posts calling for violence, but may have been unable to discern them from "bravado or constitutionally protected speech." Email from DHS to the Committees (June 3, 2021).

[188] *Examining the U.S. Capitol Attack – Part II: Joint Hearing Before the S. Comm. on Homeland Sec. & Governmental Affairs and the S. Comm. on Rules & Admin.*, 117th Cong. (2021) (testimony of Melissa Smislova, Acting Under Secretary, Office of Intelligence and Analysis, Dep't of Homeland Sec.).

[189] *Examining the U.S. Capitol Attack – Part II: Joint Hearing Before the S. Comm. on Homeland Sec. & Governmental Affairs and the S. Comm. on Rules & Admin.*, 117th Cong. (2021) (testimony of Jill Sanborn, Ass't

Ms. Sanborn also acknowledged there may be areas for improvement in dissemination of threat information.[190] When asked whether a lack of resources impacted FBI's ability to respond, Ms. Sanborn responded that the issues are twofold. First, she highlighted the challenge of trying to figure out the intent of an individual through the "volume" of rhetoric.[191]Second , she pointed out that the FBI *might* not have the ability to mitigate a threat without a chargeable offense.[192] She noted, however, that FBI did take overt action by talking to individuals the FBI was tracking who intended to come to Washington, D.C. and trying to convince them not to come.[193]

V. USCP DID NOT COMMUNICATE INTELLIGENCE WARNING OF VIOLENCE AT THE CAPITOL ON JANUARY 6

USCP's Intelligence and Interagency Coordination Division ("IICD") possessed information about the potential for violence at the Capitol on January 6, including a plot to breach the Capitol, the online sharing of maps of the Capitol Complex's tunnel systems, and other specific threats of violence. IICD, however, did not convey the full scope of information or assess the threat as likely to occur, which affected USCP's preparations. IICD also issued numerous intelligence products, but none conveyed the full scope of known information about the threat to Congress to USCP leadership, rank-and-file officers, or law enforcement partners.

A. USCP's Decentralized Intelligence Resources

Officials have noted that USCP it is not a collector of intelligence, as defined in Title 50 of the United States Code, but rather a "consumer" of intelligence that relies on the Intelligence Community and law enforcement partners to collect, analyze, and provide it with intelligence information.[194]Nonetheless, USCP has three components responsible for intelligence -related activities. These components use open sources to gather and analyze intelligence, which is

Dir., Counterterrorism Div., Fed. Bureau of Investigation). According to the Attorney General Guidelines for Domestic FBI Operations, the "guidelines do not authorize investigating or collecting or maintaining information on United States persons *solely* for the purpose of monitoring activities protected by the First Amendment or the lawful exercise of other rights secured by the Constitution or laws of the United States." However, the FBI does have existing authority to use open source information as part of its investigative efforts. DEP'T OF JUSTICE, ATTORNEY GENERAL'S GUIDELINES FOR DOMESTIC FBI OPERATIONS 13 (2008) (emphasis added). The FBI informed the Committees that the FBI does have a guiding policy related to reviewing social media, which outlines available investigative methods to collect on social media or other online forums, and varies depending on the level of investigative activity authorized. The FBI stressed that it has safeguards in place to ensure the protection of Constitutional rights. Email from the FBI to the Committees (June 3, 2021).

[190] *Examining the U.S. Capitol Attack – Part II: Joint Hearing Before the S. Comm. on Homeland Sec. & Governmental Affairs and the S. Comm. on Rules & Admin.*, 117th Cong. (2021) (testimony of Jill Sanborn, Ass't Dir., Counterterrorism Div., Fed. Bureau of Investigation).

[191] *Id.*

[192] *Id.*

[193] *Id.*

[194] *E.g.*, *Examining the U.S. Capitol Attack: Joint Hearing Before the S. Comm. on Homeland Sec. & Governmental Affairs and the S. Comm. on Rules & Admin.*, 117th Cong. (2021) (written testimony of Steven Sund, Former Chief, U.S. Capitol Police). *See also* Blanton Interview, *supra* note 48, at 43.

incorporated into written products distributed across USCP, and at times, to law enforcement partners and members of the Capitol Police Board.[195]

USCP's intelligence-related components are the Intelligence and Interagency Coordination Division ("IICD"), the Threat Assessment Section ("TAS"), and the Intelligence Operations Section ("IOS"). All three are organized within USCP's Protective Services Bureau ("PSB"); TAS and IOS are components of PSB's Investigations Division.[196] As mentioned above, Ms. Pittman was the Assistant Chief of Police for Protective and Intelligence Operations on January 6, and in that role oversaw all three of USCP's intelligence-related entities.[197]

[198]

The three intelligence entities interact, collaborate, and provide mission support to one another; however, each has a distinct mission. TAS is responsible for investigating any threat to a Member of Congress.[199] IOS agents are the "boots on the ground" during demonstrations and relay information concerning field activity to IICD, which then reports this information, along with open source information, to USCP commanders.[200]

IICD is the principal point of contact within USCP for the Intelligence Community and coordinates with the law enforcement community at the federal, state, local, and tribal levels to increase the collection and sharing of intelligence information.[201] Among other items, IICD is responsible for (1) maximizing the collection and analysis of all source information and

[195]Pittman Interview (Apr. 20, 2021), *supra* note 8, at 51:10–52:18.

[196]OFFICE OF THE INSPECTOR GEN., U.S. CAPITOL POLICE, REVIEW OF THE EVENTS SURROUNDING THE JANUARY 6, 2021 TAKEOVER OF THE U.S. CAPITOL – REPORT 2021-I-0003-C 2–3 (Feb. 2021) (on file with the Committees) [hereinafter USCP OIG FLASH REPORT 3].

[197]U.S. CAPITOL POLICE, COMMAND STAFF ON JANUARY 6, 2021 (on file with the Committees); Pittman Interview (Apr. 20, 2021), *supra* note 8.

[198]USCP OIG FLASH REPORT 3, *supra* note 196, at 3.

[199]*Id.* at 4.

[200]OFFICE OF THE INSPECTOR GEN., U.S. CAPITOL POLICE, REVIEW OF THE EVENTS SURROUNDING THE JANUARY 6, 2021 TAKEOVER OF THE U.S. CAPITOL – REPORT 2021-I-0003-A 2–3 (Feb. 2021) (on file with the Committees) [hereinafter USCP OIG FLASH REPORT 1].

[201]*Id.* at 3.

intelligence; (2) identifying potential threats; (3) disseminating products and reports on events and incidents of interest to, or that may impact, the U.S. Capitol, the legislative process, Members, staff, or visitors; and (4) briefing USCP leadership on threats.[202] IICD is small in terms of resources. Mr. Sund testified that IICD is comprised of approximately thirty to thirty-five analysts, who had been operating in a 24/7 posture since November 2020.[203] A review of USCP's employee roster as of January 6, however, found fourteen individuals listed within IICD, including the Director.[204] By comparison, IOS had twenty-four employees and TAS had thirty-three employees.[205]

As of January 6, IICD produced three key written products: (1) special event assessments, (2) daily intelligence reports, and (3) information reports. Before any major event, IICD prepares a special event assessment, which contains: (a) a Bottom Line Up Front detailing the key takeaways of the assessment; (b) an event summary; (c) detail on expected protests; (d) a threat assessment; and (e) IICD's overall analysis.[206] Daily intelligence reports ("DIRs"), by contrast, provide an overview of scheduled events, such as Committee hearings, Congressional events, and demonstration activities, and monitor relevant issues, including suspicious activity reports and domestic and international affairs.[207] Each scheduled event is assigned a "level of probability of acts of civil disobedience/arrests occurring based on current intelligence information."[208] The level of probability ranges from "remote" to "nearly certain."[209]

Remote	Highly Improbable	Improbable	Roughly Even Odds	Probable	Highly Probable	Nearly Certain
-	-	-	-	-	-	-
1 – 5%	5 – 20%	20 – 45%	45 – 55%	55 – 80%	80 – 95%	95 – 99%

[210]

The DIR also tracks DHS's National Terrorism Advisory System Level.[211] The last category of products, information papers and reports, are intended to draw attention to a particular event or security issue.[212]

202 *Id.*
203 *Examining the U.S. Capitol Attack: Joint Hearing Before the S. Comm. on Homeland Sec. & Governmental Affairs and the S. Comm. on Rules & Admin.*, 117th Cong. (2021) (testimony of Steven Sund, Former Chief, U.S. Capitol Police); OFFICE OF THE INSPECTOR GEN., U.S. CAPITOL POLICE, REVIEW OF THE EVENTS SURROUNDING THE JANUARY 6, 2021 TAKEOVER OF THE U.S. CAPITOL – REPORT 2021-I-0003-B 20 (Mar. 2021) (on file with the Committees) [hereinafter USCP OIG FLASH REPORT 2].
204 U.S. CAPITOL POLICE, ROSTER OF EMPLOYEES FOR PAY PERIOD COVER 01.06.2021 (on file with the Committees).
205 *Id.*
206 Joint Committee Briefing with Yogananda Pittman, Acting Chief, U.S. Capitol Police (Feb. 18, 2021). *See also* INTELLIGENCE & INTERAGENCY COORDINATION DIV., U.S. CAPITOL POLICE, SPECIAL EVENT ASSESSMENT 21-A-0468 (Dec. 16, 2020).
207 *See, e.g.*, INTELLIGENCE & INTERAGENCY COORDINATION DIV., U.S. CAPITOL POLICE, DAILY INTELLIGENCE REPORT (Jan. 6, 2021).
208 *See, e.g.*, *id.*
209 *See, e.g.*, *id.*
210 *See, e.g.*, *id.*
211 *See, e.g.*, *id.*
212 Pittman Interview (Apr. 22, 2021), *supra* note 20, at 55:7–15.

Although IICD's, TAS's, and IOS's responsibilities intersect, the distribution of resources across these entities creates challenges, including the timely sharing of relevant intelligence and a lack of coordination within the agency and with law enforcement partners.[213]

B. USCP Was Warned of the Likelihood of Violence on January 6

IICD was aware of the potential for violence at the Capitol on January 6 through social media posts, monitoring of relevant websites, and warnings from private citizens. Internal records and USCP officials' testimony confirm that USCP began gathering information about events planned for January 6, 2021 as soon as demonstrations to protest the Electoral College vote certification were announced in mid-December 2020. IICD analysts completed a first special event assessment on December 16, 2020 and updated the assessment on three occasions to include new information, such as recently collected intelligence and approved demonstration activity. Although these special event assessments captured some of the intelligence available about the potential for violence, none conveyed the breadth of information that IICD possessed at the time.

1. IICD Anticipated Protests Related to the Joint Session in Mid-December 2020

On December 11, IICD Director John Donohue anticipated a challenge to the electoral vote from a few Members of Congress and requested a preliminary assessment for the January 6 Joint Session of Congress.[214] Director Donohue also requested a private company that monitors social media to set an alert for the phrase, "Joint Session of Congress."[215] On December 14, Sean Gallagher, Deputy Chief for the PSB, alerted Mr. Sund and Ms. Pittman that the Joint Session on January 6 "will bring some demonstrations, with the potential for some issues on the House floor."[216] Mr. Sund responded, "Considering a significant deployment."[217]

IICD issued the first iteration of the Special Event Assessment ("Special Assessment") for the Joint Session of Congress on December 16, 2020.[218] The December 16Special Assessment indicated that USCP was aware of only two planned protests—one by a pro-Trump group and the other by a pro-Biden group.[219] The Special Assessment noted that there were no specific known threats to the Joint Session and that there were "NO social media indications for

[213]USCP OIG FLASH REPORT 1, *supra* note 200, at 8–9. The Intelligence Operations Section is within the Protective Services Bureau and is distinct from IICD. *Id.* at 2.

[214]Email from John Donohue, U.S. Capitol Police, to IICD Research Specialist (Dec. 11, 2020, 8:42 AM) (on file with the Committees).

[215]Email from John Donohue, U.S. Capitol Police, to IICD Research Specialist (Dec. 16, 2020, 8:56 AM) (on file with the Committees).

[216]Email from Sean Gallagher, U.S. Capitol Police, to Yogananda Pittman, U.S. Capitol Police, et al., forwarded to Steven Sund, U.S. Capitol Police (Dec. 14, 2020, 4:22 PM) (on file with the Committees).

[217]Email from Steven Sund, U.S. Capitol Police, to Yogananda Pittman, U.S. Capitol Police, (Dec. 14, 2020, 9:19 PM) (on file with the Committees).

[218]INTELLIGENCE & INTERAGENCY COORDINATION DIV., U.S. CAPITOL POLICE, SPECIAL EVENT ASSESSMENT 21-A-0468 (Dec. 16, 2020).

[219]*Id.*

specific threats or concerning comments directed at the Joint Session of Congress."[220]It did acknowledge, however, "the threat of disruptive actions or violence cannot be ruled out."[221] The overall analysis concluded, "At this time there are no specific known threats related to the Joint Session of Congress - Electoral College Vote Certification."[222]

In the subsequent days, members of IICD continued to prepare for the Joint Session by collecting and receiving intelligence about the growing possibility of armed protestors and likelihood of violence. Internal records reflect that on December 19, IICD learned about President Trump's tweet, "Big protest in D.C. on January 6th. Be there, will be wild!"[223] IICD also received information about a Million MAGA March tweet, "January 6 - This will be the Biggest Protest in American History," and a Parler post stating, in substance, "Occupy DC, Congress, SCOTUS, WH."[224]

On December 21, MPD circulated an email to law enforcement partners, including USCP, flagging a Million MAGA March tweet—"This is the big one! Donald Trump is calling for this March himself."[225] MPD warned, "it looks like we are going to have another big First Amendment demo on January 6thsimilar to the November 14thand December 12thevent s" and noted that permit applications had already been submitted.[226]

2. IICD Issued an Investigative Research and Analysis Report on Threats to the Tunnels

On December 21, IICD also issued a seven-page "Investigative Research and Analysis Report" (the "December 21 IICD Report") highlighting the blog thedonald.win, which referenced tunnels on Capitol grounds used by Members of Congress.[227] The report highlighted the following blog post: "There are tunnels connected to the Capitol Building! Legislators use them to avoid press, among other things! Take note."[228] The December 21 IICD Report also listed "Patriot Organizations" expected to participate in events on January 6, including Proud Boys, Oath Keepers, and Stop the Steal, and listed "Secure Communications" likely to be used, including Signal and Wickr.[229]

[220]*Id.*
[221]*Id.*
[222]*Id.*
[223]Email from U.S. Capitol Police Intelligence Operations Official to Sergeant at Arms Official, et al. (Dec. 19, 2020, 11:33 AM) (on file with the Committees); Donald J. Trump (@realDonaldTrump), TWITTER (Dec. 19, 2020), https://twitter.com/realDonaldTrump/status/1340185773220515840.
[224]Email from National Park Service Official to Metro. Police Dep't of the Dist. Of Columbia Official et al. (Dec. 19, 2020, 10:41AM) (on file with the Committees); Email from U.S. Capitol Police Intelligence Operations Private to U.S. Capitol Police Intelligence Operations Section Inbox (Dec. 19, 2020, 2:03 PM) (on file with the Committees).
[225]Email from Metro. Police Dep't of the Dist. Of Columbia Official to John Donohue, U.S. Capitol Police, et al. (Dec. 21, 2020, 8:04 AM) (on file with the Committees).
[226]*Id.*
[227]INTELLIGENCE & INTERAGENCY COORDINATION DIV., U.S. CAPITOL POLICE, INVESTIGATIVE RESEARCH AND ANALYSIS REPORT #21-TD-159 (Dec. 21, 2020).
[228]*Id.*
[229]*Id.*

The December 21 IICD Report attached a map of the Capitol campus that was posted to the blog and noted: "several comments promote confronting members of Congress and carrying firearms during the protest."[230] It flagged approximately thirty screen shots of comments on the website, including:

- "Exactly, forget the tunnels. Get into Capitol Building, stand outside congress. Be in the room next to them. They wont have time [to] run if they play dumb."

- "Deploy Capitol Police to restrict movement. Anyone going armed needs to be mentally prepared to draw down on LEOs. Let them shoot first, but make sure they know what happens if they do."

- "If they don't show up, we enter the Capitol as the Third Continental Congress and certify the Trump Electors."

- "Bring guns. It's now or never."

- "If a million patriots who up bristling with AR's, just how brave do you think they'll be when it comes to enforcing their unconstitutional laws? Don't cuck out. This is do or die. Bring your guns."

- "Surround every building with a tunnel entrance/exit. They better dig a tunnel all the way to China if they want to escape."[231]

According to Ms. Pittman, this report was distributed only to "command staff," including the deputy chiefs and assistant chiefs.[232]

IICD members continued to work on updating the Special Assessment, given that "[s]ocial media ha[d] exploded . . . with information about January 6th events."[233] On December 22, IICD received significant information about the rising likelihood of violence, including an email with the subject line: "Threats to bring guns into DC," which included the same pages from the blog, thedonald.win, and another email with the subject line: "Video promotes armed protests in DC."[234] The latter email, written to the Assistant Director of IICD, summarized a video of Sam Andrews, a former leader of the Missouri branch of Oath Keepers, and a report on the website the Hagmann Report that described Mr. Andrews as encouraging "armed conflict during the protest" on January 6, 2021.[235]

On December 23, IICD also followed up on a call from a private citizen monitoring Twitter who warned "multiple messages show that people intend to bring weapons to the Capitol

[230] *Id.*
[231] *Id.*
[232] Pittman Interview (Apr. 20, 2021), *supra* note 8, at 72:4–15.
[233] Email from IICD Official to IICD Official et al. (Dec. 22, 2020, 3:13 PM) (on file with the Committees).
[234] Email from Intelligence Operations Official to Intelligence Operations Official (Dec. 22, 2020, 10:46 AM) (on file with the Committees); Email from IICD Official to IICD Official (Dec. 22, 2020, 1:46 PM) (on file with the Committees).
[235] Email from IICD Official to IICD Official (Dec. 22, 2020, 1:46 PM) (on file with the Committees).

on January 6th."[236] In addition, IICD received an email from an intelligence analyst at the D.C. Homeland Security and Emergency Management Agency, following up on a threat report titled, "User in Far-Right Chat group threatens to 'shoot and kill' counter protestors."[237] The email linked to threads containing "threats towards the US Congress and elected officials."[238]

3. IICD Revised the Special Assessment, but Did Not Incorporate All Available Threat Information

Despite IICD's knowledge about the growing threat of violence on January 6, the December 23 Special Assessment's overall analysis read identical to the December 16 version. It concluded that there was "no information regarding specific disruptions or acts of civil disobedience targeting this function."[239]Although the " Bottom Line Up Front" noted that protestors indicated they planned to be armed, there was no reference to the December 21 IICD Report mentioning thedonald.win blog or access to tunnels on the Capitol campus.[240] In fact, IICD concluded that "[t]he protests/rallies [were] expected to be similar to the previous Million MAGA March rallies in November and December 2020."[241] The December 23 Special Assessment also found that "[d]ue to the tense political environment following the 2020 election, the threat of disruptive actions or violence cannot be ruled out. Actions of individuals or small groups are generally not broadcast publicly making them impossible to detect."[242]

When asked about the inconsistency between the December 23 Special Assessment and the information in IICD's possession at the time, Ms. Pittman acknowledged that there was a discrepancy but could not explain why the discrepancy existed:

> I cannot go into detail without having further discussions with those individuals [who wrote the reports]. I think that [at] U.S. Capitol Police, my focus was always on the January 3rd and final assessment. However, . . . we know that there are several lessons to be learned for making sure that there is not conflicting information, regardless of which version of the assessment is distributed.[243]

[236]Email from U.S. Capitol Police Operations Inbox to U.S. Capitol Police Threats Inbox (Dec. 22, 2020, 7:31 PM) (copying Sean Gallagher, Deputy Chief, Protective Services Bureau, U.S. Capitol Police) (on file with the Committees).

[237]Email from Dist. of Columbia Homeland Sec. & Emergency Mgmt. Agency Official to Protective Services Bureau Official (Dec. 23, 2020, 7:47 AM) (on file with the Committees).

[238]*Id.*

[239]INTELLIGENCE & INTERAGENCY COORDINATION DIV., U.S. CAPITOL POLICE, SPECIAL EVENT ASSESSMENT 21-A-0468 V.2 (Dec. 23, 2020).

[240]*Id. See also* USCP OIG FLASH REPORT 2, *supra* note 203, at 24. The Flash Report further states that "the IICD Assistant Director recalled discussions with PSB officials about the tunnels and the context of the report and stated that IICD mentioned 'donald.win' in its special event assessment but didn't mention tunnels. The IICD Assistant Director thought that may be because they were not contemplating anyone breaking into the tunnels." USCP OIG FLASH REPORT 2, *supra* note 203, at 24.

[241]INTELLIGENCE & INTERAGENCY COORDINATION DIV., U.S. CAPITOL POLICE, SPECIAL EVENT ASSESSMENT 21-A-0468 V.2 (Dec. 23, 2020).

[242]*Id.*

[243]Pittman Interview (Apr. 20, 2021), *supra* note 8, at 75:12–76:6.

On December 23, MPD's Intelligence Branch alerted Mr. Sund that a website named "wildprotest.com" had just "popped up for the January 6th event."[244] Mr. Sund was assured by Deputy Chief Gallagher that the "Team [was] tracking already."[245]

On December 28, an individual emailed the general mailbox of USCP's Public Information Office and warned about "countless tweets from Trump supporters saying they will be armed on January 6th" and "tweets from people organizing to 'storm the Capitol' on January 6th."[246]

4. IICD's December 30 Special Assessment Made Few Substantive Changes

As with the earlier iterations, the December 30 Special Assessment did not capture the rising likelihood of violence that was known to IICD. In fact, the December 30 Special Assessment contained the same "Bottom Line Up Front" and overall analysis as the two prior assessments.[247] Notably, in discussing the expected protests, the December 30 Special Assessment stated, "no group is expected to march and all are planning to stay in their designated areas."[248] In addition, IICD "identified more than forty social media postings promoting protests on January 6, 2021. The number of people who indicate they are going to the event listed on these social media postings is relatively low."[249] The Assessment, however, also cited data from MPD that showed a "60%-100% increase in [hotel] bookings compared to bookings for the weekend of December 12, 2020."[250] Yet, the December 30 Assessment continued to assert that the "protests [we]re expected to be similar to the previous Million MAGA March rallies in November and December 2020."[251]

5. Aware of Their Intent to Protest, IICD Prepared an Information Paper on the Proud Boys

IICD continued to receive warnings from private citizens, companies, and partners about the increasing likelihood of violence. On January 1, IICD received a warning via its tip line that "there [were] detailed plans to storm federal buildings."[252] In addition, IICD received reports that members of the Proud Boys expected to be in D.C. on January 6. Mr. Donohue asked his staff to "update" an Information Paper on the Proud Boys.[253] The report highlighted that the

[244]Email from Steven A. Sund, Chief, U.S. Capitol Police, to Sean P. Gallagher, Chad Thomas, Yogananda Pittman, U.S. Capitol Police (Dec. 23, 2020, 9:08 PM) (on file with the Committees).
[245]*Id.*
[246]Email from Private Citizen to U.S. Capitol Police Public Information Office Inbox, (Dec. 28, 2020, 11:43 AM) (on file with the Committees).
[247]INTELLIGENCE & INTERAGENCY COORDINATION DIV., U.S. CAPITOL POLICE, SPECIAL EVENT ASSESSMENT 21-A-0468 v.2 (Dec. 30, 2020).
[248]*Id.*
[249]*Id.*
[250]*Id.*
[251]*Id.*
[252]Email from Metro. Police Dep't of the Dist. of Columbia Official to National Park Service Official et al. (Jan. 1, 2021, 10:43 PM) (on file with the Committees).
[253]Email from John Donohue, U.S. Capitol Police, to IICD Official (Jan. 3, 2021, 3:43 PM) (on file with the Committees).

Proud Boys "frequently engage in violence against left-wing protestors" and that the "presence of Proud Boys at a protest increases the likelihood of violence. Officers should remain vigilant at all times as even peaceful demonstrations can quickly devolve into violent confrontations."[254]

Notably, although this six-page report profiled the Proud Boys, they were not mentioned in any detail in the January 3 Special Assessment, other than that "the Proud Boys (who intend to wear plainclothes and not their traditional yellow and black clothing), white supremacist groups, Antifa, and other extremist groups will rally on January 6, 2021."[255]This Information Paper was distributed to all USCP employees and members of the Capitol Police Board, according to Ms. Pittman.[256] One USCP Inspector, however, told the Committees that he did not recall seeing the Information Paper prior to January 6.[257]

6. IICD Issued Its Final Special Assessment on January 3

On January 3, IICD issued its final, 15-page Special Assessment for the Joint Session. As was the case with the prior assessments, the "Bottom Line Up Front" was not changed to capture the seriousness of the threat known at the time. It noted that several protests were expected on January 6, both on the Capitol grounds and across Washington, D.C.; that "some protestors have indicated they plan to be armed"; and that "white supremacist groups may be attending."[258] An overview of the expected protests highlighted that they would be similar to previous rallies and that protestors would remain in their designated areas.[259] After numerous pages detailing the location of expected protests and traffic closures and at the end of the document, IICD's overall analysis contained a starker warning:

> Due to the tense political environment following the 2020 election, the threat of disruptive actions or violence cannot be ruled out. Supporters of the current president see January 6, 2021, as the last opportunity to overturn the results of the presidential election. **This sense of desperation and disappointment may lead to more of an incentive to become violent.** Unlike previous post-election protests, the targets of the pro-Trump supporters are not necessarily the counter-protesters as they were previously, **but rather Congress itself is the target on the 6th**. As outlined above, there has been a worrisome call for protesters to come to these events armed and **there is the possibility that protesters may be inclined to become violent.** Further, unlike the events on November 14, 2020, and December 12, 2020, there are several more protests scheduled on January 6, 2021, and the majority of them will be on Capitol grounds. The two protests expected to be the largest of the day—the Women for America First protest at the Ellipse and the Stop

[254]INTELLIGENCE & INTERAGENCY COORDINATION DIV., U.S. CAPITOL POLICE, INFORMATION PAPER #21-A-0594: THE PROUD BOYS (Jan. 3, 2021).

[255]INTELLIGENCE & INTERAGENCY COORDINATION DIV., U.S. CAPITOL POLICE, SPECIAL EVENT ASSESSMENT 21-A-0468 v.3 2 (Jan. 3, 2021) (internal citations omitted) (on file with the Committees).

[256]Pittman Interview (Apr. 22, 2021), *supra* note 20, at 8:3–9.

[257]Joint Committee Interview with USCP Inspector (May 27, 2021).

[258]INTELLIGENCE & INTERAGENCY COORDINATION DIV., U.S. CAPITOL POLICE, SPECIAL EVENT ASSESSMENT 21-A-0468 v.3 (Jan. 3, 2021) (on file with the Committees).

[259]*Id.*

the Steal protest in Areas 8 and 9—**may draw thousands of participants** and both have been promoted by President Trump himself. The Stop the Steal protest in particular does not have a permit, but several high profile speakers, including Members of Congress are expected to speak at the event. **This combined with Stop the Steal's propensity to attract white supremacists, militia members, and others who actively promote violence, may lead to a significantly dangerous situation for law enforcement and the general public alike.**[260]

7. IICD Continued to Release Daily Intelligence Reports That Did Not Align with the Final Special Assessment

In the days following the issuance of the January 3 Special Assessment, IICD issued three DIRs—none of which reflected the likelihood of violence described in the January 3 Special Assessment or more broadly known within IICD. In fact, the January 4, January 5, and January 6 DIRs assessed the probability of acts of civil disobedience from the planned protests across all of Washington, D.C. as "Remote" to "Improbable."[261] Regarding a "Million MAGA March/US Capitol," the report assigned a probability of "Improbable," adding as context, "it [is] possible the Million Magi [sic] March folks could organize a demonstration on USCP grounds. Women for America First has permitted on USCP grounds and Freedom Plaza parade permit through MPD and has been the permitted portion of previous Million MAGA Marches."[262] The Stop the Steal event was assigned a probability of "Highly Improbable" given that "no further information has been found to the exact actions planned by this group."[263] The Women for America First event planned for the Ellipse also received a "Highly Improbable" rating, but the report contained no explanation or context as to why this rating was assigned.[264]

It is clear that IICD intelligence products, in particular the January 3 Special Assessment analysis that "Congress itself is the target on the 6th" and its warning about the "significantly dangerous situation for law enforcement and the general public alike," were not incorporated in subsequent intelligence documents. One explanation given to the Committees for why the

[260]*Id.* (emphasis added).
[261]Letter from Steven Sund, Former Chief, U.S. Capitol Police, to Nancy Pelosi, Speaker of the House of Representatives (Feb. 1, 2021).
[262]INTELLIGENCE & INTERAGENCY COORDINATION DIV., U.S. CAPITOL POLICE, DAILY INTELLIGENCE REPORT (Jan. 6, 2021) (on file with the Committees). To demonstrate on Capitol grounds, individuals or groups must submit a permit to and receive approval from USCP's Special Event Section, a component of USCP's Command and Coordination Bureau within the Uniformed Operations function. The Special Events Section approved six permits for January 6, each with a limit of 50 participants due to the COVID-19 pandemic. Pittman Interview (Apr. 20, 2021), *supra* note 8, at 37:10–25. IICD's Assistant Director expressed her concerns about certain permits to an Executive Officer in the Protective Services Bureau, noting that "the permit requests . . . are being used as proxies for Stop the Steal" and "may also be involved with organizations that may be planning trouble on [January 6]." Email from IICD Official to Protective Services Bureau Official (Dec. 31, 2020, 6:00 PM) (on file with the Committees). Ms. Pittman acknowledged she was aware of the concern, but she believed IICD vetted the permit requests and confirmed that the groups who had been granted permits were not affiliated with Stop the Steal. Pittman Interview (Apr. 20, 2021), *supra* note 8, at 79:1–19.
[263]*See, e.g.*, INTELLIGENCE & INTERAGENCY COORDINATION DIV., U.S. CAPITOL POLICE, DAILY INTELLIGENCE REPORT (Jan. 6, 2021).
[264]*See, e.g.*, *id.*

January 3 Special Assessment was not incorporated into the DIRs is because a single analyst prepared and disseminated the DIRs without supervisory review.[265]

C. USCP Issued Conflicting Intelligence Products in the Days Leading Up To and on January 6

Inconsistencies between intelligence products, and within the January 3 Special Assessment, led to a lack of consensus about the gravity of the threat posed on January 6, 2021. As the USCP Inspector General noted, if one "does not read the [January 3 Special Assessment] in its entirety, they could draw an inaccurate conclusion since the [Bottom Line Up Front section] is not consistent with the rest of the document."[266] One USCP Inspector expressed concern that the warnings of violence were only included at the end of the assessment, and that they appeared inconsistent with the "Bottom Line Up Front" section.[267]

Ms. Pittman did not acknowledge the internal inconsistencies, telling the Committees that she believes "anyone assessing the report would have to read the report in its entirety."[268] When pressed on whether the "Bottom Line Up Front" section captured the known likelihood of violence, as detailed in later sections of the January 3 Special Assessment, Ms. Pittman responded, "I think the report itself captures what [IICD] was trying to share with [USCP] in terms of what we may have been facing regarding the violence."[269]

To this point, the warning in the January 3 Special Assessment that the January 6 event would not be similar to prior marches appears to have been lost on USCP leadership. The January 3 Special Assessment specifically noted: (1) "**Unlike previous post-election protests**, the targets of the pro-Trump supporters are not necessarily the counter-protesters as they were previously, but rather Congress itself is the target on the 6th," and (2) "**unlike the events on November 14, 2020, and December 12, 2020**, there are several more protests scheduled on January 6, 2021, and the majority of them will be on Capitol grounds."[270]

Ms. Pittman's written statement to the House Appropriations Committee further clarifies this point:

> Based on the assessment, [USCP] understood that this demonstration would be unlike the previous demonstrations held by protesters with similar ideologies in November and December 2020. The first and second "MAGA marches" were intended to put public pressure on states where vote counting was ongoing and on the Supreme Court to intervene in the election. This event was different because all judicial remedies for opposing election results had been exhausted and the only

[265]USCP OIG FLASH REPORT 1, *supra* note 200, at 12. Acting Chief Pittman told the Committees that, since January 6, IICD has eliminated the DIRs. Pittman Interview (Apr. 22, 2021), *supra* note 20, at 28:19–20.
[266]USCP OIG FLASH REPORT 2, *supra* note 203, at 26.
[267]Joint Committee Interview with USCP Inspector (May 27, 2021).
[268]Pittman Interview (Apr. 22, 2021), *supra* note 20, at 20:21–21:7.
[269]*Id.*
[270]INTELLIGENCE & INTERAGENCY COORDINATION DIV., U.S. CAPITOL POLICE, SPECIAL EVENT ASSESSMENT 21-A-0468 V.3 (Jan. 3, 2021) (emphasis added) (on file with the Committees).

way for their candidate to win was for Congress to reject the Electoral College results. Thus, the scheduled demonstrations were intended to pressure Congress.[271]

Despite the clear distinctions between the threat assessments for January 6 and the earlier Million MAGA Marches, Mr. Sund's testimony to the Committees and his February 1 letter to Speaker Pelosi focused on the January 3 Special Assessment and the DIR's threat assessment language that anticipated similarities between January 6 and the prior events:

> As previously mentioned, the IICD intelligence assessment indicated that the January 6 protests/rallies were "expected to be similar to the previous Million MAGA March rallies in November and December 2020, which drew tens of thousands of participants." The assessment indicated that members of the Proud Boys, white supremacist groups, Antifa, and other extremist groups were expected to participate in the January 6th event and that they may be inclined to become violent. This was very similar to the intelligence assessment of the December 12, 2020, MAGA II event. In addition, on Monday, January 4, 2021, the USCP IICD published the Daily Intelligence Report which provided an assessment of all of the groups expected to demonstrate on January 6, 2021. The IICD Daily Intelligence Report assessed "the level of probability of acts of civil disobedience/arrests occurring based on current intelligence information," as "Remote" to "Improbable" for all of the groups expected to demonstrate on Wednesday, January 6, 2021. In addition, the Daily Intelligence report indicated that "The Secretary of Homeland Security has not issued an elevated or imminent alert at this time . . . ."[272]

Similarly, during the February 23 hearing, Mr. Sund described the information possessed by IICD as "very similar to the previous assessments. It was just a little bit more detailed."[273] During the hearing Senator Leahy, in reference to the January 3 Special Assessment, asked Mr. Sund, "How much more intelligence did we need than that?" Mr. Sund responded:

> Yes, sir, that is correct. That is what the intelligence assessment said. It was very similar to the intelligence assessments that we had for the November and December MAGA marches. The intelligence assessments that we had developed for the January 6 event all the way up until January 6 were all saying very much the same thing, and that is what we had planned for. We had planned for the possibility of violence, the possibility of some people being armed, not the possibility of a coordinated military style attack involving thousands against the Capitol.[274]

[271] *U.S. Capitol Police and House Sergeant at Arms, Security Failures on January 6: Hearing before the Legis. Branch Subcomm. of the H. Appropriations Comm.*, 117th Cong. (2021) (written testimony of Yogananda Pittman, Acting Chief, U.S. Capitol Police).
[272] *Examining the U.S. Capitol Attack: Joint Hearing Before the S. Comm. on Homeland Sec. & Governmental Affairs and the S. Comm. on Rules & Admin.*, 117th Cong. (2021) (written testimony of Steven Sund, Former Chief, U.S. Capitol Police).
[273] *Examining the U.S. Capitol Attack: Joint Hearing Before the S. Comm. on Homeland Sec. & Governmental Affairs and the S. Comm. on Rules & Admin.*, 117th Cong. (2021) (testimony of Steven Sund, Former Chief, U.S. Capitol Police).
[274] *Id.*

Significantly, the January 3 Special Assessment does not appear to have informed other key decision makers' perspectives. For example, Mr. Irving told the Committees, "[e]very Capitol Police daily intelligence report between January 4 and January 6, including on January 6, forecast the chance of civil disobedience or arrests during the protests as 'remote to improbable.' I relied on that intelligence when overseeing the security plan put forth by Chief Sund."[275] Former Secretary of the Army Ryan McCarthy echoed this sentiment: "the intelligence that [DOD] received was that there was no real major difference" expected between January 6 and the earlier MAGA marches.[276]DOD planning documents referenced that Proud Boys and ANTIFA members planned to attend and "confront each other" and that there was "no indication" that Oath Keepers or other militia were planning to attend the event.[277]

Months following the attack on the U.S. Capitol, there is still no consensus among USCP officials about the intelligence reports' threat analysis ahead of January 6, 2021. On January 26, Ms. Pittman testified that USCP was aware there was a "strong potential" for violence, despite IICD's DIR assessment of a low probability for civil disobedience or violence at the January 6 planned demonstrations:

> Let me be clear: [USCP] should have been more prepared for this attack. By January 4th, [USCP] knew that the January 6th event would not be like any of the previous protests held in 2020. We knew that militia groups and white supremacist[] organizations would be attending. We also knew that some of these participants were intending to bring firearms and other weapons to the event.
> We knew that there was a strong potential for violence and that Congress was the target.[278]

However, Ms. Pittman testified on February 25 that neither USCP's January 3 Special Assessment nor any intelligence received from intelligence or law enforcement partners contained a specific, credible threat that thousands of protestors would descend on the Capitol with the intent to disrupt the Electoral College vote certification.[279] The variations in Ms. Pittman's testimony reflect the lack of consensus about whether the available intelligence information contained specific threats. As the USCP Inspector General testified, "[c]ertain officials believed USCP intelligence products indicated there may be threats but did not identify

[275]*Examining the U.S. Capitol Attack: Joint Hearing Before the S. Comm. on Homeland Sec. & Governmental Affairs and the S. Comm. on Rules & Admin.*, 117th Cong. (2021) (testimony of Paul Irving, Former Sergeant at Arms, U.S. House of Representatives). Notably, Ms. Pittman did not believe that the DIRs were shared outside of USCP leadership. *See* Pittman Interview (Apr. 22, 2021), *supra* note 20, at 30:12–21.
[276]Joint Committee Interview of Ryan McCarthy, Former Sec'y, Dep't of the Army, Dep't of Def., 25:15–16 (Apr. 6, 2021) [hereinafter McCarthy Interview]; DIST. OF COLUMBIA NAT'L GUARD, 5–7 JANUARY 2021 SUPPORT PLAN (Dec. 31, 2020); DIST. OF COLUMBIA NAT'L GUARD, 5–7 JANUARY 2021 SUPPORT PLAN (Jan. 2, 2021).
[277]DIST. OF COLUMBIA NAT'L GUARD, 5–7 JANUARY 2021 SUPPORT PLAN (Dec. 31, 2020); DIST. OF COLUMBIA NAT'L GUARD, 5–7 JANUARY 2021 SUPPORT PLAN (Jan. 2, 2021).
[278]Closed Door Briefing to the H. Appropriations Comm. (Jan. 26, 2021) (written statement of Yogananda Pittman, Acting Chief, U.S. Capitol Police).
[279]*U.S. Capitol Police and House Sergeant at Arms, Security Failures on January 6: Hearing before the Legis. Branch Subcomm. of the H. Appropriations Comm.*, 117th Cong. (2021) (written testimony of Yogananda Pittman, Acting Chief, U.S. Capitol Police).

anything specific, while other officials believed it would be inaccurate to state that there were no known specific threats to the Joint Session based on those same USCP intelligence products."[280]

D. Other USCP Intelligence Entities and Employees Received Information about Potential Threats to the Capitol from the FBI, But Did Not Share This Information with IICD or USCP Leadership

As discussed above, on January 5, the FBI's Norfolk Field Office disseminated a SIR that warned of online discussions of potential violence on January 6.[281] Specifically, the SIR highlighted a particular thread stating, "Be Ready to Fight. Congress needs to hear glass breaking, doors being kicked in, and blood from their BLM and Pantifa slave soldiers being spilled. Get violent . . . stop calling this a march, or rally, or a protest. Go there ready for war . . . ."[282] FBI's Norfolk Field Office transmitted that report to the FBI Washington Field Office at 6:52 p.m. on January 5.[283] The Norfolk intelligence analyst described the SIR as relating to "potential criminal activities in the Washington DC area planned for tomorrow (01/06)."[284] At 7:37 p.m., an intelligence analyst with FBI's Washington Field Office sent the SIR to a list serve of partners in the National Capital Region, writing only, "[p]lease see the attached SIR released this evening by Norfolk for awareness."[285]

The USCP Inspector General concluded that a USCP analyst embedded with the FBI Joint Terrorism Task Force retrieved a copy of the SIR from an FBI intranet system.[286] Records provided to the Committees show that the analyst, an employee within IOS—not IICD— received the SIR via the FBI Washington Field Office's email.[287] In a February briefing with the Committees, Ms. Pittman indicated that the USCP analyst forwarded the report to his supervisor, but it was not further circulated.[288] Mr. Sund testified to the same account.[289] The USCP Inspector General, however, concluded that the USCP analyst emailed the SIR to an IOS

[280]*Oversight of the United States Capitol Police and Preparations for and Response to the Attack of January 6th: Hearing before the H. Comm. on Administration*, 117th Cong. (2021) (testimony of Michael A. Bolton, Inspector Gen., U.S. Capitol Police).
[281]*See Examining the U.S. Capitol Attack – Part II: Joint Hearing Before the S. Comm. on Homeland Sec. & Governmental Affairs and the S. Comm. on Rules & Admin.*, 117th Cong. (2021) (testimony of Jill Sanborn, Ass't Dir., Counterterrorism Div., Fed. Bureau of Investigation).
[282]FBI_SIR_000001–2. *See also* Barrett & Zapotosky, *supra* note 159.
[283]Email from FBI Norfolk JTTF Intelligence Analyst to FBI Washington Field Office Intelligence Analyst (Jan. 5, 2021, 6:52 PM) (on file with the Committees).
[284]*Id.*
[285]Email from FBI Washington Field Office Intelligence Analyst to Incident Listserv (Jan. 5, 2021, 7:37 PM) (on file with the Committees). *See also Examining the U.S. Capitol Attack – Part II: Joint Hearing Before the S. Comm. on Homeland Sec. & Governmental Affairs and the S. Comm. on Rules & Admin.*, 117th Cong. (2021) (testimony of Jill Sanborn, Ass't Dir., Counterterrorism Div., Fed. Bureau of Investigation) (indicating that the Washington Field Office disseminated the SIR within an hour of receiving it.
[286]USCP OIG FLASH REPORT 1, *supra* note 200, at 9.
[287]Email from FBI Washington Field Office Intelligence Analyst to Intelligence Operations Section Official (Jan. 5, 2021, 7:42 PM) (on file with the Committees).
[288]Joint Committee Briefing with Yogananda Pittman, Acting Chief, U.S. Capitol Police (Feb. 18, 2021).
[289]*Examining the U.S. Capitol Attack: Joint Hearing Before the S. Comm. on Homeland Sec. & Governmental Affairs and the S. Comm. on Rules & Admin.*, 117th Cong. (2021) (testimony of Steven Sund, Former Chief, U.S. Capitol Police).

distribution list.[290] USCP did not provide any documents to the Committees confirming either account. No one from IICD or USCP leadership received the SIR before January 6.[291] The USCP Inspector General's report noted that the "memorandum did not surface again until it was attached to an information package sent out late on January 6, 2021, after the security breach occurred."[292]

Also on the evening of January 5, Deputy Chief Gallagher flagged additional information concerning the Capitol campus tunnel system, including an "online tip" received by the FBI National Threat Operations Center of a "significant uptick" in new visitors to the website WashingtonTunnels.com.[293] The email attached posts from thedonald.win referencing access to tunnels and noted that the website had been very active in "promoting photos of the tunnel system and stating their goal of finding Democratic Members early to block them from entering the Capitol."[294] The email also noted a "huge uptick with reporting via open source of the groups intentions of forming a perimeter around the campus," with an image attached.[295]

Similar to the intelligence already in IICD's possession prior to January 5, the FBI SIR and the warning regarding the tunnel system were not elevated to USCP leadership. When asked why the FBI SIR was not escalated further despite the warnings it contained, Mr. Sund explained that the SIR contained information similar to the existing intelligence—a limited potential for violence between protestors.[296] Mr. Sund told the Committees that IICD had processes in place to evaluate and escalate intelligence to the Director and leadership, as needed.[297] The USCP Inspector General contradicted Mr. Sund's testimony, concluding, "there is no clear channel for the distribution of intelligence information up to the Chief and down to the line officers and across departmental entities."[298] Existing guidance on information sharing is ambiguous, such as requiring that the head of IICD "[e]nsur[e] all intelligence information is collected, processed, and disseminated in the most efficient manner possible."[299]

[290] USCP OIG FLASH REPORT 1, *supra* note 200, at 9; *Oversight of the United States Capitol Police and Preparations for and Response to the Attack of January 6th: Hearing before the H. Comm. on Administration*, 117th Cong. (2021) (written testimony of Michael A. Bolton, Inspector Gen., U.S. Capitol Police).
[291] USCP OIG FLASH REPORT 1, *supra* note 200, at 9; *Oversight of the United States Capitol Police and Preparations for and Response to the Attack of January 6th: Hearing before the H. Comm. on Administration*, 117th Cong. (2021) (written testimony of Michael A. Bolton, Inspector Gen., U.S. Capitol Police).
[292] USCP OIG FLASH REPORT 1, *supra* note 200, at 9.
[293] Email from Sean Gallagher, U.S. Capitol Police, to Senate Sergeant at Arms Official et al. (Jan. 5, 2021, 9:40 PM) (on file with the Committees).
[294] *Id.*
[295] *Id.*
[296] *Examining the U.S. Capitol Attack: Joint Hearing Before the S. Comm. on Homeland Sec. & Governmental Affairs and the S. Comm. on Rules & Admin.*, 117th Cong. (2021) (testimony of Steven Sund, Former Chief, U.S. Capitol Police).
[297] *Id.*
[298] USCP OIG FLASH REPORT 2, *supra* note 203, at 23.
[299] *Id.*

E. USCP Did Not Warn Its Officers or Law Enforcement Partners of the Gravity of the Threat

The inconsistencies in IICD's products and the lack of consensus on the nature of the threat appears to have affected leadership's perspective about the import of the January 3 Special Assessment. Although Ms. Pittman placed a great significance on the January 3 Special Assessment, noting that its issuance led to a significant number of security enhancements, it is unclear who received the January 3 Special Assessment and whether it had a meaningful impact on its law enforcement partners.[300]

USCP stated that the conclusions of the January 3 Special Assessment were discussed "with law enforcement partners externally on January 4, 2021."[301] A January 4 email memorializing notes from the call with law enforcement partners, however, does not include any discussion of the January 3 Special Assessment.[302] No member of IICD is listed as participating in the call.[303] Ms. Pittman acknowledged to the Committees that the January 3 Special Assessment was not disseminated to law enforcement partners prior to January 6, but she maintained it was discussed orally.[304]

Ms. Pittman also told the Committees that the January 3 Special Assessment was shared with members of the Capitol Police Board.[305] The Architect of the Capitol, by contrast, told the Committees that he does not remember receiving the January 3 Special Assessment or being briefed on it.[306] USCP confirmed that it does "not have any documentation that [the January 3 Special Assessment] was shared outside the Department in written form."[307]

Not only was the January 3 Special Assessment not shared widely outside of USCP, it was also not briefed to rank-and-file officers. USCP claimed that the January 3 Special Assessment was "widely distributed" "to officers at the rank of Sergeant and above internally."[308] USCP leadership expected Sergeants and Lieutenants to "brief the officers within their chain of command."[309] Mr. Sund told the Committees, "[o]n January 5th, 2021, [he] issued a directive to the two assistant chiefs and . . . Bureau Commanders where our officers in the field [were] assigned to ensure officers [were] briefed at roll calls on January 6, 2021 of the expected demonstration activity."[310] He noted that he received confirmation emails that all "officers and

[300]Letter from Office of the Gen. Counsel, U.S. Capitol Police, to the Committees 4 (Feb. 19, 2021) (listing various security measures taken as a result of the January 3, 2021 Special Event Assessment) (on file with the Committees).
[301]*Id.*
[302]Email from Intelligence Operations Official to Intelligence Operations Official et al. (Jan. 4, 2021, 4:14 PM) (on file with the Committees).
[303]*See id.*
[304]Pittman Interview (Apr. 22, 2021), *supra* note 20, at 10:10–25.
[305]*Id.* at 21:1–14.
[306]Blanton Interview, *supra* note 48, at 85:2–10.
[307]Attachment to email from Office of the Gen. Counsel, U.S. Capitol Police, to the Committees (Apr. 30, 2021).
[308]Letter from Office of the Gen. Counsel, U.S. Capitol Police, to the Committees (Feb. 19, 2021) (on file with the Committees).
[309]*Id.*
[310]Steven A. Sund, Responses to Questions for the Record (Apr. 6, 2021) (on file with the Committees).

officials" were briefed.[311] Mr. Sund did not provide the details of the brief the officers were provided.[312]

In contrast, several USCP officers have stated that they received no warning about the possibility of violent protests on January 6 from USCP officials.[313] Line officers raised concerns about USCP leadership's lack of communication about the potential threats on January 6, with some saying they did not receive the January 3 Special Assessment and others were made to feel that "it was business as usual."[314] One USCP Inspector told the Committees that they expected January 6 to be just like the previous two Million MAGA Marches in terms of crowd size and the potential for violence.[315] Multiple officers also reported that no meetings were held prior to January 6 to brief officers and provide emergency plans, which typically occurs for major events.[316] The Capitol Police Labor Committee stated, USCP leadership "failed to share key intelligence with officers in advance, they failed to prepare adequately, they failed to equip our officers with a plan and on that very day, they failed to lead."[317]

Ms. Pittman, however, told the Committees that the rank-and-file officers were briefed on the January 3 Special Assessment:

> So the leadership at Capitol Police did provide those intelligence briefings to the commanders at the rank of captain or above, and it [was] the expectation that those commanders that are responsible for their various divisions throughout the Department, that they would share that information down the chain of command to the rank-and file officers.[318]

She acknowledged that the information would have been conveyed on a non-recorded conference call and therefore, USCP does not have a record of what, if anything, was conveyed.[319] When asked to respond to the Capitol Police Labor Committee's statement, Ms. Pittman maintained that the officers she oversaw were aware of the intelligence—"having talked to commanders, and specifically being aware, for my area of responsibility, which was the Protective and Intelligence Operations, I know that those officers as well as supervisors were aware."[320] Ms. Pittman also stated IICD held briefings for officers above the rank of Captain on the Special Assessment, which provided those officers an opportunity to ask questions about the intelligence.[321] These

[311] *Id.*
[312] *Id.*
[313] Joaquin Sapien & Joshua Kaplan, *"I Don't Trust the People Above Me": Riot Squad Cops Open Up About Disastrous Response to Capitol Insurrection*, PROPUBLICA (Feb. 12, 2021).
[314] *Id.*
[315] Joint Committee Interview with USCP Inspector (May 27, 2021).
[316] Nomaan Merchant & Colleen Long, *Police Command Structure Crumbled Fast during Capitol Riot*, ASSOCIATED PRESS (Jan. 18, 2021).
[317] USCP Labor Comm. Media Release, *supra* note 78.
[318] Pittman Interview (Apr. 22, 2021), *supra* note 20, at 23:1–17.
[319] *Id.*
[320] *Id.* at 24:1–9.
[321] *U.S. Capitol Police and House Sergeant at Arms, Security Failures on January 6: Hearing before the Legis. Branch Subcomm. of the H. Appropriations Comm.*, 117th Cong. (2021) (written testimony of Yogananda Pittman, Acting Chief, U.S. Capitol Police).

conflicting accounts highlight an internal communication problem in USCP that affected the safety and security of officers and the individuals they are sworn to protect.

VI. USCP WAS NOT PREPARED FOR THE ATTACK ON THE CAPITOL, HAMPERING ITS RESPONSE

Despite the information IICD possessed, officials have stressed that none of it suggested a large, coordinated attack on the Capitol. Mr. Sund testified that the siege of the Capitol was not the result of "poor planning" by USCP, but rather a "lack of accurate and complete intelligence across several federal agencies."[322] Ms. Pittman agreed:

> [T]he intelligence wasn't there to suggest that thousands of people, insurrectionists, were going to breach the United States Capitol, attacking law enforcement officers. I believe the intelligence did advise that we should anticipate violence, that some of the violence would be directed toward the Capitol, toward Congress. But to say that any law enforcement agency in the National Capital Region had intelligence that said that tens of thousands of people were going to attack law enforcement on January 6th, I think that it's accurate to say that no law enforcement agency had that.[323]

She stressed that USCP was prepared for a significant likelihood of violence.[324]

Despite Mr. Sund's and Ms. Pittman's claims, in addition to the deficiencies in USCP's handling of available intelligence, there were also deficiencies in USCP's operational planning and response efforts. Both Ms. Pittman and Mr. Sund told the Committees that USCP made a number of adjustments to its operational posture for January 6 in light of available intelligence.[325] Yet, USCP leadership did not prepare a USCP-wide security or staffing plan. USCP officers were also not trained, equipped, or staffed to respond to the attack.

Many rank-and-file officers have expressed concerns about USCP's lack of preparations for the Joint Session. As one summarized:

> We were ill prepared. We were NOT informed with intelligence. We were betrayed. We were abandoned by ALL the deputy chiefs and above that day. We still have not been told where exactly the chiefs were that day and what their [role] was on the 6th. USCP needs to address the 6th openly and honestly. The chiefs

[322] *Examining the U.S. Capitol Attack: Joint Hearing Before the S. Comm. on Homeland Sec. & Governmental Affairs and the S. Comm. on Rules & Admin.*, 117th Cong. (2021) (testimony of Steven Sund, Former Chief, U.S. Capitol Police).

[323] Pittman Interview (Apr. 22, 2021), *supra* note 20, at 42:1–11.

[324] *Id.* at 43:4–8.

[325] *See* discussion *infra* Section V.B; Letter from Office of the Gen. Counsel, U.S. Capitol Police, to the Committees 4–5 (Feb. 19, 2021) (listing security measures taken in response to the January 3, 2021 Special Event Assessment) (on file with the Committees); *Examining the U.S. Capitol Attack: Joint Hearing Before the S. Comm. on Homeland Sec. & Governmental Affairs and the S. Comm. on Rules & Admin.*, 117th Cong. (2021) (written testimony of Steven Sund, Former Chief, U.S. Capitol Police).

> need to be held accountable[.] [T]hey need to be under investigation for failure to supervise and failure to take police action.[326]

Another officer stated, "1/6 was not only a result of a few months of intelligence not being analyzed and acted upon, but more so decades of failing to take infrastructure, force protection, emergency planning, and training seriously."[327]

A. USCP Lacked Detailed Operational Plans for January 6

1. USCP Did Not Prepare a Department-Wide Operational Plan

USCP did not prepare a department-wide operational plan for January 6.[328] Prior to January 6, Mr. Sund believed USCP would need support to secure the Capitol perimeter in light of the large number of expected protestors at the Capitol and he had informal discussions with the House and Senate Sergeants at Arms concerning National Guard assistance.[329] One USCP Inspector noted the significance of these discussions, as he was not aware of National Guard assistance at the Capitol having been discussed since the September 11, 2001 terrorist attacks.[330] Despite these concerns, Mr. Sund did not direct the creation of a department-wide operational plan for January 6. Ms. Pittman told the Committees that USCP creates department-wide plans for large events, but no such plan was prepared for the January 6 Joint Session.[331] When asked to explain why no such plan was created, Ms. Pittman stated that it would have been the Chief of Police's responsibility to request that operational commanders prepare such a plan and that she could not explain why the then-Chief of Police chose not to do so before January 6.[332] The USCP Inspector General noted, "USCP did not have policies and procedures in place that communicated which personnel were responsible for operational planning, what type of operational planning documents [USCP] personnel should prepare, or when [USCP] personnel should prepare operational planning documents."[333]

The most comprehensive description of USCP's operational plans for the Joint Session was a four-page document prepared for USCP leadership to brief Members about security enhancements ("Leadership Briefing document").[334] The Leadership Briefing document

[326] Officer Statement #6 provided to the Committees (on file with the Committees).
[327] Officer Statement #10 provided to the Committees (on file with the Committees).
[328] *See* Pittman Interview (Apr. 22, 2021), *supra* note 20, at 45:5–7; *see also* USCP OIG FLASH REPORT 1, *supra* note 200, at 5.
[329] *Examining the U.S. Capitol Attack: Joint Hearing Before the S. Comm. on Homeland Sec. & Governmental Affairs and the S. Comm. on Rules & Admin.*, 117th Cong. (2021) (written testimony of Steven Sund, Former Chief, U.S. Capitol Police). Mr. Sund disputes the characterization of the discussions as "informal," but has acknowledged he did not communicate with the full Capitol Police Board or make a request in writing. *See id.*; Steven A. Sund, Responses to Questions for the Record (Apr. 6, 2021) (on file with the Committees).
[330] Joint Committee Interview with USCP Inspector (May 27, 2021).
[331] *See* Pittman Interview (Apr. 22, 2021), *supra* note 20, at 45:1–7.
[332] *See id.* at 45:8–17.
[333] USCP OIG FLASH REPORT 1, *supra* note 200, at 7.
[334] *See* U.S. CAPITOL POLICE, DEMONSTRATION ACTIVITY & USCP RESPONSE SURROUNDING THE 1/6/21 JOINT SESSION OF CONGRESS TO CERTIFY THE ELECTORAL COUNT (Jan. 5, 2021) (on file with the Committees); SMS Message from Steven Sund to Yogananda Pittman (Jan. 4, 2021, 10:41 AM) ("Good morning chad. and Ananda, I

described at a high-level the intelligence information informing USCP's security preparations: (1) the "March for Trump" rally on the Ellipse and a Stop the Steal event planned on Capitol grounds were "expected to draw thousands"; (2) members of the Proud Boys and Antifa were expected to attend; (3) hotels were reporting a 60 to 100 percent increase in bookings; and (4) USCP was tracking social media posts encouraging attendees to be armed.[335] Based on this information, USCP's security preparations for January 6 included:

- Restricting the Capitol buildings and plaza to Members, staff, and visitors on official business;
- Deploying bike racks;
- Increasing exterior patrols;
- Posting additional officers at barricades, tunnels, and other select locations within the Capitol Complex;
- Activating seven civil disturbance platoons;
- Enhancing protection for Congressional leadership teams; and
- Placing the Investigations Division into an "all hands on deck" posture and having USCP analysts working "24/7 all week."[336]

2. Division-Specific Operational Plans Were Not Detailed

Although USCP did not prepare a department-wide plan, at least two entities created division-specific plans: the Uniformed Services Bureau ("USB") and the CDU.[337] Neither document laid out in detail staffing or officer assignments for the Joint Session. For example, the two-page "USB Operational Posture" document described certain "beyond routine in-session COVID posts and staffing."[338] It stated that there would be "increased exterior patrols" and officers stationed at particular traffic barricades and other office building locations.[339] The operational plan, however, did not describe the overall numbers of officers on duty on January 6; where these officers would be stationed; the officers' responsibilities; the command-and-control system for January 6; or any contingencies in the event of emergencies.[340]

am starting to receive multiple requests for briefing calls to members and committees. I would like to put together a one pager front and back overview of the events as we know them and our department preparation.").

[335] *See* U.S. CAPITOL POLICE, DEMONSTRATION ACTIVITY & USCP RESPONSE SURROUNDING THE 1/6/21 JOINT SESSION OF CONGRESS TO CERTIFY THE ELECTORAL COUNT 2 (Jan. 5, 2021) (on file with the Committees).

[336] *See id.* at 2–4.

[337] The U.S. Capitol Police Inspector General identified a one-page Plan of Action for the Hazardous Materials Response Team. USCP OIG FLASH REPORT 1, *supra* note 200, at 5. USCP was unable to locate this document for the Committees.

[338] U.S. CAPITOL POLICE, USB OPERATIONAL POSTURE FOR THE JOINT SESSION OF CONGRESS ON JANUARY 6, 2021, at 1 (Jan. 2021) (on file with the Committees).

[339] *Id.*

[340] *Id.*

The CDU began preparing a Joint Session Operation Plan as early as December 28, 2020 and finalized the plan on January 5, 2021.[341] Among other items, the seventeen-page plan contained sections on command-and-control; mission objectives; staffing plan; deployment strategies; and directives on use of force and crowd management tactics.[342] The CDU Operational Plan also included a section on tactical response/counter-sniper over-watch, which highlighted the deployment of the Containment Emergency Response Team (CERT), described as an eight person "counter-assault ground team" staged around the Capitol Complex.[343]

The CDU Operational Plan, however, was not informed by the January 3 Special Assessment.[344] The CDU Operational Plan's description of expected protests stated that the "protests/rallies are expected to be similar to the previous Million MAGA March rallies," in contrast to the differentiating details included in the January 3 Special Assessment.[345] The CDU Operational Plan also stated that "[a]t this time there are no specific known threats related to the Joint Session of Congress," but did not specifically acknowledge or reference the January 3 Special Assessment's warning that "Congress itself is the target."[346] The CDU Plan contained no detail concerning the significance of the threat, apart from noting that the protests were expected to be similar to previous Million MAGA Marches, which ended in clashes between protestors and resulted in individuals being charged with "assault with a dangerous weapon, assault on police, simple assault, weapons violations, riotous acts, and destruction of property, disorderly conduct, resisting arrest, and crossing a police line."[347] When asked to reconcile the CDU Operational Plan's statement regarding "no specific known threats" and the January 3 Special Assessment's overall conclusions, Ms. Pittman emphasized the word "specific," arguing that "for an intelligence analyst, it is in terms of the . . . who, where, when, and how" and that much of the information in IICD's possession was "raw information" that needed "to be vetted."[348] However, Ms. Pittman insisted that USCP made security enhancements based on the information contained in the January 3 Special Assessment, including increasing the number of CDU platoons available for January 6.[349]

Notably, USCP did not coordinate between its protective and intelligence operations and its uniformed operations. When asked if she thought it was odd that no department-wide plan was prepared for the Joint Session, Ms. Pittman explained that, in her role as Assistant Chief for the Protective and Intelligence Operations, she was commonly not involved in planning and operations.[350] For example, the postings of officers within the USB was between the Chief and

[341] *See* U.S. CAPITOL POLICE, CDU OPERATIONAL PLAN (Dec. 28, 2020) (on file with the Committees); U.S. CAPITOL POLICE, CDU OPERATIONAL PLAN (Jan. 5, 2021) (on file with the Committees).
[342] U.S. CAPITOL POLICE, CDU OPERATIONAL PLAN 2–10 (Jan. 5, 2021) (on file with the Committees).
[343] *Id.* at 7.
[344] *Compare id. with* INTELLIGENCE & INTERAGENCY COORDINATION DIV., U.S. CAPITOL POLICE, SPECIAL EVENT ASSESSMENT 21-A-0468 V.3 (Jan. 3, 2021) (on file with the Committees).
[345] *Id.*
[346] *Id.*
[347] U.S. CAPITOL POLICE, CDU OPERATIONAL PLAN 1 (Jan. 5, 2021) (on file with the Committees).
[348] Pittman Interview (Apr. 22, 2021), *supra* note 20, at 33:10–35:4.
[349] *Id.* at 35:23–36:1.
[350] *Id.* at 45:21–46:10.

the Assistant Chief for Uniformed Services; Ms. Pittman was not consulted.[351] Ms. Pittman also acknowledged that CDU did not consult IICD when drafting its operational plan.[352]

3. USCP Did Not Document a Comprehensive Staffing Plan for January 6

A department-wide operational plan should have detailed the number of sworn officers on duty for the Joint Session, where those officers would be positioned, and the command-and-control plan.[353] USCP, however, did not prepare a staffing plan prior to January 6.[354]As noted above, USCP employed 1,840 officers on January 6.[355] Ms. Pittman told the Committees that USCP was in an "all hands . . . on deck" posture that day.[356] One Inspector, however, clarified that leave was not cancelled for officers and described that staffing was at standard levels.[357]

Documents provided to the Committees reflect that USCP had 1,214 sworn officers "on site" at 2:00 p.m. on January 6 and 1,457 sworn officers "on site" across the entire 24 hour-period.[358] Although USCP conveyed the overall number of officers "on site," it could not explain where these officers were located or the breakdown of officers by division. Ms. Pittman acknowledged that she did not know where officers were posted throughout the day, aside from that they were "deployed throughout the campus."[359] USCP has no official record listing the exact number of sworn officers that were posted in or around the Capitol Building when those positions were attacked. The most detailed response USCP could provide to the Committees was that "[o]f those officers in the Uniformed Services Bureau . . . approximately 195 were assigned to interior or exterior posts at the U.S. Capitol and 276 were assigned to the Department's seven [CDU] platoons."[360]USCP was only able to account for the location of 417 officers; it could not account for the remaining 797 officers.[361] USCP was also unable to show how many officers were re-missioned or called in to reinforce other positions throughout the day.

As noted above, the division-specific operational planning and briefing documents did not mention the total number of officers and their assigned locations, with one exception—they both referenced the number of CDU personnel activated for January 6. Notably, each contained a different figure. The USB Operational Posture document listed 242 officers, as well as 29

[351]*See id.* at 48:5–15.
[352]*Id.* at 31:16–21.
[353]*Id.* at 55:5–9.
[354]*Id.* at 45:5–7.
[355]U.S. CAPITOL POLICE, SWORN STAFFING – JANUARY 6, 2021 INSURRECTION (on file with the Committees).
[356]Pittman Interview (Apr. 22, 2021), *supra* note 20, at 52:9–53:4. USCP staggered officers' reporting times to ensure around-the-clock coverage. *Id.* at 52:14–20.
[357]Joint Committee Interview with USCP Inspector (May 27, 2021); *see also* U.S. CAPITOL POLICE, SWORN STAFFING – JANUARY 6, 2021 INSURRECTION (on file with the Committees).
[358]U.S. CAPITOL POLICE, SWORN STAFFING – JANUARY 6, 2021 INSURRECTION (on file with the Committees). U.S. Capitol Police also had 43 sworn officers "at alternative facility/travel" and teleworking. *Id.* As noted above, *supra* note 356, U.S. Capitol Police staggered officers' shifts to ensure coverage for the entire day.
[359]Pittman Interview (Apr. 22, 2021), *supra* note 20, at 53:13–25.
[360]Letter from Office of the Gen. Counsel, U.S. Capitol Police, to the Committees 9 (Feb. 19, 2021) (on file with the Committees).

[361]*Id.*

lieutenants, sergeants, and acting sergeants, for a total of 271 CDU personnel.[362] The CDU Operational Plan, by contrast, listed 233 CDU personnel activated for January 6.[363] The Leadership Briefing document, circulated on January 5, referenced 236 CDU officers.[364] In explaining the discrepancies, one USCP official explained to the Committees, "it's common practice on CDU to not know how many people you have until the day of. So while there may not be a document from before that reflects the number," USCP documents the number after the fact.[365]

B. USCP Officers Were Not Trained or Equipped to Defend Against the January 6 Attack

Even with the security enhancements USCP implemented for January 6, the officers on duty were unprepared to defend themselves and the Capitol on January 6. One security enhancement was to activate "the largest number of CDU platoons possible,"—seven platoons, four of which were "hard" platoons.[366] Four was the maximum number of hard platoons USCP could staff because it included all the officers trained in the tactics and equipment of hard platoons.[367] Only officers in hard platoons received training on how to "handle more aggressive riot type of situations."[368] According to the USCP Inspector General, "[t]he majority of [hard platoon CDU] officers, however, have not completed the [annual refresher] training during the past few years," and recent USCP recruits "did not complete the usual required 40 hours of [civil disturbance] training."[369]

Hard platoon officers were provided additional protective gear, including helmets, hardened plastic gear, and shields, among other equipment. According to Mr. Sund, USCP "took a number of steps to outfit [CDU] personnel with additional hard gear" and "enhanced access to the property management division, in the event officers needed replacement uniforms or equipment, and vehicle services."[370] Mr. Sund further testified to efforts he made to improve officer access to protective equipment in the year prior, stating:

> During my time as the Chief, I had directed enhancements to the protective equipment being issued to our sworn employees. In 2020, I directed the procurement of riot helmets for all of the sworn members of [USCP]. Prior to this

[362] U.S. CAPITOL POLICE, USB OPERATIONAL POSTURE FOR THE JOINT SESSION OF CONGRESS ON JANUARY 6, 2021, at 2 (Jan. 2021) (on file with the Committees).
[363] U.S. CAPITOL POLICE, CDU OPERATIONAL PLAN 6 (Jan. 5, 2021) (on file with the Committees).
[364] *See* U.S. CAPITOL POLICE, DEMONSTRATION ACTIVITY & USCP RESPONSE SURROUNDING THE 1/6/21 JOINT SESSION OF CONGRESS TO CERTIFY THE ELECTORAL COUNT 2 (Jan. 5, 2021) (on file with the Committees).
[365] Pittman Interview (Apr. 22, 2021), *supra* note 20, at 60:1–4.
[366] *Examining the U.S. Capitol Attack: Joint Hearing Before the S. Comm. on Homeland Sec. & Governmental Affairs and the S. Comm. on Rules & Admin.*, 117th Cong. (2021) (testimony of Steven Sund, Former Chief, U.S. Capitol Police).
[367] Pittman Interview (Apr. 22, 2021), *supra* note 20, at 60:19–61:3.
[368] *Id.* at 61:13–15.
[369] USCP OIG FLASH REPORT 2, *supra* note 203, at 13.
[370] *Examining the U.S. Capitol Attack: Joint Hearing Before the S. Comm. on Homeland Sec. & Governmental Affairs and the S. Comm. on Rules & Admin.*, 117th Cong. (2021) (testimony of Steven Sund, Former Chief, U.S. Capitol Police).

> time, riot helmets were only issued to members assigned to [USCP's] Civil Disturbance Units (CD) [*sic*]. The delivery of the helmets from the manufacturer had been delayed over the past several months due to the effects of COVID-19, but we had been pushing for delivery by the Inauguration. As helmets became available, we pushed for their expedited delivery due to the upcoming demonstration and approximately 104 of the helmets were delivered on Monday, January 4.[371]

Despite the arrival of approximately 100 new helmets on January 5, the USCP Inspector General found that CDU was "operating at a decreased level of readiness as a result of a lack of standards for equipment."[372] USCP officers, for example, were given defective riot shields that had been improperly stored and, as a result, "shatter[ed] upon impact."[373] Not only was certain equipment defective, but USCP did not authorize CDU officers to wear the gear at the beginning of their shift.[374] The CDU operational plan required that protective gear be "pre-stage[d]" in proximity to the platoons' staging locations, and the CDU field commander would instruct officers to retrieve that gear "depending on the presence of counter-groups and the reported interactions between the opposing groups."[375] In at least once instance, USCP protective shields were locked in a bus during the riot so that a CDU platoon was unable to access them, and as a result, the platoon was required to respond to the crowd without the protection of their riot shields."[376]

USCP also did not authorize its CDU forces to use all available less-than-lethal munitions. This included grenade launchers and sting ball grenades that USCP officials acknowledged "may have enhanced CDU's ability to push back the rioters . . . ."[377] The CDU plan only authorized the use of the FN-303 system and pepper balls.[378] When asked why additional less-than-lethal munitions in USCP's possession were not authorized, Ms. Pittman explained that USCP did not have sufficient personnel trained to deploy those various types of weapons systems.[379]

The training and equipment requirements applied to fewer than 300 of the 1,200 officers on duty during the height of the attack. The remaining 900 officers had even less training and equipment to defend themselves and the buildings and individuals they are sworn to protect.

[371] *Id.*
[372] USCP OIG FLASH REPORT 2, *supra* note 203, at 1, 6.
[373] *Id.* at 10.
[374] One officer attributed this decision to concerns about the "appearance" of CDU officers in hard gear. Joint Committee Interview with USCP Inspector (May 27, 2021).
[375] U.S. CAPITOL POLICE, CDU OPERATIONAL PLAN 10 (Jan. 5, 2021) (on file with the Committees). *See also* Pittman Interview (Apr. 22, 2021), *supra* note 20, at 63:15–65:1.
[376] USCP OIG FLASH REPORT 2, *supra* note 203 at 13.
[377] *Id.* at 12–13 (noting that the use of Sting Ball pellets by MPD and flashbangs by the Virginia State Police were "particularly effective in neutralizing and removing combative individuals").
[378] U.S. CAPITOL POLICE, CDU OPERATIONAL PLAN 3 (Jan. 5, 2021) (on file with the Committees). *See also* Pittman Interview (Apr. 22, 2021), *supra* note 20, at 67:16–24. According to Ms. Pittman, USCP also used "the MK-9, which is just a more powerful OC spray, as well as the MK-46, another type of OC spray, and their PR-24 batons, which is a larger type of stick baton." Pittman Interview (Apr. 22, 2021), *supra* note 20, at 67:16–24.
[379] Pittman Interview (Apr. 22, 2021), *supra* note 20, at 68:5–13.

Officers in soft platoons or those not in the CDU received some basic CDU training when they first joined the force. Consequently, the officers may have gone years since receiving any formal CDU training. In terms of equipment, the officers were outfitted in their regular uniforms.[380] Officers stationed at security posts in Capitol office buildings and around the security perimeter also had "OC spray as well as batons available to them. . . . [W]hether or not those [officers] actually had it on, someone would have to physically look at them and see."[381]

C. USCP Leaders Failed to Communicate with Front-Line Officers During the Attack

USCP uses an incident command system ("ICS") to respond to any "occurrence or event . . . that requires a response to protect life or property."[382] The USCP's Incident Command System Directive, which was last updated in October 2018, defines the command system as that for "command, control, and coordination of a response that provides a means to coordinate the efforts of individuals and agencies as they work toward the common goal of stabilizing an incident while protecting life, property, and environment."[383] One of the primary rationales for using the ICS is to "increase the efficiency of incident management and allow for rapid and seamless integration with stakeholders, military command, and other government partners."[384]

The ICS provides that USCP will implement an "incident action plan" that includes the overall incident objectives and the strategies to "ensure incident objectives are met."[385] Incident objectives "are based on realistic expectations of what can be accomplished when all allocated resources have been effectively deployed."[386] As noted above, USCP did not prepare a department-wide operational plan prior to January 6.[387] USCP also did not document incident objectives for the Joint Session. Mr. Sund testified that he and others established the following priorities for other agencies:

(1) Secure the perimeter and foundation of the Capitol; and

(2) Assist USCP in removing unauthorized persons from the Capitol and conduct a top to bottom sweep of the building to ensure no unauthorized persons, or hazardous devices remained in the building.[388]

While the Incident Command System Directive generally describes the role of the different divisions in the ICS, it does not detail how an ICS is established or how it operates during an

[380] *Id.* at 56:23–57:6.
[381] *Id.* at 57:2–22.
[382] U.S. CAPITOL POLICE, DIRECTIVE 1052.003 – INCIDENT COMMAND SYSTEM 2 (Oct. 2018) (on file with the Committees) [hereinafter DIRECTIVE 1052.003 – INCIDENT COMMAND SYSTEM].
[383] *Id.*
[384] *Id.* at 3.
[385] *Id.* at 2.
[386] *Id.*
[387] *See supra* Part VI.A.1.
[388] *Examining the U.S. Capitol Attack: Joint Hearing Before the S. Comm. on Homeland Sec. & Governmental Affairs and the S. Comm. on Rules & Admin.*, 117th Cong. (2021) (written testimony of Steven Sund, Former Chief, U.S. Capitol Police).

incident.[389] It does not detail how incident commanders should communicate priorities, strategies, or tactics to front-line officers.[390]

According to Mr. Sund, in advance of January 6 there were two designated incident commanders—one was to monitor the Capitol Grounds and the other was to monitor the Capitol Building, including the Joint Session.[391] Mr. Sund further explained that these incident commanders were responsible for communicating with front-line officers via one of two radio channels—one for each commander.[392] Designating incident commanders as those who are to be issuing directions is intended to reduce confusion and provide the most direct information.[393] One of the officers identified to the Committees as a designated incident commander was listed in the CDU operational plan.[394] The other officer, however, is not specified in any document provided to the Committees as having been formally designated as an incident commander prior to January 6.[395] According to that officer, the designation would have been made in a department-wide operational plan.[396]

According to information provided to the Committees, officers received little-to-no communication from senior officers during the attack and at no point did USCP leadership take over the radios to communicate with front-line officers.[397] As one officer noted, "[t]here was very little direction, if any, provided by ranking members of the USCP throughout the whole day - mid-level and senior leadership was providing very little, if any, direction. I felt like I was alone and I felt like I had to make my own decisions."[398] Another officer explained,

> I was horrified that NO deputy chief or above was on the radio or helping us. For hours the screams on the radio were horrific[,] the sights were unimaginable[,] and there was a complete loss of control. . . . For hours NO Chief or above took command and control. Officers were begging and pleading for help for medical triage.[399]

One officer publicly stated "we heard nothing that day" and another officer reported, "We were on our own. Totally on our own."[400] Ms. Pittman attributed the lack of communication to the

[389] DIRECTIVE 1052.003 – INCIDENT COMMAND SYSTEM, *supra* note 382, at 3.
[390] *Id.*
[391] *Examining the U.S. Capitol Attack: Joint Hearing Before the S. Comm. on Homeland Sec. & Governmental Affairs and the S. Comm. on Rules & Admin.*, 117th Cong. (2021) (written testimony of Steven Sund, Former Chief, U.S. Capitol Police); Steven A. Sund, Responses to Questions for the Record (Apr. 6, 2021) (on file with the Committees).
[392] *Examining the U.S. Capitol Attack: Joint Hearing Before the S. Comm. on Homeland Sec. & Governmental Affairs and the S. Comm. on Rules & Admin.*, 117th Cong. (2021) (written testimony of Steven Sund, Former Chief, U.S. Capitol Police).
[393] *Cf. id.*
[394] U.S. CAPITOL POLICE, CDU OPERATIONAL PLAN 2 (Jan. 5, 2021) (on file with the Committees).
[395] Joint Committee Interview with USCP Inspector (May 27, 2021).
[396] *Id.*
[397] *Id.*; Officer Statements #6, 20 provided to the Committees (on file with the Committees).
[398] Officer Statement #20 provided to the Committees (on file with the Committees).
[399] Officer Statement #6 provided to the Committees (on file with the Committees).
[400] Sapien & Kaplan, *supra* note 313; Merchant & Long, *supra* note 316.

incident commanders being overwhelmed and engaging with rioters, rather than issuing orders over the radio.[401]

Despite incident commanders being overwhelmed, USCP leadership never took control of the radio to communicate with responding officers. Officers did not recall hearing Mr. Sund on the radio at any point during the attack and only recalled hearing Ms. Pittman once—when she ordered a lockdown of the Capitol Building at 2:00 p.m.[402] The Capitol Police Labor Committee explained that Inspector Tom Loyd issued the lockdown order an hour prior to Ms. Pittman doing so, and based on information provided to the Committees, Ms. Pittman's later statement came without any further direction.[403] Chad Thomas, Assistant Chief of Police for Uniformed Operations, reportedly told officers he tried but was unable to get on the radio to communicate to officers.[404] Neither Mr. Sund nor Ms. Pittman provided an explanation for why USCP leadership did not directly communicate with officers. One officer attributed this failure to a lack of operational experience among USCP leadership and suggested that the promotion process at USCP should be reevaluated.[405] In the absence of communication, officers lacked clarity about whether to respond to calls for "all available units."[406] An officer reported hearing a Lieutenant repeatedly ask over the radio, "[d]oes anybody have a plan?"[407]

VII. OPAQUE CAPITOL POLICE BOARD PROCESSES SLOWED REQUESTS FOR NATIONAL GUARD SUPPORT

As described above, USCP is overseen by the Capitol Police Board—comprised of the House and Senate Sergeants at Arms and the Architect of the Capitol.[408] The purpose of the Board is to "direct, oversee and support the Capitol Police in its mission, as well as to advance coordination between Congress, the Capitol Police, the Sergeants at Arms of the House and the Senate and the Architect of the Capitol."[409] Mr. Stenger told the Committees that the Capitol Police Board is intended to be a "clearinghouse of information" and ensure coordination between the House and Senate, rather than an "operational" entity.[410] The Capitol Police Board, however, has broad authority and control over key operational decisions.[411] One of those responsibilities is declaring emergencies for the purpose of accepting support services[412] and approving the

[401] Joint Committee Briefing with Yogananda Pittman, Acting Chief, U.S. Capitol Police (Feb. 18, 2021).
[402] Officer Statements #27, 30 provided to the Committees (on file with the Committees); U.S. CAPITOL POLICE, TIMELINE OF EVENTS, *supra* note 61, at 15.
[403] USCP Labor Comm. Media Release, *supra* note 78; *see also* Officer Statement #30 provided to the Committees (on file with the Committees).
[404] Sapien & Kaplain, *supra* note 313.
[405] Joint Committee Interview with USCP Inspector (May 27, 2021).
[406] Sapien & Kaplain, *supra* note 313.
[407] Merchant & Long, *supra* note 316.
[408] CAPITOL POLICE BD. MANUAL, *supra* note 24, at §§ 1.1, 1.2. The USCP Chief serves on the Board as an *ex-officio*, non-voting member. *Id.*
[409] *Id.* at § 1.1.
[410] Joint Committee Briefing with Michael Stenger, Former Sergeant at Arms, U.S. Senate (Feb. 18, 2021).
[411] *See supra* Part III.A.1.b. For example, Mr. Sund testified that he "could not deliver water to [USCP officers] on a hot day" without Capitol Police Board approval. *See Examining the U.S. Capitol Attack: Joint Hearing Before the S. Comm. on Homeland Sec. & Governmental Affairs and the S. Comm. on Rules & Admin.*, 117th Cong. (2021) (testimony of Steven Sund, Former Chief, U.S. Capitol Police).
[412] 2 U.S.C. § 1970; CAPITOL POLICE BD. MANUAL, *supra* note 24, at §§ 6.1–6.3.

appointment of special officers.[413] Yet, none of the members of the Capitol Police Board appeared fully familiar with the process or requirements relating to emergency declarations or requesting external support. This lack of familiarity with the process delayed requests for National Guard assistance on and before January 6.

A. Capitol Police Board Members Did Not Understand the Statutory and Regulatory Authorities of the Capitol Police Board

Pursuant to 2 U.S.C. § 1970, "Executive departments and Executive agencies may assist the United States Capitol Police in the performance of its duties . . . when requested by *the Capitol Police Board.*"[414] The Capitol Police Board must submit a written request for external assistance; however, during emergencies, the House and Senate SAAs may authorize the request for their respective chambers.[415] A separate statutory provision, 2 U.S.C. § 1974, authorizes the USCP Chief to appoint special officers "in the event of an emergency, as determined by the Capitol Police Board . . . ."[416] Although there is a statutory requirement that any Capitol Police Board request for external assistance be in writing, Capitol Police Board members informed the Committees that a Board vote on or request for support from external agencies may be done orally and subsequently documented.[417]

Thus, the USCP Chief may not directly request support from Executive agencies, including the National Guard. Instead, the USCP Chief of Police submits a written request to the Capitol Police Board, seeking (1) an emergency declaration and (2) approval to request external assistance.[418] Capitol Police Board members disagreed as to whether a vote needs to be unanimous. Mr. Stenger informed the Committees that unanimity is required,[419] whereas Mr. Blanton indicated that only a majority vote was needed—if two Board members agreed, the request would be approved.[420] By statute, the Capitol Police Board would need to consult with

[413] 2 U.S.C. § 1974; CAPITOL POLICE BD. MANUAL, *supra* note 24, at § 5.3.
[414] 2 U.S.C. § 1970(a)(1) (emphasis added). The statute also provides that the Capitol Police Board must consult with Congressional leaders in non-emergency situations. *Id.*
[415] 2 U.S.C. § 1970(a)(4)(B).
[416] 2 U.S.C. § 1974(a). Alternatively, the USCP Chief may appoint special officers pursuant to a concurrent resolution of Congress. *Id.* Such appointments are subject to Capitol Police Board approval. 2 U.S.C. § 1974(c)(2); CAPITOL POLICE BD. MANUAL, *supra* note 24, at § 5.3.
[417] *Health and Wellness of Employees and State of Damage and Preservation as a Result of the January 6 Insurrection: Hearing Before the Legislative Branch Subcomm. of the H. Comm. on Appropriations*, 117th Cong. (2021) (testimony of J. Brett Blanton, Architect of the Capitol) ("[W]e can do a verbal vote on the Board. So, if [Chief Sund] goes to the . . . chairman of the Police Board [Michael Stenger] and says, 'I—I want to do this. We need to do it now.' [W]e can have a verbal vote and get it done . . . and then follow it with the written paperwork so there's nothing slowing anything down."); Joint Committee Briefing with Steven Sund, Former Chief, U.S. Capitol Police (Feb. 17, 2021).
[418] Joint Committee Briefing with Michael Stenger, Former Sergeant at Arms, U.S. Senate (Feb. 18, 2021); CAPITOL POLICE BD. MANUAL, *supra* note 24, at § 6.3.20 (providing that the USCP Chief must provide a written communication to the Board of the existence of an emergency necessitating support services).
[419] Joint Committee Briefing with Michael Stenger, Former Sergeant at Arms, U.S. Senate (Feb. 18, 2021).
[420] Blanton Interview, *supra* note 48, at 28:13–21. The Capitol Police Board Manual states, "Unless specifically stated otherwise in this Manual, the Board will strive for a consensus in all decisions." It further provides an exception allowing a majority of the Board to take action on matters involving the "safety, welfare and preservation of the Capitol complex . . . ." CAPITOL POLICE BD. MANUAL, *supra* note 24, at § 2.4.

Congressional leadership, except in an emergency.[421] In emergency situations, the USCP Chief need only secure the approval of the House or Senate SAAs to be able to request external assistance on their behalf in matters relating their respective chambers; however, the request for assistance must still be obtained from the SAAs in writing.[422] There is no corresponding statutory provision providing the USCP Chief with direct and independent authority to request external assistance in emergency situations.

None of the Capitol Police Board members on January 6 could fully explain in detail the statutory requirements for requesting National Guard assistance.[423] For example, when asked by Senator Blunt why he felt that he needed the approval of Mr. Stenger and Mr. Irving to request National Guard assistance, Mr. Sund testified, "that has always been the case."[424] Mr. Stenger told the Committees that he did not know if Capitol Police Board approval was required before requesting external assistance, "but that's what we thought and we were more than happy to go along with that."[425]

Members of the Capitol Police Board also indicated that there was no formal process for such requests. Mr. Stenger indicated that "typically" the USCP Chief would send a written request to the Capitol Police Board, but "in some cases, [the Chief] may approach" a Board member individually "to get a feel for what support may or may not" exist.[426] Mr. Sund acknowledged that he typically went directly to the House and Senate SAAs, rather than submitting a formal request to the entire Board.[427] When discussing the approval process, the Capitol Police Board members did not distinguish between emergency or non-emergency situations.[428]

The Architect of the Capitol also expressed concern about transparency and accountability of the Capitol Police Board. Specifically, he informed the Committees that the Board "overclassif[ies] things that do not need to be classified. . . . Even looking at old security assessments, they were classified at such a high level."[429] According to Mr. Blanton, the Board does not circulate an unclassified summary of the relevant information, as occurs in Executive

[421] 2 U.S.C. § 1970(a)(1).
[422] 2 U.S.C. § 1970(a)(4)(B).
[423] *Examining the U.S. Capitol Attack: Joint Hearing Before the S. Comm. on Homeland Sec. & Governmental Affairs and the S. Comm. on Rules & Admin.*, 117th Cong. (2021) (testimony of Steven Sund, Former Chief, U.S. Capitol Police) ("I would have to go back and look at the specific rule, but it is a standard—it is a standing rule that we have. I cannot request the National Guard without a declaration of emergency from the Capitol Police Board. . . . It is just a process that is in place.").
[424] *Id.*
[425] Joint Committee Briefing with Michael Stenger, Former Sergeant at Arms, U.S. Senate (Feb. 18, 2021).
[426] *Id.*
[427] *Examining the U.S. Capitol Attack: Joint Hearing Before the S. Comm. on Homeland Sec. & Governmental Affairs and the S. Comm. on Rules & Admin.*, 117th Cong. (2021) (testimony of Steven Sund, Former Chief, U.S. Capitol Police).
[428] Joint Committee Briefing with Michael Stenger, Former Sergeant at Arms, U.S. Senate (Feb. 18, 2021); Joint Committee Briefing with Steven Sund, Former Chief, U.S. Capitol Police (Feb. 17, 2021); Blanton Interview, *supra* note 48, at 28:8–10.

[429] Blanton Interview, *supra* note 48, at 90:8–25.

branch agencies. This over-classification can hinder conversations about proposed requests and oversight of the Capitol Police Board's decision-making:

> The transparency aspect is even more troubling because when everything is classified, you can't enter into a logical discussion with leadership and oversight [about] the proposals. . . . [I]t reduces the ability of people in my office . . . [and] in oversight of the Capitol Police Board [to review relevant information]. Not everybody [is] read into particular programs. Not everybody has top secret clearance.[430]

All members of the Capitol Police Board as constituted on January 6 later agreed that reforms were necessary to clarify, streamline, and make the approval process "more nimble."[431] As Mr. Stenger testified, "there are a lot of statutes out there on the Capitol Police Board that go back many, many years. Things have changed . . . ."[432]

B. USCP Did Not Submit a Formal Request for National Guard Assistance to the Capitol Police Board Prior to January 6

Prior to January 6, Mr. Sund failed to submit a formal request for National Guard support to all members of the Capitol Police Board and thus, never sought nor received authority from the Board to make any such request. His interactions were limited to informal conversations with Mr. Irving, and Mr. Stenger. In fact, no one ever discussed the possibility of National Guard support with the Board's third voting member, the Architect of the Capitol, Brett Blanton.[433]

Mr. Sund testified that he asked the two SAAs to declare an emergency and authorize National Guard assistance on Monday, January 4, but that this request was denied.[434] Mr. Sund testified to the Committees that on January 4 around 11:00 a.m., he met in person with Mr. Irving to request that the Capitol Police Board make an emergency declaration and authorize the

[430]*Id.* at 91:6–9, 106:17–21.

[431]*Examining the U.S. Capitol Attack: Joint Hearing Before the S. Comm. on Homeland Sec. & Governmental Affairs and the S. Comm. on Rules & Admin.*, 117th Cong. (2021) (testimonies of Steven Sund, Former Chief, U.S. Capitol Police; Paul Irving, Former Sergeant at Arms, U.S. House of Representatives; and Michael Stenger, Former Sergeant at Arms, U.S. Senate).

[432]*Examining the U.S. Capitol Attack: Joint Hearing Before the S. Comm. on Homeland Sec. & Governmental Affairs and the S. Comm. on Rules & Admin.*, 117th Cong. (2021) (testimony of Michael Stenger, Former Sergeant at Arms, U.S. Senate).

[433]Blanton Interview, *supra* note 48, at 27:5–10 ("I actually have to correct what you said, because Chief Sund has said that he has talked directly to the House Sergeant at Arms and later to the Senate Sergeant at Arms, he never asked the Board. And that is a very important distinction because there was never a request for declaration of an emergency until the evening of the 6th.").

[434]*Examining the U.S. Capitol Attack: Joint Hearing Before the S. Comm. on Homeland Sec. & Governmental Affairs and the S. Comm. on Rules & Admin.*, 117th Cong. (2021) (testimony of Steven Sund, Former Chief, U.S. Capitol Police). Mr. Sund has subsequently communicated to the Committees that he believes this discussion took place on January 3, not January 4. Steven A. Sund, Responses to Questions for the Record (Apr. 6, 2021) (on file with the Committees).

assistance of the National Guard.[435] Mr. Sund testified that Mr. Irving "was concerned with the 'optics' of having National Guard present," did not believe the intelligence warranted assistance from the National Guard, and therefore did not support the request.[436] Mr. Sund further testified that Mr. Irving referred him to Mr. Stenger to discuss the request. According to Mr. Sund, Mr. Stenger did not approve the request, and instead suggested that Mr. Sund "lean forward" and contact the National Guard to determine how quickly and what kind of assistance could be provided if needed.[437]

Acting on Mr. Stenger's advice, Mr. Sund testified that he called General Walker, the Commander of DCNG, around 6:45 p.m. on January 4; explained that he did not have the authority to request assistance; and asked how quickly DCNG could respond to a request.[438] According to Mr. Sund, General Walker informed Mr. Sund that he had 125 National Guard troops supporting COVID response in Washington, D.C. that could be repurposed if necessary.[439]Mr. Sund testified that he met in person with Mr. Stenger on January 5 around 12:00 p.m. and reported the conversation with General Walker.[440]Mr. Sund also testified that later in the day he told Mr. Irving about the conversation with General Walker.[441]Mr. Sund di d not contact Mr. Blanton, the third voting member of the Capitol Police Board, regarding the request.[442]

General Walker corroborated the majority of Mr. Sund's account. However, General Walker testified that he spoke with Mr. Sund on January 3 and asked Mr. Sund whether he would be requesting assistance from DCNG.[443]According to General Walker, Mr. Sund told him he was not allowed to request support, but asked: "if I do call you, will you be able to support me?"[444] General Walker testified that he responded, "[y]es, but I have to get approval from the Secretary of the Army and ultimately the Secretary of Defense because it is a [f]ederal request."[445]

Mr. Irving and Mr. Stenger disputed Mr. Sund's testimony about his request for emergency authorization for DCNG assistance. Neither Mr. Irving nor Mr. Stenger perceived the conversations with Mr. Sund as a formal request to the Board.[446]Mr. Irving testified that on

[435]*Examining the U.S. Capitol Attack: Joint Hearing Before the S. Comm. on Homeland Sec. & Governmental Affairs and the S. Comm. on Rules & Admin.*, 117th Cong. (2021) (testimony of Steven Sund, Former Chief, U.S. Capitol Police).
[436]*Id.*
[437]*Id.*
[438]*Id.*
[439]*Id.*
[440]*Id.*
[441]*Id.*
[442]*Id.*
[443]*Examining the U.S. Capitol Attack – Part II: Joint Hearing Before the S. Comm. on Homeland Sec. & Governmental Affairs and the S. Comm. on Rules & Admin.*, 117th Cong. (2021) (testimony of Maj. Gen. William Walker, Commanding Gen., Dist. of Columbia Nat'l Guard).
[444]*Id.*
[445]*Id.*
[446]*Examining the U.S. Capitol Attack: Joint Hearing Before the S. Comm. on Homeland Sec. & Governmental Affairs and the S. Comm. on Rules & Admin.*, 117th Cong. (2021) (testimonies of Paul Irving, Former Sergeant at Arms, U.S. House of Representatives, and Michael Stenger, Former Sergeant at Arms, U.S. Senate).

January 4, he spoke by phone with Mr. Sund, on a call that later included Mr. Stenger, about an offer from the National Guard to provide 125 unarmed troops for traffic duty near the Capitol.[447] Mr. Irving testified that he, Mr. Sund, and Mr. Stenger collectively agreed the available intelligence did not warrant having troops at the Capitol.[448] Mr. Irving further testified that the decision was not based on the optics of National Guard troops at the Capitol, contrary to Mr. Sund's testimony.[449]

Mr. Blanton confirmed to the Committees that Mr. Sund never sought Capitol Police Board approval to request National Guard presence in the days before January 6.[450] Notably, according to the Department of Defense ("DOD") timeline, DOD officials confirmed with USCP on January 3 and January 4 that USCP was not requesting National Guard support.[451]

C. The USCP Chief of Police Lacked Authority to Unilaterally Request National Guard Support Even in the Midst of the Attack

As described above, before National Guard assistance can be requested, the Capitol Police Board must issue an emergency declaration and approve a request for National Guard assistance.[452] The statute governing assistance from Executive departments and agencies provides that the House and Senate SAAs may request assistance from "Executive departments and Executive agencies" for their respective chambers in an emergency.[453] Therefore, as the attack unfolded, Mr. Sund needed Mr. Stenger's and Mr. Irving's approval before he could formally request DCNG assistance.[454]

After discussing the need for National Guard support on January 4 and relaying the subsequent conversation with General Walker on January 5, the topic was not revisited by the Capitol Police Board until the afternoon of January 6.[455] By 12:50 p.m., Mr. Sund understood

[447] *Examining the U.S. Capitol Attack: Joint Hearing Before the S. Comm. on Homeland Sec. & Governmental Affairs and the S. Comm. on Rules & Admin.*, 117th Cong. (2021) (testimony of Paul Irving, Former Sergeant at Arms, U.S. House of Representatives) ("On January 4, I spoke with USCP Chief Sund and Senate Sergeant at Arms Stenger about a National Guard offer to incorporate 125 unarmed troops into the security plan to work traffic duty near the Capitol, with the expectation that those troops would free up Capitol Police officers to be at the Capitol.").

[448] *Id.* Mr. Irving did not specify which intelligence products he, Mr. Stenger, and Mr. Sund relied on—the January 3 Special Assessment, the Daily Intelligence Reports, or other products.

[449] *Id.*

[450] Blanton Interview, *supra* note 48, at 27 ("I actually have to correct what you said, because Chief Sund has said that he has talked directly to the House Sergeant at Arms and later to the Senate Sergeant at Arms, he never asked the Board. And that is a very important distinction because there was never a request for declaration of an emergency until the evening of the 6th.").

[451] DEP'T OF DEF. TIMELINE, *supra* note 86.

[452] 2 U.S.C. §§ 1970, 1974; CAPITOL POLICE BD. MANUAL OF PROCEDURES, *supra* note 24, at §§ 6.1–6.3. By contrast, the Committees were informed that USCP has mutual aid agreements with law enforcement agencies; the USCP Chief does not need the Capitol Police Board's approval to activate those agreements. *See* Letter from Steven Sund to the Committees 4 (Feb. 26, 2021) (on file with the Committees).

[453] 2 U.S.C. § 1970(a)(4)(B)(ii).

[454] 2 U.S.C. § 1970(a). As discussed *infra*, once the request is made, the Department of Defense must assess and approve the request.

[455] *See, e.g.*, *Examining the U.S. Capitol Attack: Joint Hearing Before the S. Comm. on Homeland Sec. & Governmental Affairs and the S. Comm. on Rules & Admin.*, 117th Cong. (2021) (written testimonies of Steven Sund, Former Chief, U.S. Capitol Police; and Paul Irving, Former Sergeant at Arms, U.S. House of

that "the situation was deteriorating rapidly" and that outside law enforcement and National Guard assistance was necessary.[456] Mr. Sund testified that he first contacted MPD, followed closely by the U.S. Secret Service Uniformed Division.[457] Mr. Sund testified to the Committees that he "notified the two Sergeant[s] at Arms by 1:09 p.m. that [he] urgently needed support and asked them to declare a State of Emergency and authorize the National Guard."[458]Mr. Sund later corrected his testimony, informing the Committees that his initial call to Mr. Irving requesting an emergency declaration and National Guard assistance occurred at 12:58 p.m.[459] Mr. Sund testified that Mr. Irving stated he needed to "run it up the chain of command," that Mr. Sund followed up about the status of the request on multiple occasions, and that Mr. Irving stated he was waiting to hear back from congressional leadership.[460]

Mr. Irving disputed Mr. Sund's description of events—particularly that Mr. Sund first requested DCNG assistance at 1:09 p.m. Mr. Irving testified that he had "no memory of a call at 1:09 p.m. and [based on a review of his phone records], there [was] no call from Mr. Sund (or any other person) at that time."[461] According to Mr. Irving, the first call he received after 1:00 p.m. from Mr. Sund was at 1:28 p.m., during which Mr. Sund described the conditions outside the Capitol as deteriorating and indicated that he might make a request for the National Guard in the future.[462] Mr. Irving testified that Mr. Sund did not formally request an emergency declaration or National Guard authorization until after 2:00 p.m., a request that was immediately approved.[463] Mr. Stenger informed the Committees that he met with Mr. Irving sometime between 1:30 p.m. and 2:00 p.m. and that Mr. Irving was "waiting for approval from House leadership to move forward with the request."[464] Mr. Sund informed the Committees that Mr.

Representatives); Joint Committee Briefing with Michael Stenger, Former Sergeant at Arms, U.S. Senate (Feb. 18, 2021).

[456]*Examining the U.S. Capitol Attack: Joint Hearing Before the S. Comm. on Homeland Sec. & Governmental Affairs and the S. Comm. on Rules & Admin.*, 117th Cong. (2021) (written testimony of Steven Sund, Former Chief, U.S. Capitol Police). *See also* Joint Committee Briefing with Steven Sund, Former Chief, U.S. Capitol Police (Feb. 17, 2021).

[457]*Examining the U.S. Capitol Attack: Joint Hearing Before the S. Comm. on Homeland Sec. & Governmental Affairs and the S. Comm. on Rules & Admin.*, 117th Cong. (2021) (written testimony of Steven Sund, Former Chief, U.S. Capitol Police). USCP's timeline of events reflects that Mr. Sund called MPD for assistance at 12:58 p.m. and Secret Service at 1:01 p.m. *See* U.S. CAPITOL POLICE, TIMELINE OF EVENTS, *supra* note 61, at 11–12. Following his sworn testimony to the Committees, Mr. Sund reviewed his phone records and clarified that he called MPD for assistance at 12:55 p.m. and Secret Service at 1:08 p.m. *See* Letter from Steven Sund to the Committees 3 (Feb. 26, 2021) (on file with the Committees).

[458]*Examining the U.S. Capitol Attack: Joint Hearing Before the S. Comm. on Homeland Sec. & Governmental Affairs and the S. Comm. on Rules & Admin.*, 117th Cong. (2021) (written testimony of Steven Sund, Former Chief, U.S. Capitol Police). *See also* Joint Committee Briefing with Steven Sund, Former Chief, U.S. Capitol Police (Feb. 17, 2021).

[459]*See* Letter from Steven Sund to the Committees 3 (Feb. 26, 2021) (on file with the Committees).

[460]*Examining the U.S. Capitol Attack: Joint Hearing Before the S. Comm. on Homeland Sec. & Governmental Affairs and the S. Comm. on Rules & Admin.*, 117th Cong. (2021) (written testimony of Steven Sund, Former Chief, U.S. Capitol Police).

[461]*Examining the U.S. Capitol Attack: Joint Hearing Before the S. Comm. on Homeland Sec. & Governmental Affairs and the S. Comm. on Rules & Admin.*, 117th Cong. (2021) (written testimony of Paul Irving, Former Sergeant at Arms, U.S. House of Representatives).

[462]*Id.*

[463]*Id.*

[464]Joint Committee Briefing with Michael Stenger, Former Sergeant at Arms, U.S. Senate (Feb. 18, 2021).

Irving approved the request at 2:07 p.m.; Mr. Sund conveyed the approval to Mr. Stenger and, and upon his agreement, USCP memorialized that the Capitol Police Board's official approval was given at 2:10 p.m.[465]

Phone records provided to the Committees show a number of calls between Mr. Sund and Mr. Irving or Mr. Stenger between 12:00 p.m. and 2:10 p.m. on January 6.[466]

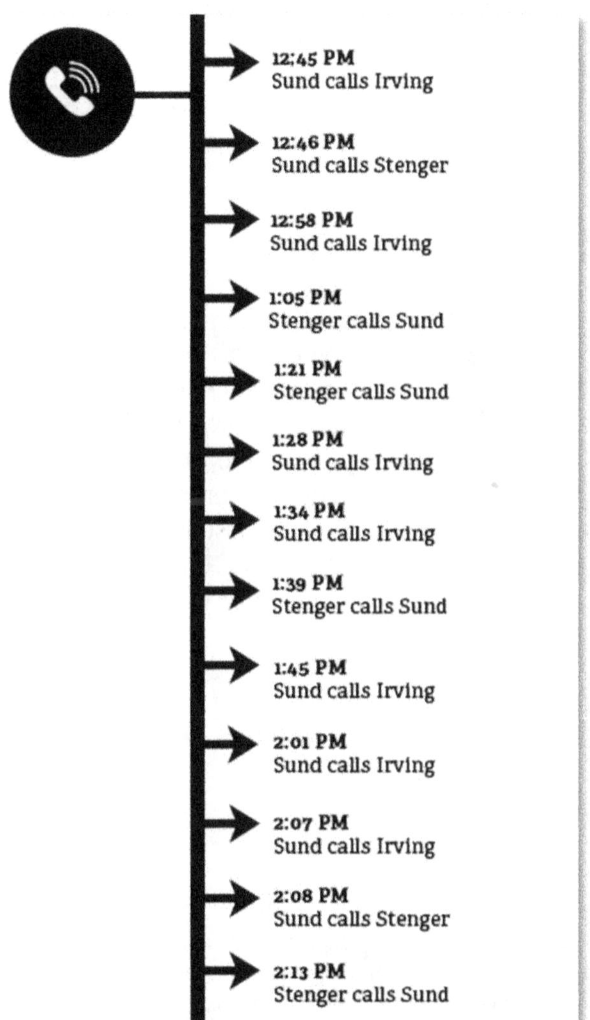

The phone records reveal only the timing, originator, and recipient of the call. They cannot corroborate the various accounts of Mr. Stenger, Mr. Irving, or Mr. Sund. Text messages provide more insight. A review of Mr. Sund's text messages on January 6 reveal no messages to or mentions of Mr. Irving.[467]There is a single message to Mr. Stenger. At 12:48 p.m.—two minutes after Mr. Sund called Mr. Stenger—Mr. Sund texted Mr. Stenger, "FYI we're running a

[465]*See* Letter from Steven Sund to the Committees 4–5 (Feb. 26, 2021) (on file with the Committees).
[466]Graphic derived from phone records provided by Steven Sund and U.S. Capitol Police (on file with the Committees). These records are consistent with information Mr. Irving provided to the Committees. *See* Letter from Counsel for Mr. Irving to the Committees (Mar. 29, 2021) (on file with the Committees).
[467]*See* SMS Content of Steven Sund for January 6–7, 2021 (on file with the Committees).

concerning suspicious package over by the Republican club by the S. Capitol St. metro."[468] The only other mention of Mr. Stenger occurred at 1:07 p.m., nine minutes after Mr. Sund claims he requested an emergency declaration.[469] At that time, Mr. Sund texted Jennifer Hemingway, then the Deputy Senate SAA, "just briefed Stenger we had a breach of the fence line on the west front by several thousand protestors."[470] There is no mention of the National Guard.[471]

Regardless of when the request was made, Mr. Sund acknowledged that he made the request orally to Mr. Irving and Mr. Stenger.[472] He did not submit a formal request to the Capitol Police Board.[473] This need to await Capitol Police Board approval during an emergency hindered Mr. Sund's ability to quickly request the assistance of the D.C. National Guard. Even when under attack, the USCP Chief still needed an emergency declaration from the Capitol Police Board before requesting National Guard assistance.[474]

VIII. DEPARTMENT OF DEFENSE AND DISTRICT OF COLUMBIA NATIONAL GUARD ASSISTANCE ON JANUARY 6

On January 6, DCNG had 154 personnel on duty at 37 locations in the National Capital Region, including 40 personnel comprising the Quick Reaction Force ("QRF") stationed at Joint Base Andrews, to assist MPD with crowd control.[475] DOD's decision to provide DCNG support to the D.C. government was influenced by lessons learned following DCNG deployment during the summer of 2020 to civil disturbances related to the murder of George Floyd.[476] As a result, the Acting Secretary of Defense imposed a series of control measures on DCNG deployment, including that the Secretary of Defense approve the issuance of weapons, batons, and protective equipment and that the QRF be used as "a last resort;" the Secretary of the Army imposed an additional control measure that he approve a "concept of operations" before the use of the QRF."[477]

[468] *See id.*
[469] *See id.*
[470] *See id.*
[471] *See id.*
[472] *Examining the U.S. Capitol Attack: Joint Hearing Before the S. Comm. on Homeland Sec. & Governmental Affairs and the S. Comm. on Rules & Admin.*, 117th Cong. (2021) (written testimonies of Steven Sund, Former Chief, U.S. Capitol Police, and Paul Irving, Former Sergeant at Arms, U.S. House of Representatives).
[473] *Cf. id.*
[474] *Examining the U.S. Capitol Attack: Joint Hearing Before the S. Comm. on Homeland Sec. & Governmental Affairs and the S. Comm. on Rules & Admin.*, 117th Cong. (2021) (written testimony of Steven Sund, Former Chief, U.S. Capitol Police). As discussed more below, once a request for National Guard assistance is made, that request must go through the Department of Defense's vetting and approval processes. Those processes and how they relate to the January 6 attack are discussed *infra* Part VIII.
[475] DEP'T OF THE ARMY, DEP'T OF DEF., REPORT OF U.S. ARMY OPERATIONS ON JANUARY 6, 2021, at 6 (Mar. 18, 2021) (on file with the Committees) [hereinafter DEP'T OF THE ARMY REPORT].
[476] *Id.*
[477] SEC'Y OF DEFENSE MEM., EMPLOYMENT GUIDANCE FOR THE DISTRICT OF COLUMBIA NATIONAL GUARD (Jan. 4, 2021).

Although USCP did not seek DCNG assistance in advance of January 6, as the attack unfolded, both USCP and MPD pleaded for DCNG assistance.[478] DOD officials claimed they did not receive a "workable" request until approximately 2:30 p.m.[479] DCNG personnel did not arrive at the Capitol until approximately 5:20 pm—nearly three hours later.[480] DOD officials stressed that, during this period, DOD officials and DCNG were preparing their personnel— assessing the situation, determining how best to provide assistance, instructing personnel, and ensuring personnel were properly equipped. The two key DOD decision-makers on January 6— Christopher Miller, Acting Secretary of Defense, and Ryan McCarthy, Secretary of the Army— told the Committees that this planning was vital to DCNG's success in carrying out its mission.[481] The Chief of the Staff of the Army —General James McConville—echoed this sentiment.[482] The Commanding General of DCNG, however, stated that DCNG was ready to assist USCP and criticized DOD's delay in authorizing DCNG deployment.[483]

The below section describes actions taken by DOD and DCNG in advance of and on January 6. It provides background on DCNG, discusses DOD's assessment of the D.C. Mayor's request for assistance, analyzes the control measures imposed on DCNG deployment in the days leading up to January 6, and discusses the actions DOD and DCNG officials took during the attack.

A. Background

DCNG is composed of more than 2,700 soldiers and airmen and provides mission-capable personnel in times of war or national emergency.[484] Whereas state and other territorial National Guards report to the state or territorial executive official,[485] D.C.'s unique position as a federal district makes DCNG the only National Guard unit that reports solely to the President.[486] The President, however, has delegated the authority to activate DCNG to the Secretary of

[478] *Examining the U.S. Capitol Attack – Part II: Joint Hearing Before the S. Comm. on Homeland Sec. & Governmental Affairs and the S. Comm. on Rules & Admin.*, 117th Cong. (2021) (testimony of Maj. Gen. William Walker, Commanding Gen., Dist. of Columbia Nat'l Guard).
[479] Joint Committee Interview of Christopher Miller, Former Acting Sec'y, Dep't of Def., 95:21-25 (Apr. 16, 2021) [hereinafter Miller Interview].
[480] DEP'T OF DEF. TIMELINE, *supra* note 86.
[481] *See, e.g.*, McCarthy Interview, *supra* note 276; Miller Interview, *supra* note 479, at 141:14–142:2.
[482] *Cf.* Joint Committee Interview of Gen. James McConville, Chief of Staff, Dep't of the Army, Dep't of Def. 33:9–35:2 (May 27, 2021) [hereinafter Gen. McConville Interview].
[483] *Examining the U.S. Capitol Attack – Part II: Joint Hearing Before the S. Comm. on Homeland Sec. & Governmental Affairs and the S. Comm. on Rules & Admin.*, 117th Cong. (2021) (testimony of Maj. Gen. William Walker, Commanding Gen., Dist. of Columbia Nat'l Guard).
[484] DIST. OF COLUMBIA NAT'L GUARD, *About Us*, https://dc.ng.mil/About-Us/.
[485] U.S. NAT'L GUARD, *Federal Mission*, https://www.nationalguard.mil/About-the-Guard/Army-National-Guard/About-Us/Federal-Mission/.
[486] D.C. CODE § 49-409; DEP'T OF THE ARMY REPORT, *supra* note 475, at 1; DIST. OF COLUMBIA NAT'L GUARD, *About Us*, https://dc.ng.mil/About-Us/.

Defense, who has further delegated some authority to the Secretary of the Army.[487]These delegations of authority were in place on January 6 and were relied upon by DOD officials.[488]

Upon a request by the D.C. Mayor, DCNG can support the D.C. Government after obtaining approval from the Secretary of the Army, who must seek approval from the Secretary of Defense.[489]When requested by the D.C. Mayor, DCNG can provide assistance on any land belonging to the City of Washington, D.C., which excludes federal territory such as the Capitol Complex and the National Mall.[490]

DCNG may also support federal agencies.[491] However, it must first receive a request for assistance ("RFA") from a proper civilian authority.[492] For the Capitol Complex, such a requesting party could include the Capitol Police Board or the USCP Chief.[493] After a civilian authority submits an RFA to DCNG, the request is sent to the Secretary of the Army.[494] The RFA is evaluated according to six criteria: (1) legality (compliance with the laws), (2) lethality (the potential use of deadly force by or against DOD Forces), (3) risk (the safety of DOD Forces), (4) cost (including the source of funding and the effect on the DOD budget), (5) appropriateness (whether the requested support is in the interest of the DOD), and (6) readiness (impact on DOD's ability to perform its other primary missions).[495]

After initial analysis, the Secretary of the Army consults with the Office of the Secretary of Defense, including the Office of the General Counsel. The Secretary of the Army also consults with the Deputy Attorney General ("DAG"), and thereafter approves the request, if appropriate. Upon approval, DCNG Commanding General informs the requesting civilian authority.[496]The process is similar if the RFA requires Secretary of Defense approval . The Secretary of the Army will brief the Secretary of Defense on the plan of action. The Secretary of Defense, in turn, typically confers with the DOD General Counsel, the Chairman of the Joint

[487]Exec. Order No. 11485, 34 Fed. Reg. 15411 (Oct. 1, 1969) (authorizing and directing the Secretary of Defense to "supervise, administer, and control" DCNG); SEC'Y OF DEFENSE MEM., SUPERVISION AND CONTROL OF THE NATIONAL GUARD OF THE DISTRICT OF COLUMBIA (OCT. 10, 1969) (further delegating supervision, administration, and control of DCNG to the Secretary of the Army).

[488]McCarthy Interview, *supra* note 276, at 125:23–126:3; Miller Interview, *supra* note 479, at 36:20–37:2, 38:19–25.

[489]Exec. Order No. 11485, 34 Fed. Reg. 15411 (October 1, 1969) (authorizing and directing the Secretary of Defense to "supervise, administer, and control" DCNG); SEC'Y OF DEFENSE MEM., SUPERVISION AND CONTROL OF THE NATIONAL GUARD OF THE DISTRICT OF COLUMBIA (OCT. 10, 1969) (further delegating supervision, administration, and control of DCNG to the Secretary of the Army).

[490]*Cf. Examining the U.S. Capitol Attack: Joint Hearing Before the S. Comm. on Homeland Sec. & Governmental Affairs and the S. Comm. on Rules & Admin.*, 117th Cong. (2021) (written testimony of Robert Contee III, Acting Chief, Metro. Police Dep't of the Dist. of Columbia).

[491]Exec. Order No. 11485, 34 Fed. Reg. 15411 (Oct. 1, 1969).

[492]*Id.*; McCarthy Interview, *supra* note 276, at 14:15–15:18.

[493]McCarthy Interview, *supra* note 276, at 16:5–11 (indicating there would be no difference between a request submitted by the Capitol Police Board and the USCP Chief). Although Mr. McCarthy did not distinguish between the Capitol Police Board and USCP, as described above, the Capitol Police Board is responsible for requesting assistance from Executive agencies and departments, or authorizing the USCP Chief to do so. *See supra* Part VII.A; Pittman Interview (Apr. 20, 2021), *supra* note 8, at 30:3–5.

[494]DEP'T OF THE ARMY REPORT, *supra* note 475, at 7.

[495]*Id.*

[496]*Id.*

Chiefs of Staff, and the Chief of the National Guard Bureau. The Secretary of Defense then decides whether to authorize the use of DCNG.[497] The DCNG Commanding General informs the requesting civilian authority of the approval.[498] According to officials, as was the case on January 6, DOD only serves to support the requesting authority.[499]

B. DOD's Posture Following the Events of Summer 2020

In the summer of 2020, DCNG was activated to support local and federal law enforcement officers in responding to civil disturbances related to the murder of George Floyd. On May 31, 2020, President Trump, then-Secretary of Defense Mark Esper, and Chairman of the Joint Chiefs of Staff General Mark Milley conducted a conference call with "all 50 governors to try to get additional Guard support to come to the Capitol," resulting in the National Guard's full mobilization of over 5,000 National Guard personnel.[500] As part of its response, DCNG employed certain tactics that drew "considerable scrutiny" including flying medical evacuation helicopters near crowds of protestors.[501]

Mr. McCarthy noted that the concern about the perception of troops on American streets was discussed during the summer of 2020 by all key decision makers, including the Secretary of Defense, the Chairman of the Joint Chiefs, the Army Chief of Staff, the Chief of the National Guard Bureau, the Deputy Secretary of Defense, and the General Counsels.[502] General McConville also told the Committees that these concerns were discussed within DOD leadership and reiterated that the military should only be used as a "last resort" in domestic law enforcement operations.[503] When General Walker was asked whether the issue of "optics" of a uniformed presence was "ever brought up by Army leadership when the DC National Guard was deployed during the summer of 2020," he responded, "[i]t was never discussed [in] June. It was never discussed July 4th when we were supporting the city. It was never discussed August 28th when we supported the city."[504]

The U.S. Army ("Army") acknowledged that "the preparations for the events of January 6 were informed by the considerable scrutiny received after the federal response to protests in summer 2020."[505] Accordingly, after the June 2020 events, Mr. Esper and Mr. McCarthy "determined that any future requests from civil authorities for DCNG support during planned

[497] DEP'T OF DEF. TIMELINE, *supra* note 86, at 3.
[498] DEP'T OF THE ARMY REPORT, *supra* note 475, at 3.
[499] McCarthy Interview, *supra* note 276, at 13:17–14:14.
[500] *Id.* at 18:4–15. According to then-Secretary Esper, "at the peak of the response efforts in the District of Columbia, more than 5,100 National Guard personnel from the [DCNG] and 11 states . . . were authorized by their respective Governors to provide support." *Department of Defense Authorities and Roles Related to Civilian Law Enforcement: Hearing before the H. Armed Services Comm.*, 116th Cong. (2020) (written testimony of Mark T. Esper, Secretary of the Defense).
[501] DEP'T OF THE ARMY REPORT, *supra* note 475, at 3.
[502] McCarthy Interview, *supra* note 276, at 48:4–15, 48:23–24.
[503] Gen. McConville Interview, *supra* note 482, at 68:17–24.
[504] *Examining the U.S. Capitol Attack – Part II: Joint Hearing Before the S. Comm. on Homeland Sec. & Governmental Affairs and the S. Comm. on Rules & Admin.*, 117th Cong. (2021) (testimony of Maj. Gen. William Walker, Commanding Gen., Dist. of Columbia Nat'l Guard).
[505] DEP'T OF THE ARMY REPORT, *supra* note 475, at 2.

protests required thorough scrutiny by both of them to ensure that the use of the National Guard was necessary; and that if so, the mission was narrowly tailored and appropriate for military forces."[506]

Mr. Miller, who was appointed as Acting Secretary of Defense in November 2020, told the Committees that there was an "undercurrent" of conversation about the lessons learned from the summer, such as "don't fly helicopters over crowds for crowd control."[507] Mr. Miller elaborated:

> [The events of the summer] reiterated things that we already know, which is the United States Armed Forces should only be used as a last resort in domestic law enforcement after all other capabilities have been expended. And the use of force and the use of the military in domestic law enforcement needs to be extremely thoughtful and carefully planned and done with deliberation, because at the end of the day, the Armed Forces of the United States, as you all know, is—it's very important when we use Armed Forces in a domestic situation.[508]

Similarly, Mr. McCarthy, who was the Secretary of the Army during the summer protests and on January 6, told the Committees that DOD's leadership was aware of the "history of military involvement on American streets" and that "if we were going to put troops on American streets . . . we wanted to be very clear about what we were doing."[509] "We're very conscious of that any time we [put troops on American streets], because of the history, and ultimately the perception that forms."[510]

Other events also informed DOD's posture in the days leading up to January 6. For example, during the summer 2020 protests, Guardsmen were not required to clearly identify themselves during the summer protests, which was addressed in the FY 2021 National Defense Authorization Act that included a provision requiring Guardsmen to clearly identify themselves when deployed domestically.[511] Further, on January 3, ten former Secretaries of Defense released a public letter warning DOD about using the military to resolve election disputes. Mr. McCarthy explained that "[the] hyperbole . . . about martial law and [the] 10 Sec Def letter" were "discussed in the entire Pentagon."[512]

When asked whether the public criticism about DOD's role during the summer 2020 civil disturbances or the other events led to any reluctance by leadership to participate in or assist on January 6, Mr. McCarthy responded: "No, just a lot of questions, a lot of rigor. We never said

[506] *Id.* at 3.
[507] Miller Interview, *supra* note 479, at 26:22–25, 27:1–6.
[508] *Id.* at 15:3–11.
[509] McCarthy Interview, *supra* note 276, at 26:4–15, 22:12–16.
[510] *Id.* at 47:15–20.
[511] *Id.* at 21:20–25. *See also* National Defense Authorization Act for Fiscal Year 2021, Pub. L. No. 116-283, § 1064. The provision was included in response to allegations that federal law enforcement and National Guard were not appropriately identified during the summer 2020 events. Ellen Mitchell, *Murphy Reminds Defense Leaders that Forces in DC Protests Must Visibly ID Themselves*, THE HILL (Jan. 6, 2021).
[512] McCarthy Interview, *supra* note 276, at 22:4-5, 24:4–11; *Opinion: All 10 Living Former Defense Secretaries: Involving the Military in Election Disputes Would Cross into Dangerous Territory*, WASH. POST (Jan. 3, 2021).

no; it was just we wanted to put the conditions in place to be successful. And we learned a lot from last summer about things that would go well and things that didn't," adding that "it was very important that we got [deployment of DCNG] right."[513] Further, in explaining the difference between DOD's response during the summer compared to January 6, Mr. McCarthy stressed that the two events had different timelines—the civil disturbances during the summer occurred over a series of days, whereas the events of January 6 "cooked off in minutes."[514] Mr. McCarthy viewed this difference in time as one that impacted DOD's "ability to prepare and marshal the capability to support" law enforcement on January 6.[515]

C. Events Leading Up to January 6

1. D.C. Government's Request for Assistance

On December 31, 2020, Mayor Bowser and the D.C. Homeland Security and Emergency Management Agency ("HSEMA") submitted a formal request for DCNG assistance on January 5 and January 6, 2021 to support the Metropolitan Police Department and other D.C. entities.[516] The HSEMA letter, directed to General William Walker, stated that the mission for DCNG would "primarily be crowd management and assistance with blocking vehicles at traffic posts" and requested "1) Six (6) crowd management teams to manage crowds at specified Metro stations and prevent overcrowding on Metro platforms and 2) A team to assist at thirty (30) designated traffic posts."[517] Both letters requested that DCNG be unarmed during the mission.[518]

On January 1, General Walker sent a letter to Secretary McCarthy recommending approval of the D.C. Government's request.[519] In the letter, General Walker stated that he had "analyzed the request for support" and "determined the support constitute[d] valid training and operational practices."[520] Mr. McCarthy told the Committees that, upon receiving General Walker's letter, Army leadership spent the next few days deliberating about how to support the request and conducting a mission analysis in consultation with DCNG and MPD to identify the "task organization" and logistics.[521] Mr. McCarthy believed certain conditions needed to be satisfied before he could approve the request, including the designation of a lead federal agency to support the operation and a concept of operations.[522] Mr. McCarthy memorialized his

[513] McCarthy Interview, *supra* note 276, at 23:13–20.
[514] *Id.* at 48:9–14.
[515] *Id.*
[516] Letter from Muriel Bowser, Mayor, Dist. of Columbia, to Maj. Gen. William Walker, Commanding Gen., Dist. of Columbia Nat'l Guard (Dec. 31, 2020); Letter from Dr. Christopher Rodriguez, Dir., Dist. of Columbia Homeland Sec. & Emergency Mgmt. Agency, to Maj. Gen. William Walker, Commanding Gen., Dist. of Columbia Nat'l Guard (Dec. 31, 2020).
[517] Letter from Dr. Christopher Rodriguez, Dir., Dist. of Columbia Homeland Sec. & Emergency Mgmt. Agency, to Maj. Gen. William Walker, Commanding Gen., Dist. of Columbia Nat'l Guard (Dec. 31, 2020).
[518] *Id.*; Letter from Muriel Bowser, Mayor, Dist. of Columbia, to Maj. Gen. William Walker, Commanding Gen., Dist. of Columbia Nat'l Guard (Dec. 31, 2020).
[519] Letter from Maj. Gen. William Walker, Commanding Gen., Dist. of Columbia Nat'l Guard, to Ryan McCarthy, Sec'y, Dep't of the Army, Dep't of Def. (Jan. 1, 2021).
[520] *Id.*
[521] McCarthy Interview, *supra* note 276, at 29:5–13.
[522] *Id.* at 30:2–5, 30:16–23, 31:1–8.

concerns in an undated and unsigned letter.[523] Mr. McCarthy explained a lead federal agency was necessary to deal with the "tension" that arises "between the Mayor and the federal" side, particularly noting the challenges of coordinating the Park Police, Capitol Police, MPD, and FBI, which necessitated an "architecture for the command and control."[524]

On Saturday January 2, 2021, Mr. McCarthy, Mr. Miller, and General Milley conferred about the D.C. Government's request for assistance.[525] Mr. Miller told the Committees that the conversation focused on understanding the roles of the local and federal law enforcement and discussing the "concern about using the Armed Forces for domestic law enforcement."[526] During the January 2 meeting, all agreed that the mission analysis needed to be finalized and would be presented for final decision on January 4.[527]

2. USCP Confirmed It Was Not Requesting DCNG Assistance

Mr. Sund and General Walker discussed the potential need for DCNG assistance as early as January 3.[528] General Walker told the Committees that he asked Mr. Sund if USCP planned to request DCNG assistance, and explained that such a request had to be in writing because the Secretary of Defense had to approve it.[529] Mr. Sund informed General Walker that he was not authorized to request DCNG support, but asked informally, "if I do call you, will you be able to support me?"[530] General Walker responded in the affirmative but reminded Mr. Sund that he would still have to seek approval from the Secretary of the Army and the Secretary of Defense because it was a federal request.[531]

On January 3, an employee within DOD's Office of Homeland Defense and Global Security confirmed with USCP that it was not requesting support from DOD.[532] DOD again sought and received confirmation on January 4 that USCP was not seeking DOD assistance.[533] According to Mr. McCarthy, because DOD received a request from Mayor Bowser's office, it wanted to confirm whether other law enforcement entities would also need assistance.[534] As he explained,

> That's why people called and asked. They were trying to . . . when I get back to the [concept of operations] and the command and control, all of the really meaty military tactical stuff, if you don't understand the concept of how the day is going

[523]Draft Memorandum from the Sec'y of the Army to the Acting Sec'y of Def. (Undated).
[524]McCarthy Interview, *supra* note 276, at 31:7–25, 32:1–3.
[525]DEP'T OF DEF. TIMELINE, *supra* note 86, at 1.
[526]Miller Interview, *supra* note 479, at 25:8–16, 19–22.
[527]*Id.* at 24:19–24.
[528]*Examining the U.S. Capitol Attack – Part II: Joint Hearing Before the S. Comm. on Homeland Sec. & Governmental Affairs and the S. Comm. on Rules & Admin.*, 117th Cong. (2021) (testimony of Maj. Gen. William Walker, Commanding Gen., Dist. of Columbia Nat'l Guard).
[529]*Id.*
[530]*Id.*
[531]*Id.*
[532]OFFICE OF THE SEC'Y OF DEF. MEMORANDUM FOR THE RECORD, *supra* note 114, at 1.
[533]*Id.* at 2.
[534]McCarthy Interview, *supra* note 276, at 44:7–15.

> to go, what your mission is going to be, who are you supporting—we are a supporting function. That's why they made all the calls and made sure everybody has the support they need. So that was critically important to codify.[535]

General McConville summarized the events leading up to January 6: "the Capitol Police had no plan for military to be involved around the Capitol. The only agency . . . that had a request for military was the Metro Police. No one else did."[536] Acting Chief Pittman testified that she was unaware of both calls from DOD, but that she would have stated that USCP needed the assistance of the National Guard, as she had previously told Mr. Sund.[537]

3. Coordination with Cabinet and White House Officials

Around 1:00 p.m. on January 3, Mr. Miller hosted a "Cabinet-level synchronization and coordination call."[538] Mr. Miller told the Committees that he initiated the call for two reasons, "[o]ne was to share information so we could coordinate and synchronize, and number two, I wanted to make sure that . . . they knew that any request for Department of Defense support, that it was legit, I was happy to provide."[539] Generally, Mr. Miller "wanted to make sure everybody was talking and that we weren't going to get surprised."[540] Mr. Miller stated that during this meeting, DOJ was reminded that it typically serves as the lead federal agency for domestic law enforcement activities.[541]

Later that afternoon, Mr. Miller and General Milley met with President Trump, who concurred in the activation of DCNG to support law enforcement.[542] According to Mr. Miller, the meeting with the President was scheduled to discuss a separate issue, unrelated to the January 6 Joint Session of Congress.[543] At the end of the meeting, President Trump brought up the Joint Session, asking Mr. Miller whether they were prepared.[544] Mr. Miller told the Committees that the conversation with President Trump about January 6 was "a 15-second, 30-second conversation. It was an in passing, kind of what else is going on type thing."[545]

When asked whether President Trump had a role in the approval process for the Mayor's request, Mr. Miller told the Committees no, because President Trump "had delegated that authority and authorization to me" so there was no requirement for Mr. Miller to get the

[535] *Id.* at 44:7–15.
[536] Gen. McConville Interview, *supra* note 482, at 19:9–12.
[537] Pittman Interview (Apr. 22, 2021), *supra* note 20, at 27:3, 9–11.
[538] Miller Interview, *supra* note 479, at 30:21–24. According to DOD records, the meeting included the Acting Attorney General, Secretary of the Interior, Acting Secretary of the Department of Homeland Security, and National Security Advisor. OFFICE OF THE SEC'Y OF DEF. MEMORANDUM FOR THE RECORD, *supra* note 114, at 1. Mr. Miller recalled that a senior official "from [DHS's] operations side" joined the call, but he did not remember if the Acting Secretary of Defense also joined the call. Miller Interview, *supra* note 479, at 31:8–17.
[539] Miller Interview, *supra* note 479, at 33:17–21.
[540] *Id.* at 34:14–15.
[541] *Id.* at 35:4–8. When asked whether DOJ was the lead Federal agency during the summer 2020 protests, Mr. Miller stated that he did not know, but he assumed so based on "standard practices." *Id.* at 35:9–14.
[542] DEP'T OF DEF. TIMELINE, *supra* note 86, at 1.
[543] Miller Interview, *supra* note 479, at 36:16–19.
[543] Miller Interview, *supra* note 479, at 36:16–19. [544] *Id.* at 37:15–24.
[544] *Id.* at 37:15–24.
[545] *Id.* at 37:22–24.

President's approval.[546] Mr. McCarthy, who did not attend the meeting with the President, suggested to the Committees that the President delegated authorization authority to Mr. Miller during the meeting, adding that "[i]t's the President's ultimate authority to put Guardsmen in D.C., so yes. Normally you inform [the President], at least some communication, a courtesy, to either the President directly or to the Chief of Staff to let him know, and if the President wants to discuss, obviously it is his discretion."[547]

On January 4, Mr. Miller convened a second conference call with Cabinet members.[548] Mr. Miller told the Committees that in the time leading up to January 6 he recognized that "the tone and rhetoric of the more aggressive demonstrators--Boogaloo Boys, Proud Boys . . . had changed in the last couple months . . . ." and that while he "didn't have any indicators of an assault on the Capitol," he recognized "that 6 January was the critical day in many of these conspiratorial-minded folks' narrative, and that [it] . . . could be a pretty dramatic day."[549] According to Mr. Miller, these concerns were raised internally in DOD and in inter-agency calls.[550] On the January 4 call, according to Mr. Miller, he and General Milley voiced concern about the permits that had been issued, questioning whether there was a mechanism to revoke permits for the 1,000 to 2,000 people who had been granted permission to gather on Capitol grounds.[551] The Department of the Interior and D.C. officials assured DOD leadership that the protests were constitutionally protected activities.[552] During the call, according to Mr. Miller, he and General Milley also suggested locking down D.C. to avoid potential violence; however, the idea was not pursued.[553] Mr. Miller described that the consensus from law enforcement was that, given the current threat picture, they believed they had all "resources and capability they needed to control the demonstration."[554] Mr. Miller testified that he "felt comfortable" about the mission planning and believed they were "all operating off a common operating picture."[555]

4. Designation of a Lead Federal Agency

All DOD officials interviewed stressed the importance of the designation of a lead federal agency to support operations on January 6. The lead federal agency is "the nexus and locus for all information flow" and ensures that everything is coordinated and synchronized across federal agencies and departments.[556] Mr. Miller noted that DOD "should never, ever be the lead federal agency for domestic law enforcement," except for the establishment of martial law.[557]Indeed, Mr. McCarthy required an agency to be designated before supporting the Mayor's request for

[546]*Id.* at 36:20–25, 37:1–2.
[547]McCarthy Interview, *supra* note 276, at 46:5–10, 15–25.
[548]DEP'T OF THE ARMY REPORT, *supra* note 475, at 13.
[549]Miller Interview, *supra* note 479, at 73:1–4, 12–15.
[550]*Id.* at 73:19–23.
[551]*Id.* at 74:1–16.
[552]*Id.* at 74:17–20.
[552]*Id.* at 74:1–20.
[553]*Id.* at 74:22–76:5.
[554]*Id.* at 76:1–5, 77:10–15.
[555]*Id.* at 78:8–12.
[556]*Id.* at 43:21–25.
[557]*Id.* at 44:1–7.

National Guard assistance.[558] According to Mr. McCarthy, on January 4, the White House designated DOJ as the lead federal agency for January 6: "Sunday evening, after Acting Secretary Miller and General Milley met with the President, they got the lead [f]ederal agency established, all of the pieces started coming together."[559] Mr. Miller also recalled that DOJ was designated as the lead federal agency at some point prior to January 6, but he did not know what role the White House played in the decision.[560]

Although DOD understood that DOJ was designated as the lead federal agency, there appears to have been no clearly established point of contact within the department, according to Mr. McCarthy, which he found "concerning."[561] Prior to January 6, Mr. McCarthy sent a letter to Acting Attorney General Jeffrey Rosen outlining the Army's operational plan in support of the Mayor's request and reached out informally to David Bowdich, FBI Deputy Director, because the two had worked together previously.[562] But Mr. McCarthy claimed, even during the attack, he was never provided an official point of contact at DOJ and had no contact with DOJ or FBI officials until approximately 4:00 p.m.[563] General McConville also stated that DOJ was designated as the lead federal agency; however, he noted that DOJ did not conduct any interagency rehearsals or have an integrated security plan, as DOJ did during the summer 2020 protests when it had also been designated as the lead federal agency.[564] General McConville stressed the importance of integrated security plans and acknowledged that had there been one on January 6, DOD's response time would have been quicker.[565]

In contrast, Mr. Miller stated Richard Donoghue, Acting Deputy Assistant Attorney General, served as DOJ's operational lead on January 6.[566] Notably, however, Mr. Miller acknowledged that, during the attack, he convened calls with Cabinet members to share information and ensure everyone was on the same page.[567] When asked why he convened the calls, as opposed to the lead federal agency, Mr. Miller responded, "somebody needed to do it."[568] Mr. Miller was not familiar with any actions DOJ took to coordinate the federal response on January 6.[569]

On May 12, 2021, Jeffrey Rosen, the Acting Attorney General on January 6, testified at a House Oversight hearing that it was "not accurate" that DOJ was the lead federal agency for security preparations on January 6.[570] He stated that DOJ's responsibilities were specific to

[558]McCarthy Interview, *supra* note 276, at 30:1–6.
[559]*Id.* at 35:11–14.
[560]Miller Interview, *supra* note 479, at 42:1–16.
[561]McCarthy Interview, *supra* note 276, at 37:12–23.
[562]*Id.* at 38:1–20.
[563]*Id.* at 38:1–20.
[564]Gen. McConville Interview, *supra* note 482, at 32:17–25, 85:15–24.
[565]*Id.* at 66:11–23.
[566]Miller Interview, *supra* note 479, at 46:1–47:1.
[567]*See, e.g., id.* at 148:9–16.
[568]*Id.* at 148:17–20.
[569]*Id.* at 149:12–16.
[570]*The Capitol Insurrection: Unexplained Delays and Unanswered Questions Hearing before the H. Comm. on Oversight and Reform*, 117th Cong. (2021) (testimony of Jeffrey Rosen, former Acting Att'y Gen., Dep't of Justice).

intelligence coordinating and information sharing.[571] DOJ has not acknowledged that it was designated the lead federal agency for January 6 and has yet to fully comply with the Committees' requests for information.[572]

5. Approval of D.C.'s Request and Control Measures for DCNG Deployment

On January 4, Mr. McCarthy recommended that Mr. Miller approve the D.C. Government's request for DCNG assistance. To formalize the recommendation, Mr. McCarthy sent a letter to Mr. Miller recommending the following assignments:

- Traffic Control Points: 90 personnel (180 total/2 shifts);
- Metro station support: 24 personnel (48 total/2 shifts);
- Weapons of Mass Destruction Civil Support Team: 20 personnel; and
- Internal Command and Control: 52 personnel.[573]

The recommendation also included the support of the Quick Reaction Force of 40 personnel staged at Joint Base Andrews.[574]

Mr. Miller, in consultation with Mr. McCarthy, the DOD General Counsel, and General Milley, approved the plan to deploy DCNG to assist the D.C. government.[575] Control measures, however, were imposed over the deployment of DCNG. In a memo dated January 4 (the "January 4 Memo"), Mr. Miller outlined the following:

> Without my subsequent, personal authorization, the DCNG is not authorized the following:
>
> - To be issued weapons, ammunition, bayonets, batons, or ballistic protection equipment such as helmets and body armor.
> - To interact physically with protestors, except when necessary in self-defense or defense of others, consistent with the DCNG Rules for the Use of Force.
> - To employ any riot control agents.
> - To share equipment with law enforcement agencies.

[571] *Id.*
[572] *Id.*
[573] Letter from Ryan McCarthy, Sec'y, Dep't of the Army, Dep't of Def., to Christopher Miller, Acting Sec'y, Dep't of Def. (Jan. 4, 2021).
[574] Letter from Ryan McCarthy, Sec'y, Dep't of the Army, Dep't of Def., to Christopher Miller, Acting Sec'y, Dep't of Def. (Jan. 4, 2021).
[575] DEP'T OF DEF. TIMELINE, *supra* note 86, at 1.

- To use Intelligence, Surveillance, and Reconnaissance (ISR) assets or to conduct ISR or Incident, Awareness, and Assessment activities.

- To employ helicopters or any other air assets.

- To conduct searches, seizures, arrests, or other similar direct law enforcement activity.

- To seek support from any non-DCNG National Guard units.[576]

Mr. Miller explained to the Committees the reasoning behind each control measure. For example, the purpose of the measure regarding the issuance of protection equipment was two-fold, "[o]ne was to make sure we presented an image of support as opposed to aggressiveness, and number two was at that particular point [we] did not want to provide an opportunity for . . . some of these people to take advantage of the situation."[577] Mr. McCarthy explained the purpose of the restriction as being "able to control the escalation of capability and the employment of that capability with civilians."[578] Mr. McCarthy further explained that DOD,

> want[s] to do everything [it] can to calm the crowd. When you come out there with body armor and shields and weapons, it sends a message very quickly. If you're going to take those measures, it obviously has to be done in the most extreme cases. So they just wanted to be very conscious of the decision making in the lead-up to those types of events.[579]

Mr. Miller described the second listed control measure on physical interaction with protestors as a "classic statement of intent" that the mission is to "support domestic law enforcement in a non-aggressive, non-kinetic way."[580] Mr. Miller explained that the third measure about riot control agents was to make sure that the commanders on the ground knew it was not going to be "an aggressive mission."[581]

Mr. McCarthy told the Committees that Mr. Esper and General Milley had issued guidance following the summer 2020 events incorporating lessons learned from those events.[582] Mr. McCarthy noted that the riot gear control measure was a "carbon copy" of this previously issued guidance.[583] Mr. McCarthy acknowledged that none of the control measures in the

[576]Memorandum from Christopher Miller, Acting Sec'y, Dep't of Def., to Ryan McCarthy, Sec'y, Dep't of the Army, Dep't of Def. (Jan. 4, 2021). Secretary McCarthy also sent a letter to Deputy Attorney General Jeffrey Rosen memorializing DOD's plan, which was discussed on conference calls on January 5 and 6. Letter from Ryan McCarthy, Sec'y, Dep't of the Army, Dep't of Def., to Jeffrey A. Rosen, Deputy Attorney Gen., Dep't of Justice (Jan. 4, 2021). Mr. Miller was not aware of the letter to DOJ, but he did participate in a conference call with Acting Attorney General Rosen in the evening of January 4. Miller Interview, *supra* note 479, at 69:18–70:13.
[577]Miller Interview, *supra* note 479, at 51:21–25, 52:1.
[578]McCarthy Interview, *supra* note 276, at 61:12–15.
[579]*Id.* at 62:15–22.
[580]Miller Interview, *supra* note 479, at 54:7–15.
[581]*Id.* at 54:20–25.
[582]McCarthy Interview, *supra* note 276, at 61:8–20.
[583]*Id.* at 61:15–20.

January 4 Memo was in effect during the summer protests.[584] Notably, Mr. Miller stated that there was no discussion of any prior guidance issued by Mr. Esper.[585] When asked for a copy of this guidance, the Department of Defense indicated no such document existed.[586]

The January 4 Memo also provided guidance on the use of the QRF:

> You may employ the DCNG Quick Reaction Force (QRF) only as a last resort and in response to a request from an appropriate civil authority. If the QRF is so employed, DCNG personnel will be clearly marked and/or distinguished from civilian law enforcement personnel, and you will notify me immediately upon your authorization.

When asked why the language regarding a "last resort" was included, Mr. Miller responded that it was "[s]tandard military doctrine and procedures for utilizing quick reaction forces and capabilities in military operations."[587]

On January 5, upon receiving Mr. Miller's approval, Mr. McCarthy conveyed the approval to General Walker, outlining General Walker's authorities and control measures for DCNG in a letter.[588] In addition to the control measures outlined in the January 4th Memo, Mr. McCarthy added an additional requirement that a "concept of operations" be submitted prior to the deployment of the QRF.[589] Mr. McCarthy testified that the restriction was needed to know "how we're going to employ the capability and ultimately support them and command and control them."[590] Mr. McCarthy also testified that the restriction on the movement of troops was critical if General Walker was "re-missioning" the troops.[591] Mr. McCarthy explained that this control measure was also in place during the summer of 2020.[592] Further, Mr. McCarthy emphasized that if troops were "creeping towards the Capitol," Mr. McCarthy wanted to communicate that to Congress because of the "impressions that would be made."[593] Mr. Miller never reviewed Mr. McCarthy's January 5 letter and was unaware that Mr. McCarthy added these additional measures, but noted that he deferred to operational leaders to impose any control measures deemed necessary.[594]

When asked about the January 6 control measures in comparison to the summer protests, Mr. McCarthy stated he did not remember if General Walker had deployed the QRF prior to January 6 and explained that during the summer, he and General Walker were co-located

[584] *Id.* at 68:8–12.
[585] Miller Interview, *supra* note 479, at 53:5–7.
[586] Email from Office of Legislative Affairs, Dep't of Def., to Committee Staff (Apr. 19, 2021).
[587] Miller Interview, *supra* note 479, at 56:20–25, 57:1–2.
[588] Letter from Ryan McCarthy, Sec'y, Dep't of the Army, Dep't of Def., to Maj. Gen. William Walker, Commanding Gen., Dist. of Columbia Nat'l Guard (Jan. 5, 2021).
[589] *Id.*
[590] McCarthy Interview, *supra* note 276, at 69:19–21.
[591] *Id.* at 74:17–21.
[592] *Id.* at 74:8–16.
[593] *Id.* at 74:21–25.
[594] Miller Interview, *supra* note 479, at 70:17–23, 71:1–12.

together—implying that there was no need for a "concept of operations."[595] When asked about the measure regarding the movement of Guardsmen from one corner to another, Mr. McCarthy gave a similar response stating, "Well, the summer, I was sitting side by side with him. It was very different."[596]

In his testimony to the Committees on March 3, General Walker described the control measures differently from Mr. McCarthy and Mr. Miller, stating:

> The Secretary of the Army's January 5th letter withheld authority for me to employ the Quick Reaction Force. In addition, the Secretary of the Army's memorandum to me required that a "concept of operation" (CONOP) be submitted to him before any employment of the QRF. I found that requirement to be unusual as was the requirement to seek approval to move Guardsmen supporting MPD to move from one traffic control point to another.[597]

As General Walker further described, "[b]y definition, a QRF is an *in extremis* force, a break glass in case of need element, postured to respond to an immediate and urgent need by friendly forces. Such requirement that a CONOP be staffed to higher headquarters during an emergency situation would inevitably delay implementation of the QRF."[598] Mr. McCarthy, by contrast, told the Committees he did not find the requirement to be unusual, stressing that "we gave [Walker] everything he requested."[599]

D. As the Attack Unfolded, DOD's Mission Planning Efforts Resulted in DCNG Not Arriving Until After Both Chambers Had Already Been Secured

On the morning of January 6, DCNG had 154 personnel on duty at 37 locations in the National Capital Region, including 40 personnel comprising the QRF stationed at Joint Base Andrews.[600] DOD officials have stressed that, on the morning of January 6, "DCNG was prepared to provide the limited support requested by HSEMA and nothing more."[601] As Mr. Miller described, as of the morning of January 6, "[e]veryone had what they needed, and had no additional requests. And it was very clear that domestic law enforcement felt they [had] all the resources and capability they needed to control the demonstration."[602]

[595] McCarthy Interview, *supra* note 276, at 69:22–25, 70:3–11.
[596] *Id.* at 71:17–25, 72:1–2.
[597] *Examining the U.S. Capitol Attack – Part II: Joint Hearing Before the S. Comm. on Homeland Sec. & Governmental Affairs and the S. Comm. on Rules & Admin.*, 117th Cong. (2021) (written testimony of Maj. Gen. William Walker, Commanding Gen., Dist. of Columbia Nat'l Guard).
[598] Maj. Gen. William Walker, Questions for the Record (on file with the Committees).
[599] McCarthy Interview, *supra* note 276, at 72:24–25, 73:1–13.
[600] DEP'T OF THE ARMY REPORT, *supra* note 475, at 6. Additional personnel were assigned to the night shift, meaning they were at home or in hotels during the day. Further, "100 personnel were on 3-hour recall, 250 personnel on 6-hour recall, and 350 personnel on 12-hour recall." *Id.* at 7.
[601] *Id.* at 7.
[602] Miller Interview, *supra* note 479, at 77:12–15.

Yet, as the Capitol attack unfolded, USCP and MPD pleaded for DCNG assistance.[603] DOD officials spent the afternoon assessing the situation, determining how best to provide assistance, instructing personnel on the mission, and ensuring personnel were properly equipped.[604] DCNG personnel ultimately did not arrive at the Capitol until approximately 5:20 p.m., nearly three hours after DOD officials acknowledged receipt of a workable request for DCNG assistance.[605] By that time, both the House and Senate chambers had already been declared secure.[606]

1. Initial Requests for Assistance Were Muddled

DOD officials were monitoring the events and receiving updates on the crowds at the Capitol throughout the morning of January 6.[607] That afternoon, Mayor Bowser first called Mr. McCarthy at approximately 1:34 p.m.[608] The call, however, was not a direct request for DCNG assistance; rather, according to Mr. McCarthy, Mayor Bowser said "'are you getting requests or anything from the Capitol? It appears the crowd's getting out of hand,' and there [were] no specifics. We didn't know if anything was breached or any of that, but it was just more of a '[a] re you getting requests?'"[609]

Mr. Sund called General Walker at 1:49 p.m.[610] Mr. McCarthy and the Department of the Army recognize this as the first request on January 6 for DCNG assistance.[611] According to

[603]*Examining the U.S. Capitol Attack – Part II: Joint Hearing Before the S. Comm. on Homeland Sec. & Governmental Affairs and the S. Comm. on Rules & Admin.*, 117th Cong. (2021) (testimony of Maj. Gen. William Walker, Commanding Gen., Dist. of Columbia Nat'l Guard).

[604]*See, e.g.*, McCarthy Interview, *supra* note 276; Miller Interview, *supra* note 479, at 108:22–109:15 (ordering activation of DCNG at 3:04 p.m., with the understanding that Mr. McCarthy and General Walker would continue mission planning for DCNG's deployment); *Examining the U.S. Capitol Attack – Part II: Joint Hearing Before the S. Comm. on Homeland Sec. & Governmental Affairs and the S. Comm. on Rules & Admin.*, 117th Cong. (2021) (written testimony of Robert Salesses, Senior Official Performing the Duties of the Ass't Sec'y for Homeland Def. & Global Sec., Dep't of Def.).

[605]OFFICE OF THE SEC'Y OF DEF. MEMORANDUM FOR THE RECORD, *supra* note 114, at 7.

[606]U.S. CAPITOL POLICE, TIMELINE OF EVENTS, *supra* note 61, at 20 (indicating the Senate chamber was secure by 4:19 p.m. and the House chamber was secure by 4:28 p.m.).

[607]*See* DEP'T OF DEF. TIMELINE, *supra* note 86, at 2 (indicating the Acting Secretary of Defense was receiving updates on demonstrator movements); Gen. McConville Interview, *supra* note 482, at 17:25–18:2.

[608]DEP'T OF DEF. TIMELINE, *supra* note 86, at 2. The D.C. Government indicated that Mayor Bowser first spoke with Mr. McCarthy sometime after 1:49 p.m. GOV'T OF THE DIST. OF COLUMBIA TIMELINE, *supra* note 76, at 4. Mr. McCarthy could not recall the exact time at which he spoke with Mayor Bowser, but agreed it was sometime in "that window." McCarthy Interview, *supra* note 276, at 81:12–20.

[609]McCarthy Interview, *supra* note 276, at 81:3–8, 100:16–18 ("That's when the Mayor first contacted us, but it was not clear what was going to be required of us."). *See also Examining the U.S. Capitol Attack – Part II: Joint Hearing Before the S. Comm. on Homeland Sec. & Governmental Affairs and the S. Comm. on Rules & Admin.*, 117th Cong. (2021) (written testimony of Robert Salesses, Senior Official Performing the Duties of the Ass't Sec'y for Homeland Def. & Global Sec., Dep't of Def.) ("[T]he Mayor of DC called the Secretary of the Army to request an unspecified number of additional DC National Guard personnel.").

[610]U.S. CAPITOL POLICE, TIMELINE OF EVENTS, *supra* note 61, at 14; *Examining the U.S. Capitol Attack – Part II: Joint Hearing Before the S. Comm. on Homeland Sec. & Governmental Affairs and the S. Comm. on Rules & Admin.*, 117th Cong. (2021) (written testimony of Maj. Gen. William Walker, Commanding Gen., Dist. of Columbia Nat'l Guard).

[611]McCarthy Interview, *supra* note 276, at 82:9–11; DEP'T OF THE ARMY REPORT, *supra* note 475, at 7 (treating the 1:49 p.m. phone as 0:00).

General Walker, he "immediately" conveyed the request to Army officials.[612] "[I]t was right after we got off the phone [with General Walker] that it was literally—we found out on TV that the Capitol had been breached."[613] Mr. McCarthy described the time around the initial request as one of "tremendous confusion."[614] Mr. McCarthy and Army officials were trying to acquire additional information from D.C. officials and DCNG regarding what assistance was needed and what the situation was at the Capitol.[615]

2. Army Staff Reportedly Advised Against Approving D.C.'s Request

According to Army records, Mr. McCarthy "made several attempts to elicit additional information from DCNG."[616] Around 2:20 p.m., Mr. McCarthy asked DCNG to "establish a conference call between USCP, MPD, and DCNG to help DOD better understand the situation on the Capitol grounds."[617] Shortly into that call, Mr. McCarthy claims he came to appreciate the gravity of the situation and "knew mentally whatever we could bring in the next minutes or hours, we had to go get the authority to go."[618] He added, DOD "knew there was an extraordinary event happening . . . at the Capitol, and [DOD] needed to respond."[619] Although the call with D.C. and USCP officials continued, Mr. McCarthy left to seek the Acting Secretary of Defense's approval to activate DCNG.[620]

Before leaving to speak with the Acting Secretary of Defense, Mr. McCarthy told members of his staff—led by Lieutenant General Walter Piatt, Director of the Army Staff, and Lieutenant General Charles Flynn, Director of Army Operations and Plans—to "take the call" and "figure [this] out."[621] Mr. McCarthy explained to the Committees that he expected the parties to address "simple things. How big is the crowd? Are they in the buildings? Where are they? What [did they] need from [DNCG]? How do[es] [DCNG] configure themselves? What kind of equipment do[es] [DCNG] need?"[622]

[612]*Examining the U.S. Capitol Attack – Part II: Joint Hearing Before the S. Comm. on Homeland Sec. & Governmental Affairs and the S. Comm. on Rules & Admin.*, 117th Cong. (2021) (written testimony of Maj. Gen. William Walker, Commanding Gen., Dist. of Columbia Nat'l Guard).
[613]McCarthy Interview, *supra* note 276, at 82:15–18.
[614]*Id.* at 82:19–25.
[615]*Id.* at 82:19–25; DEP'T OF THE ARMY, DEP'T OF THE ARMY REPORT, *supra* note 475, at 7.
[616]DEP'T OF THE ARMY, DEP'T OF THE ARMY REPORT, *supra* note 475, at 7.
[617]*Id.*
[618]McCarthy Interview, *supra* note 276, at 82:24–83:1. *See also Examining the U.S. Capitol Attack – Part II: Joint Hearing Before the S. Comm. on Homeland Sec. & Governmental Affairs and the S. Comm. on Rules & Admin.*, 117th Cong. (2021) (written testimony of Robert Salesses, Senior Official Performing the Duties of the Ass't Sec'y for Homeland Def. & Global Sec., Dep't of Def.) ("Following a call with the Mayor of DC and her staff, the Secretary of the Army met with the Acting Secretary of Defense and the Chairman of the Joint Chiefs of Staff to discuss the requests of the U.S. Capitol Police and the Mayor of DC (at approximately 2:30 p.m.)."). General McConville also recalled being informed of the request around 2:25 p.m. Gen. McConville Interview, *supra* note 482, at 22:25–26:4 ("There was -- I think that's probably the best way to describe it, when there was an official request, that we were taking that request and going to the Secretary of Defense and saying that they need National Guard to respond to the Capitol.").
[619]McCarthy Interview, *supra* note 276, at 88:25–89:2.
[620]*Id.* at 101:6–15.
[621]*Id.* at 82:23–24, 83:23–84:1, 84:10–15, 86:8–13.
[622]*Id.* at 85:12–18.

Mr. Sund and Acting MPD Chief Contee testified to the Committees that, during the conversation, Army officials expressed reluctance and hesitation to send DCNG to the Capitol. According to Acting MPD Chief Contee, Army officials cited the importance of planning and public perception: "the response was more asking about the plan; you know, what was the plan for the National Guard? The response was more focused on, in addition to the plan, the optics, you know, how this looks with boots on the ground on the Capitol."[623] Acting MPD Chief Contee testified that Army officials stated that they "did not like the optics of boots on the ground at the Capitol."[624] Mr. Sund characterized General Piatt as saying, "I don't like the visual of the National Guard standing a line with the Capitol in the background. I would much rather relieve USCP officers from other posts so they can handle the protestors" and that his "recommendation would be not to support the request."[625] General Walker also testified that General Flynn and General Piatt expressed concern about the "optics" during the call, adding that General Flynn and General Piatt "both said it would not be in their best military advice to advise the Secretary of the Army to have uniformed Guard's members at the Capitol during the election confirmation."[626]

The Army has denied its officials mentioned optics. According to Army records, after Mr. Sund requested immediate assistance, General Piatt "calmly stated that the Army needed help understanding the situation and needed to clarify what specific task(s) the USCP wanted DCNG to perform."[627] The Army acknowledged that General Piatt "expressed concern about Army soldiers clearing the Capitol Building, recommending that the National Guard assist with crowd control while law enforcement cleared the Capitol Building."[628] According to Army records, and as described more below, the Mayor and Acting MPD Chief Contee interpreted this as a denial of support; General Piatt explained multiple times that DOD was not denying the request but that a basic plan needed to be developed "before rushing into an unclear and dynamic situation."[629] Army records do not reference General Piatt's purported statement that it would not be his best military advice to send DCNG personnel to the Capitol.

Neither Mr. McCarthy nor Mr. Miller participated in the phone call with General Piatt, Army staff, D.C. officials, and Mr. Sund. Both Mr. McCarthy and Mr. Miller, however, strongly denied mentioning or discussing the role of optics in assessing whether to provide DCNG

[623] *Examining the U.S. Capitol Attack: Joint Hearing Before the S. Comm. on Homeland Sec. & Governmental Affairs and the S. Comm. on Rules & Admin.*, 117th Cong. (2021) (testimony of Robert Contee III, Acting Chief, Metro. Police Dep't of the Dist. of Columbia).
[624] *Id.*
[625] *Examining the U.S. Capitol Attack: Joint Hearing Before the S. Comm. on Homeland Sec. & Governmental Affairs and the S. Comm. on Rules & Admin.*, 117th Cong. (2021) (written testimony of Steven Sund, Former Chief, U.S. Capitol Police).
[626] *Examining the U.S. Capitol Attack – Part II: Joint Hearing Before the S. Comm. on Homeland Sec. & Governmental Affairs and the S. Comm. on Rules & Admin.*, 117th Cong. (2021) (testimony of Maj. Gen. William Walker, Commanding Gen., Dist. of Columbia Nat'l Guard).
[627] DEP'T OF THE ARMY REPORT, *supra* note 475, at 8.
[628] *See id.*; *Examining the U.S. Capitol Attack – Part II: Joint Hearing Before the S. Comm. on Homeland Sec. & Governmental Affairs and the S. Comm. on Rules & Admin.*, 117th Cong. (2021) (testimony of Robert Salesses, Senior Official Performing the Duties of the Ass't Sec'y for Homeland Def. & Global Sec., Dep't of Def.) ("General Piatt told me yesterday that he did not say anything about optics.").
[629] DEP'T OF THE ARMY REPORT, *supra* note 475, at 8.

assistance to USCP or MPD.[630] When asked whether he disagreed with General Piatt's purported statements that sending DCNG personnel would not be his best military advice, Mr. McCarthy responded "at that moment, absolutely" noting that he "ran down the hallway" and "interrupted a meeting with the Secretary of Defense to get the authority to go."[631] Mr. Miller also downplayed General Piatt's purported belief that sending DCNG personnel was not the best military advice: "Their best military advice is theirs. The best military advice that I take is from the Chairman of the Joint Chiefs of Staff, statutorily. So the best military advice that I received was, 'Let's go. Agree.'"[632] When asked to explain the Army officials' purported statements, Mr. McCarthy explained his view that the parties "were clearly talking past each other . . . and created a lot of confusion," and as described more below, required a "a lot of clean-up . . . ."[633]

3. DOD Senior Officials Consider D.C.'s Request for Assistance

Beginning around 2:30 p.m., as General Piatt continued to speak with MPD, USCP, and other officials, Mr. McCarthy briefed Mr. Miller on the unfolding situation at the Capitol.[634] Mr. Miller recalled not receiving a "workable request" until that time.[635] In Mr. Miller's view, the breach of the Capitol building and the shooting of a woman inside the Capitol building marked a fundamental change in that it was clear that law enforcement could no longer handle the situation and DOD would be required to play a much bigger role.[636] At 3:04 p.m., Mr. Miller approved the activation of the full DCNG, "although [DOD] did not know exactly what was going to be required of [DOD] to support operations at the Capitol."[637] General McConville described Mr. Miller's decision as immediate and stated that no one advised against sending support.[638] Mr. McCarthy conveyed Mr. Miller's authorization to General Walker, directing him to recall all personnel and to initiate movement to posture forces to support MPD.[639]

Mr. Miller's 3:04 p.m. authorization was to activate the National Guard in preparation to support domestic law enforcement at the Capitol.[640] It was not an instruction for DCNG personnel to deploy to the Capitol, but rather an instruction to personnel to convene at the Armory, get outfitted with the appropriate equipment, and be briefed on the new mission. Mr. Miller understood that Mr. McCarthy and General Walker would continue mission planning.[641] Conducting mission analysis, however, was initially delayed as a result of confusion following

[630]Miller Interview, *supra* note 479, at 98:20–22; McCarthy Interview, *supra* note 276, at 86:24–87:9.
[631]McCarthy Interview, *supra* note 276, at 128:25–129:3.
[632]Miller Interview, *supra* note 479, at 99:18–21.
[633]McCarthy Interview, *supra* note 276, at 129:4–7.
[634]*Id.* at 101:6–15.
[635]Miller Interview, *supra* note 479, at 95:21–25.
[636]*Id.* at 94:15–23, 139:17–140:1.
[637]McCarthy Interview, *supra* note 276, at 101:6–15. *See also* DEP'T OF DEF. TIMELINE, *supra* note 86, at 2; *Examining the U.S. Capitol Attack – Part II: Joint Hearing Before the S. Comm. on Homeland Sec. & Governmental Affairs and the S. Comm. on Rules & Admin.*, 117th Cong. (2021) (written testimony of Robert Salesses, Senior Official Performing the Duties of the Ass't Sec'y for Homeland Def. & Global Sec., Dep't of Def.). Mr. Miller authorized the deployment of Maryland and Virginia's National Guard units to the Capitol at 4:18 p.m., almost an hour after authorizing all DCNG units to protect the Capitol. DEP'T OF DEF. TIMELINE, *supra* note 86, at 2.
[638]Gen. McConville Interview, *supra* note 482, at 36:16–17, 37:24–38:2.
[639]DEP'T OF DEF. TIMELINE, *supra* note 86, at 2.
[640]Miller Interview, *supra* note 479, at 108:22–109:15.
[641]*Id.* at 109:6–110:12, 114:7–21.

the call with General Piatt, USCP, MPD, and other officials. According to the Army, D.C. officials interpreted General Piatt's comments as "a denial of support" and threatened to "go to the media."[642] General Walker confirmed that a D.C. official "threatened to have the Mayor hold a press conference" to announce that DOD refused to support its request for assistance.[643] At 2:55 p.m., a reporter tweeted that DOD "had just denied a request by D.C. officials to deploy the National Guard to the US Capitol."[644] Mr. McCarthy explained to the Committees that, by the time he finished meeting with Mr. Miller, "they were tweeting . . . it was on the news that we weren't coming, we had declined support, which we hadn't. We never had. So there was tremendous confusion" between 3:00 p.m. and 3:30 p.m.[645] In that time, Mr. McCarthy had to "talk to the Mayor as well as [C]ongressional leaders, other members of the media, to tell them, 'No, we are indeed coming,' because there was a perception that we declined the request for support, and that was never the case."[646] Although Mr. McCarthy told those with whom he spoke that DCNG was "coming," he did not explain that the Army needed to complete a "mission analysis" before DCNG were authorized to leave the Armory.[647]

4. Mission Analysis

After Mr. Miller's 3:04 p.m. authorization for DCNG to activate and fully mobilize, DCNG personnel—those assisting MPD at traffic control points and the Quick Reaction Force—began to reassemble at the Armory. There, DCNG personnel were briefed on their new mission and equipped with the necessary protection. According to Mr. Miller, in the time needed for the personnel to assemble, he continued to perform "mission analysis"—assessing where DCNG personnel would be staged, what they would be doing, and what equipment they would need. Mr. McCarthy chose to relocate to MPD Headquarters, where he could discuss the mission plan with Mayor Bowser and Acting MPD Chief Contee face-to-face.[648] Mr. McCarthy arrived at MPD Headquarters around 4:10 p.m.[649]

According to an Army report, "a critical planning factor was to specify unit-level tasks to employ the DCNG . . . because . . . the Army does not respond to crises as individuals, but instead by small units such as squads and platoons."[650] General McConville informed the Committees that DCNG personnel were originally assigned to assist with traffic control points, and that if that purpose were to change, "ideally, you'd want to have a task and purpose for what

[642] DEP'T OF THE ARMY REPORT, *supra* note 475, at 8. According to the Army, Lt. Gen. Piatt explained at least three times during the call that DOD was not denying the request for assistance, but that it needed to develop a plan before "rushing into an unclear and dynamic situation." *Id.*
[643] Joint Committee Briefing with Maj. Gen. William Walker, Commanding Gen., Dist. of Columbia Nat'l Guard (Feb. 26, 2021).
[644] *See* Aaron C. Davis (@byaaroncdavis), TWITTER (Jan. 6, 2021, 2:55 PM), https://twitter.com/byaaroncdavis/status/1346908166030766080?lang=en ("BREAKING: A source tells me the Defense Department has just denied a request by DC officials to deploy the National Guard to the US Capitol.").
[645] McCarthy Interview, *supra* note 276, at 87:15–23.
[646] *Id.* at 102:7–11.
[647] *Id.* at 106:18–107:3.
[648] *Id.* at 102:21, 104:16-17, 105:23.
[649] *See* DEP'T OF DEF. TIMELINE, *supra* note 86, at 2. *See also* DEP'T OF THE ARMY REPORT, *supra* note 475, at 9 (indicating Mr. McCarthy arrived at approximately 4:05 p.m.); McCarthy Interview, *supra* note 276, at 102:21– 103:1 (placing his arrival time around 4:00 p.m.).
[650] DEP'T OF THE ARMY REPORT, *supra* note 475, at 9.

they would do" and that "you would want to make sure that they had they had the appropriate qualifications for the task and purpose" given.[651] Another important aspect was determining the appropriate equipment for the mission. In addition, DCNG personnel had to re-group—those on duty were stationed at 37 separate locations around the National Capital Region. Mr. McCarthy summarized:

> They didn't have their equipment. They weren't together, they didn't have their equipment, and they didn't know—I mean, these guys are on street corners. You had to bring them back to the Armory. The Capitol [was] under attack. We need[ed] to put their body armor on, put [their] equipment on, [tell them] you're going to link up at the corner First and D, you're going to be inserted by the Capitol Police, you're going to lay in a perimeter out in front of the building. They had to be informed of what they are about to go do. These guys were 20 blocks away, controlling traffic.[652]

By contrast, General Walker believed that DCNG personnel at traffic control points had the equipment necessary to respond to the Capitol, testifying that "[t]hey had gear in the vehicle. They were equipped with force protection, helmets, shin guards, and body protection."[653] Mr. McCarthy told the Committees that he understood that DCNG personnel had helmets and vests in their vehicles, but he noted that they did not have shields and batons, which were necessary to respond to control the growing crowd at the Capitol.[654] Mr. Miller testified that he was not aware that guardsmen had equipment in their vehicles, but that he was "gratified" to know that "subordinate commanders" had the "latitude to do what they needed."[655]

By 4:32 p.m., Mr. McCarthy and his D.C. counterparts had agreed upon a "task and purpose" for DCNG, "identif[ied] link-up locations, and confirm[ed] key leaders at each site."[656] Accounts differ as to who within DOD needed to approve the final plan in order to deploy DCNG troops to the Capitol. Mr. McCarthy briefed Mr. Miller on the plan, who raised no objections.[657] But Mr. Miller informed the Committees that he did not need to approve the plan—in his view, his 3:04 p.m. authorization was all encompassing and as soon as Mr. McCarthy and General Walker finished their mission analysis, DCNG had all necessary

[651]Gen. McConville Interview, *supra* note 482, at 24:15–20.
[652]McCarthy Interview, *supra* note 276, at 92:16–93:1.
[653]*Examining the U.S. Capitol Attack – Part II: Joint Hearing Before the S. Comm. on Homeland Sec. & Governmental Affairs and the S. Comm. on Rules & Admin.*, 117th Cong. 131–32 (2021) (testimony of Maj. Gen. William Walker, Commanding Gen., Dist. of Columbia Nat'l Guard).
[654]McCarthy Interview, *supra* note 276, at 96:9–14, 98:4–14.
[655]Miller Interview, *supra* note 479, at 65:14–20.
[656]DEP'T OF THE ARMY REPORT, *supra* note 475, at 9.
[657]*Cf.* OFFICE OF THE SEC'Y OF DEF. MEMORANDUM FOR THE RECORD, *supra* note 114, at 6; Miller Interview, *supra* note 479, at 131:20–24; DEP'T OF DEF. TIMELINE, *supra* note 86, at 3; DEP'T OF THE ARMY REPORT, *supra* note 475, at 9, 10.

authorizations to deploy.[658] General McConville informed the Committees that, although he did not know for sure, he believed Mr. Miller did need to approve the deployment plan.[659]

Mr. McCarthy told the Committees that he authorized General Walker to depart the Armory for the Capitol at 4:35 p.m.[660] In contrast, General Walker testified that he did not receive authorization to depart the Armory until 5:08 p.m.[661] DCNG records indicate that General McConville conveyed the deployment instruction.[662] General McConville explained that he joined an in-progress video conference and "said you have all the authorities you need to move, you moving? And [General Walker] said yeah."[663] General McConville believed that General Walker had received the direction to deploy prior to their 5:08 p.m. conversation, noting that he does not have the authority to order deployment in his advisory position.[664]

These discrepancies reflect the breakdown in communication between DOD and DCNG officials, who were all located in different parts of the District. When asked about the discrepancy between DCNG's timeline and the Army's timeline, Mr. Miller pointed to the "fog and friction of chaotic situations."[665] General McConville also referenced "fog and friction," adding that the Pentagon is "an administrative headquarters" rather than a tactical "command and control headquarters that's actually fighting a battle" and it's "not unusual in crisis situations to have times that are not exact."[666]

While there are conflicting reports as to when DCNG left the Armory, all agree that it occurred shortly after 5:00 p.m.[667] Neither Mr. Miller, Mr. McCarthy, nor General McConville could explain why it took DCNG more than 30 minutes after the deployment directive to leave the Armory. Mr. Miller speculated that this time may have been used to provide personnel final instructions.[668] General McConville noted that "it takes time to move people" and also believed that it may have been used to finalize logistics.[669]

[658] Miller Interview, *supra* note 479, at 109:23–110:12, 114:7–11.
[659] Gen. McConville Interview, *supra* note 482, at 51:13–14.
[660] McCarthy Interview, *supra* note 276, at 108:8–22. *See also* OFFICE OF THE SEC'Y OF DEF. MEMORANDUM FOR THE RECORD, *supra* note 114, at 6; DEP'T OF THE ARMY, DEP'T OF THE ARMY REPORT, *supra* note 475, at 10.
[661] *Examining the U.S. Capitol Attack – Part II: Joint Hearing Before the S. Comm. on Homeland Sec. & Governmental Affairs and the S. Comm. on Rules & Admin.*, 117th Cong. (2021) (written testimony of Maj. Gen. William Walker, Commanding Gen., Dist. of Columbia Nat'l Guard).
[662] DIST. OF COLUMBIA NAT'L GUARD, TIMELINE FOR REQUEST FOR ASSISTANCE DURING CIVIL UNREST ON 6 JANUARY 2021 AND D.C. NATIONAL GUARD AUTHORIZATION TO RESPOND 4 (2021).
[663] Gen. McConville Interview, *supra* note 482, at 56:11–14.
[664] *Id.* at 56:23, 60:22–24, 61:1–8.
[665] Miller Interview, *supra* note 479, at 135:9–136:1. "Fog . . . refers to the ambiguous nature of information in war and the difficulties encountered in maximizing good information. According to [military theorist, General Carl Philipp Gottfried von] Clausewitz, friction 'is the force that makes the apparently easy so difficult.' Friction is the interaction of chance and action and can be caused by many factors, including enemy forces, friendly actions, or the environment." Capt. Philip Lere, *Fog, Friction, and Logistics*, ARMY SUSTAINMENT MAGAZINE (2017), *available at* https://www.army.mil/article/185864/fog_friction_and_logistics.
[666] Gen. McConville Interview, *supra* note 482, at 83:20–24, 84:13–15.
[667] DEP'T OF THE ARMY REPORT, *supra* note 475, at 10.
[668] Miller Interview, *supra* note 479, at 133:25–135:7.
[669] Gen. McConville Interview, *supra* note 482, at 55:6, 14–17.

DCNG arrived at the Capitol around 5:20 p.m.[670] Even if Mr. Miller and Mr. McCarthy did not become aware of the request or urgency for DCNG assistance until approximately 2:30 p.m., nearly three hours elapsed between that awareness and arrival of DCNG. General Walker testified that "it should not take 3 hours to either say yes or no to an urgent request . . . [i]n an event like that where everybody saw it, it should not take 3 hours."[671]

General Walker testified that his "'concept of operation' [would have been] simple, to immediately deploy as many civil disturbance equipped DCNG personnel to the Capitol as possible in direct support of MPD."[672] He "would have immediately pulled all the guardsmen that were supporting the Metropolitan Police Department," whom General Walker believed had the necessary equipment in their vehicles and 150 Guardsmen could have arrived in 20 minutes.[673] He noted that, shortly after 3:00 p.m., he directed the QRF to move from Andrews Air Force base to the Armory, noting that the QRF "returned to the Armory in about 20 minutes, so we had them sit there waiting [until] we [got] the approval . . . ."[674] General Walker noted that DCNG was "ready to go" before 5:00 p.m.[675] General Walker stressed that DCNG was "prepared to come to the Capitol":

> [I]t is a mandate that all National Guard practices civil disturbance. We are equipped for it, we train for it, and we are prepared to do it when called upon. So if we had been approved to do it, we would have got there and helped the United States Capitol Police.[676]

When asked about the apparent three-hour delay, however, Mr. McCarthy noted DOD took more than two days to conduct mission analysis for the D.C. Government's December 31, 2020 request and took less than two hours to prepare a plan on January 6.[677] Mr. Miller also stressed that it typically takes active duty forces—"people specifically sitting in their areas before they deploy"—three hours minimum to mission plan, get outfitted, and briefed on the mission.[678] He attributed criticism to "either hyper-politicization of the situation or an ignorance of how military operations work."[679]

670 *See, e.g.*, McCarthy Interview, *supra* note 276, at 104:8–12; *Examining the U.S. Capitol Attack – Part II: Joint Hearing Before the S. Comm. on Homeland Sec. & Governmental Affairs and the S. Comm. on Rules & Admin.*, 117th Cong. (2021) (written testimony of Maj. Gen. William Walker, Commanding Gen., Dist. of Columbia Nat'l Guard); DEP'T OF THE ARMY REPORT, *supra* note 475, at 10.

671 *Examining the U.S. Capitol Attack – Part II: Joint Hearing Before the S. Comm. on Homeland Sec. & Governmental Affairs and the S. Comm. on Rules & Admin.*, 117th Cong. (2021) (testimony of Maj. Gen. William Walker, Commanding Gen., Dist. of Columbia Nat'l Guard).

672 Maj. Gen. William Walker, Questions for the Record (on file with the Committees).

673 *Examining the U.S. Capitol Attack – Part II: Joint Hearing Before the S. Comm. on Homeland Sec. & Governmental Affairs and the S. Comm. on Rules & Admin.*, 117th Cong. (2021) (testimony of Maj. Gen. William Walker, Commanding Gen., Dist. of Columbia Nat'l Guard).

674 *Id.*

675 *Id.*

676 *Id.*

677 McCarthy Interview, *supra* note 276, at 24:23–25. Mr. McCarthy also described the two-day period as "pretty quick." *Id.*

678 Miller Interview, *supra* note 479, at 114:22–115:4.

679 *Id.* at 140:8–10.

General McConville, Mr. McCarthy, and Mr. Miller also stressed the differences between the National Guard and law enforcement, including that National Guard personnel are not first responders who can show up in minutes, and the importance of "mission planning" before dispatching DCNG personnel. General McConville explained:

> But there's a difference, maybe getting a couple hours or couple things of doing civil disturbance training than actually clearing a building with all these important people here in contact or in a contested environment. You want to make sure you're using the right people with the right skill set to do that. And that's why you plan. That's why you prepare. That's why you rehearse. And that's my best military advice on all these things.[680]

According to Mr. McCarthy, in all situations—emergency or otherwise—DOD needs to understand how DCNG "would be inserted in the operation" to ensure the best conditions for them to be successful.[681] Mr. McCarthy added:

> You know, much of how well you're going to do in our profession, 90 percent of how well you do is decided before you ever go wheels up, your preparation and the lead-up to operations. When the intel says there's no threat, when you're not requested to support, we're not like law enforcement where we were there in a matter of minutes, that they're postured throughout the city. It takes time to spin up our personnel to support operations. They were re-missioned from doing traffic control. You know, these are the sorts of things that had it been different in the way you were postured for that day, the performance would have been different. But the Guard is normally the last resort in support for any of these domestic type of operations in support of law enforcement.[682]

Mr. McCarthy also explained that the mission analysis must be performed in all situations, including during a crisis or emergency.[683]

Mr. Miller echoed Mr. McCarthy's statements noting that time and resources would be wasted without planning, coordinating, and synchronizing and sending people into a situation without understanding what's happening on the ground "doesn't work" and is "not effective."[684] He explained that he had an "obligation" to DOD personnel and their families to ensure personnel "are employed in a manner that protects them to the greatest extent possible."[685] He added:

> So when I see this timeline, this isn't a video game. This isn't Halo where, you know, Master Chief gets to just teleport himself across town. We have got forces in contact. We have to pull them out of contact. We have to prepare them. And, yes, I've been in my share of shows, where it doesn't work out that way, and the

[680]Gen. McConville Interview, *supra* note 482, at 35:7–15.
[681]McCarthy Interview, *supra* note 276, at 14:24–15:13, 96:2–8.
[682]*Id.* at 109:21–110:10.
[683]*Id.* at 50:2–14.
[684]Miller Interview, *supra* note 479, at 141:14–142:2.
[685]*Id.* at 140:10–13.

> one thing I've learned is I have a moral and a professional obligation to the citizens of this country that when we employ military force that we do it in a very mature, deliberate, and well-planned way.
>
> So that is why I am always kind of like, less than 90 minutes? . . . I [previously mentioned] our premier counterterrorism force in the United States military that has been doing this for 40 years, has a three-hour period. The fact that the National Guard was able to move this fast is unprecedented in the history of the National Guard. So I see it fundamentally different than this criticism that there was some sort of conspiracy to slow down the deployment.[686]

When asked the risk of deploying DCNG earlier, Mr. Miller warned it would have been "uncoordinated," "unsynchronized," and "not effective."[687] He continued, explaining what might have happened if DCNG had deployed without planning:

> I've been in a few riots and just having people show up without a plan and without mission intent, and having understanding of what is happening on the ground—you can just run to the sound of the gunfire, but usually it just doesn't work. It's not effective.
>
> So taking that time to make sure you have as much information as you can and making sure that your people—most importantly, that your soldiers have the information they need is pretty much the fundamental nature of these things. Unless you're an extremely well-trained organization that has practiced and trained and educated and experienced at just coming in—and we have some of those. It's not the D.C. National Guard, I just want to tell you that, and it's not a criticism of them. That's not their mission.[688]

E. Deployment of the QRF

As noted above, DCNG had a 40-person QRF staged at Joint Base Andrews on January 6.[689] A QRF is a standard element of "guardsmen held in reserve equipped with civil disturbance response equipment (helmets, shields, batons, etc.) and postured to quickly respond to an urgent and immediate need for assistance by civilian authorities."[690] On January 4, Mr. Miller directed that the QRF could be employed "only as a last resort and in response to a request from an appropriate civil authority."[691] On January 5, Mr. McCarthy reiterated this control

[686] *Id.* at 140:14–141:8.
[687] *Id.* at 141:14–19.
[688] *Id.* at 141:22–142:11.
[689] *Examining the U.S. Capitol Attack – Part II: Joint Hearing Before the S. Comm. on Homeland Sec. & Governmental Affairs and the S. Comm. on Rules & Admin.*, 117th Cong. (2021) (written testimony of Robert Salesses, Senior Official Performing the Duties of the Ass't Sec'y for Homeland Def. & Global Sec., Dep't of Def.).
[690] *Examining the U.S. Capitol Attack – Part II: Joint Hearing Before the S. Comm. on Homeland Sec. & Governmental Affairs and the S. Comm. on Rules & Admin.*, 117th Cong. (2021) (written testimony of Maj. Gen. William Walker, Commanding Gen., Dist. of Columbia Nat'l Guard).
[691] Memorandum from Christopher Miller, Acting Sec'y, Dep't of Def., to Ryan McCarthy, Sec'y, Dep't of the Army, Dep't of Def. (Jan. 4, 2021); *Examining the U.S. Capitol Attack – Part II: Joint Hearing Before the S. Comm.*

measure, withheld General Walker's ability to deploy the QRF, and directed that any consideration of QRF deployment must be preceded by a "concept of operations."[692] General Walker described these directives as "unusual."[693]

General Walker also testified that the QRF was outfitted with all the equipment needed to go to the Capitol and was "ready to go" before 5:00 p.m.[694] General McConville stated that "there was never an intent to have a quick reaction force going in to clear the Capitol."[695] Neither Mr. McCarthy nor Mr. Miller recalled whether the QRF had its civil disturbance gear available at Joint Base Andrews. Mr. McCarthy also noted that he was never informed that the QRF was at the Armory, equipped, and prepared to depart for the Capitol.[696] When asked whether the QRF was properly equipped to respond to the Capitol, even if that was not the original intent, General McConville reiterated the importance of the assigned mission: "it depends on what the mission was."[697]

Mr. McCarthy also acknowledged that, even if properly equipped, the QRF still needed to be briefed on the new mission.[698] "I wanted to be clear of the concept for operations and how we were going to bring these [available DCNG personnel, including the QRF] together, make sure they ha[d] the right equipment, a clear understanding of their mission, and then link up with an organization and contact. So, you know, it was ultimately my call, and I wanted to make sure we got it right."[699] General McConville reiterated the same point:

> But the bottom line is, is when you commit some type of quick reaction force, at least from a military standpoint, what we always do is, ideally, we rehearse it. We have a plan. We have an idea of what we want to do so you can tell the soldiers and the leaders, "This is where you need to go. This is what you can expect to do. This is the equipment you need to have." And then you can make sure that that quick reaction force has the capabilities to actually do that.[700]

When asked if he believed the concept of operations requirement slowed QRF deployment, Mr. Miller clarified that the "concept of operations" provided did not need to be a detailed presentation, it need only describe the plan of action.[701] He also could not assess

on Homeland Sec. & Governmental Affairs and the S. Comm. on Rules & Admin., 117th Cong. (2021) (written testimony of Robert Salesses, Senior Official Performing the Duties of the Ass't Sec'y for Homeland Def. & Global Sec., Dep't of Def.).

[692]Letter from Ryan McCarthy, Sec'y, Dep't of the Army, Dep't of Def., to Maj. Gen. William Walker, Commanding Gen., Dist. of Columbia Nat'l Guard (Jan. 5, 2021).

[693]*Examining the U.S. Capitol Attack – Part II: Joint Hearing Before the S. Comm. on Homeland Sec. & Governmental Affairs and the S. Comm. on Rules & Admin.*, 117th Cong. (2021) (written testimony of Maj. Gen. William Walker, Commanding Gen., Dist. of Columbia Nat'l Guard).

[694]*Id.*

[695]Gen. McConville Interview, *supra* note 482, at 41:24–42:1.

[696]McCarthy Interview, *supra* note 276, at 125:18–21.

[697]Gen. McConville Interview, *supra* note 482, at 42:4.

[698]McCarthy Interview, *supra* note 276, at 100:7–9.

[699]*Id.* at 124:1–13.

[700]Gen. McConville Interview, *supra* note 482, at 25:4–12.

[701]Miller Interview, *supra* note 479, at 156:11–25.

whether deployment of the QRF prior to 5:00 p.m. would have made a difference without knowing the situation on the ground and how they were to be used.[702]

General Walker and Robert Salesses, Deputy Assistant Secretary of Defense for Homeland Defense Integration and Defense Support of Civil Authorities, testified that they believed the attack on the Capitol constituted a last resort and that QRF deployment would have been appropriate.[703] When asked for his view, Mr. Miller told the Committees that General Walker never expressed his view that it was a last resort situation, and Mr. Miller stressed that he delegated all necessary approvals to General Walker: "If he felt it was a last resort[,] he had all the authority he needed [to deploy the QRF to the Capitol]."[704]

IX. CONCLUSION

January 6, 2021 marked not only an attack on the Capitol Building—it marked an attack on democracy. The entities responsible for securing and protecting the Capitol Complex and everyone onsite that day were not prepared for a large-scale attack, despite being aware of the potential for violence targeting the Capitol. The Committees' investigation to-date makes clear that reforms to USCP and the Capitol Police Board are necessary to ensure events like January 6 are never repeated.

The failures leading up to and on January 6 were not limited to legislative branch entities. As has been made clear in the Committees' two public hearings on the subject, failures extended to a number of executive branch agencies. A key contributing factor to the tragic events of January 6 was the failure of the Intelligence Community to properly analyze, assess, and disseminate information to law enforcement regarding the potential for violence and the known threats to the Capitol and the Members present that day. Further scrutiny of these failures and the preparations and response of federal agencies will continue.

[702] *Id.* at 157:3–22.
[703] *Examining the U.S. Capitol Attack – Part II: Joint Hearing Before the S. Comm. on Homeland Sec. & Governmental Affairs and the S. Comm. on Rules & Admin.*, 117th Cong. (2021) (written testimony of Maj. Gen. William Walker, Commanding Gen., Dist. of Columbia Nat'l Guard, and testimony of Robert Salesses, Senior Official Performing the Duties of the Ass't Sec'y for Homeland Def. & Global Sec., Dep't of Def.).
[704] Miller Interview, *supra* note 479, at 60:3–25.

Appendix A: USCP Inspector General Recommendations

OPERATIONAL PLANNING AND INTELLIGENCE RECOMMENDATIONS

(1) **Recommendation 1: Establish policies and procedures requiring documentation for supervisory review and approval, standardized planning document formats, and communication to personnel of criteria for determining the level of operational planning documentation necessary for each anticipated event.**

(2) **Recommendation 2: Establish policies and procedures designating the specific entity or entities responsible for overseeing the operational planning and execution process for each anticipated event.**

(3) **Recommendation 3: Establish policies and procedures requiring that individual units develop operational plans and coordinate those plans with other units for a comprehensive, Department-wide effort.**

(4) **Recommendation 4: Implement formal guidance requiring that employees communicate any intelligence reports and concerns from external sources to appropriate commanders.**

(5) **Recommendation 5: Implement detailed policies and procedures requiring any threat analysis included in operational planning is coordinated with Department entities having intelligence analysis and dissemination responsibilities.**

(6) **Recommendation 6: Provide training to its personnel on how better to understand and interpret intelligence assessments.**

(7) **Recommendation 7: Revise relevant Standard Operating Procedure to require supervisory review and approval for intelligence products to ensure its products are supported by relevant intelligence information and internally consistent.**

(8) **Recommendation 8: Require sworn and operational civilian employees to obtain a Top Secret clearance and require that administrative civilian employees obtain a minimum of a Secret clearance.**

CIVIL DISTURBANCE UNIT AND INTELLIGENCE RECOMMENDATIONS

(1) **Recommendation 1: Develop policies and procedures that identify and formalize the Civil Disturbance Unit's (CDU) mission, objectives, roles, and responsibilities.**

(2) **Recommendation 2: Update relevant Standard Operating Procedures relating to assignment of CDU personnel and use of less-lethal munitions to reflect current practices.**

(3) **Recommendation 3: Develop policies and procedures that identify and formalize the CDU's training standards, requirements, and responsibilities.**

(4) **Recommendation 4: Develop a Leadership CDU training program that focuses on command tactics and responsibilities.**

(5) **Recommendation 5: Develop policies and procedures for CDU equipment standards and lifecycle management.**

(6) **Recommendation 6: Store riot shields in a temperature-stable area with conditions designed to maximize the life of the shield, and the CDU should create a process for reporting when the shields are not stored within the guidelines of the manufacturer such as but not limited to direct sunlight, temperature-stable environment and when they have been exposed to petrol, diesel, solvents, and exhaust fumes.**

(7) **Recommendation 7: Develop policies and procedures for outlining the deploying and/or staging all available types of less-lethal weapon systems during CDU operations.**

(8) **Recommendation 8: Increase its number of less-lethal weapon systems and explore additional less lethal options.**

(9) **Recommendation 9: Train and certify additional CDU grenadiers.**

(10) **Recommendation 10: Prepare and stage necessary operational equipment for events.**

(11) **Recommendation 11: Immediately update relevant Standard Operating Procedure regarding use of PepperBall system to reflect current manufacturer recommendations and requirements and ensure that grenadiers received the training within the frequency specified in the updated policy.**

(12) **Recommendation 12: Develop a Standard Operating Procedure that identifies and formalizes the roles, responsibilities, and reporting requirements for employee listings for the CDU.**

(13) **Recommendation 13: Explore incentivizing the CDU program.**

(14) **Recommendation 14: Ensure that CDU liaisons are accountable for properly completing the CDU audit each quarter and providing it to the Commander of the CDU.**

(15) **Recommendation 15: Implement a process that will ensure that procedures for CDU inventory and reconciliation are fully functioning and operating as required. Specifically, the CDU must conduct physical inventories annually, perform reconciliations, resolve discrepancies, and provide an updated listing to the property custodian.**

(16) **Recommendation 16: Implement an inventory control for the armory and also recommend a Check-In/Out Log Book that requires approval by a supervisor for munitions and weapons.**

(17) **Recommendation 17: Either acquire an updated version of the 37mm less-lethal weapon or retire the weapon entirely because the current training for the 37mm weapon system is included in the certification process grenade launcher type weapon systems.**

(18) **Recommendation 18: Immediately enforce relevant policy that requires Intelligence and Interagency Coordination Division (IICD) prepare an Intelligence Priorities Framework annually and subsequently review the Intelligence Priorities Framework quarterly.**

(19) **Recommendation 19: Seek approval from the Capitol Police Board and its Congressional Oversight Committees to elevate and reorganize its intelligence resources into a Bureau level entity.**

(20) **Recommendation 20: Immediately codify a formal intelligence training program and enforce relevant Standard Operating Procedure requiring that the IICD Commander review and maintain the Intelligence Training Program for all IICD employees.**

(21) **Recommendation 21: Develop guidance that clearly documents channels for efficiently and effectively disseminating intelligence information to all of its personnel.**

(22) **Recommendation 22: Review the relevant draft Standard Operating Procedure regarding open source guidance for protest tracking and determine if the draft Standard Operating Procedure includes all required elements related to the IICD's open source intelligence work, and implement a comprehensive policy that covers open source intelligence efforts.**

(23) **Recommendation 23: Implement formal guidance that will ensure consistent and unified operational reporting across all intelligence and event planning documents.**

(24) **Recommendation 24: Refine document reporting that better captures operational impact to include improbable outcomes based on intelligence, trend data, threats to members, and information analysis.**

(25) **Recommendation 25: Implement guidance that will ensure consistency between analyst assessments and document summaries within its intelligence products.**

(26) **Recommendation 26: Require the Director of the IICD develop an action plan within 45 calendar days to improve the Department's capability to effectively collect, process, and disseminate intelligence information.**

COUNTER-SURVEILLANCE AND THREAT ASSESSMENT RECOMMENDATIONS

(1) **Recommendation 1: Update the relevant Standard Operating Procedures of the Criminal Investigations Section, Intelligence Operations Section (IOS) and Threat Assessment Section (TAS) to reflect current practices.**

(2) **Recommendation 2: Establish a formal policy detailing communication procedures for Counter-Surveillance Agents including how and what detailed Information is communicated through the chain of command and throughout the Department.**

(3) **Recommendation 3: Establish a formal policy detailing basic and advanced training requirements for the TAS and IOS.**

(4) **Recommendation 4: Enforce its policies regarding completion of form for stops or contacts officers initiate.**

(5) **Recommendation 5: Establish a standalone entity with a defined mission dedicated to counter-surveillance activities in support of protecting the Congressional Community and that is adequately staffed to accomplish its mission.**

(6) **Recommendation 6: Use Investigative Analysts to augment its counter-surveillance resources.**

(7) **Recommendation 7: Establish a central desk staffed with analysts, agents, and officers that can exploit, investigate, disseminate and triage information for counter-surveillance activities in real time. The desk should have a dedicated commander whose focus is on that process and providing guidance and direction to agents in the field.**

(8) **Recommendation 8: Increase the number of Threat Assessment Agents as the caseload increase.**

(9) **Recommendation 9: Use Investigative Analysts to augment its TAS at an analyst-to-agent ratio comparable to its partnering agencies.**

(10) **Recommendation 10: Consider providing more of their highest priority threat cases to the Federal Bureau of Investigation's Behavioral Analysis Unit Task Force for in-depth analysis of their priority subjects.**

CONTAINMENT EMERGENCY RESPONSE TEAM AND FIRST RESPONDERS UNIT RECOMMENDATIONS

(1) **Recommendation 1: Realign the Containment and Emergency Response Team (CERT) from the Operational Services Bureau Special Operations Division to the Protective Services Bureau and define a mission for CERT that better supports USCP's primary mission of security and protection of Congress.**

(2) **Recommendation 2: Pursue additional mission-driven training opportunities for the CERT from Federal partner agencies.**

(3) **Recommendation 3: Develop and implement recurring training between the CERT and other USCP elements such as the Dignitary Protection Division, Civil Disturbance Unit, First Responders Unit, Crisis Negotiation Team, and any other elements CERT may deploy to support.**

(4) **Recommendation 4: Update Standard Operating Procedure regarding noise flash diversionary devices.**

(5) **Recommendation 5: Establish policies that outline its procedures for completing advances and other recurring responsibilities it may have when supporting Dignitary Protection Division protective operations.**

(6) **Recommendation 6: Enforce compliance with Standard Operating Procedure requirements to have a CERT Commander present in the Command Post during high-risk events to include during any Joint Sessions of Congress.**

(7) **Recommendation 7: Ensure that the CERT Supervisors are held accountable for completing the bi-annual equipment checks including communication device function checks.**

(8) **Recommendation 8: Determine the number of CERT instructors needed relative to the size of the unit and ensure that only certified instructors are conducting CERT training. Additionally, the Department should consolidate all CERT training under the Training Services Bureau.**

(9) **Recommendation 9: Immediately enforce weapons qualification requirements for CERT officers on all assigned weapons as detailed in Standard Operating Procedure relating to CERT operators who fail to meet weapons qualifications.**

(10) **Recommendation 10: Ensure that CERT Supervisors are held accountable for completing monthly equipment inventories for all Property and Asset Management Division issued equipment for each CERT officer.**

(11) **Recommendation 11: Update relevant Standard Operating Procedure to identify which mountain bike programs meet the Department requirement for mountain bike training.**

(12) **Recommendation 12: Establish a Standard Operating Procedure that identifies the procedures for maintaining an inventory and proper storage of ballistic helmets and vests strategically placed around the Capitol Complex.**

(13) **Recommendation 13: Update relevant Standard Operating Procedure to identify the procedure for documenting the performance of the semi-annual inspections of remote locking devices.**

(14) **Recommendation 14: Establish a Standard Operating Procedure that reflects a requirement that First Responder Unit (FRU) officers be M4 certified.**

(15) **Recommendation 15: Explore options to secure ballistic helmets and vests at FRU posts.**

(16) **Recommendation 16: Train and provide FRU officers with additional less lethal weapon systems.**

(17) **Recommendation 17: Provide the FRU with additional bicycles.**

(18) **Recommendation 18: Provide FRU officers with advanced medical training similar to Emergency Medical Technicians.**

(19) **Recommendation 19: Train FRU together as a unit concerning M4 long rifle tactics.**

(20) **Recommendation 20: Coordinate with personnel from the Architect of the Capitol to resolve physical access issues.**

(21) **Recommendation 21: Ensure that FRU management are held accountable for completing and documenting remote locking device drills.**

Appendix B: Transcript of President Trump's Speech at the "Save America Rally" on January 6

Well, thank you very much. This is incredible.

Media will not show the magnitude of this crowd. Even I, when I turned on today, I looked, and I saw thousands of people here. But you don't see hundreds of thousands of people behind you because they don't want to show that.

We have hundreds of thousands of people here and I just want them to be recognized by the fake news media. Turn your cameras please and show what's really happening out here because these people are not going to take it any longer. They're not going to take it any longer. Go ahead. Turn your cameras, please. Would you show? They came from all over the world, actually, but they came from all over our country.

I just really want to see what they do. I just want to see how they covered. I've never seen anything like it. But it would be really great if we could be covered fairly by the media. The media is the biggest problem we have as far as I'm concerned, single biggest problem. The fake news and the Big tech.

Big tech is now coming into their own. We beat them four years ago. We surprised them. We took them by surprise and this year they rigged an election. They rigged it like they've never rigged an election before. And by the way, last night they didn't do a bad job either if you notice.

I'm honest. And I just, again, I want to thank you. It's just a great honor to have this kind of crowd and to be before you and hundreds of thousands of American patriots who are committed to the honesty of our elections and the integrity of our glorious republic.

All of us here today do not want to see our election victory stolen by emboldened radical-left Democrats, which is what they're doing. And stolen by the fake news media. That's what they've done and what they're doing. We will never give up, we will never concede. It doesn't happen. You don't concede when there's theft involved.

Our country has had enough. We will not take it anymore and that's what this is all about. And to use a favorite term that all of you people really came up with: We will stop the steal. Today I will lay out just some of the evidence proving that we won this election and we won it by a landslide. This was not a close election.

You know, I say, sometimes jokingly, but there's no joke about it: I've been in two elections. I won them both and the second one, I won much bigger than the first. OK. Almost 75 million people voted for our campaign, the most of any incumbent president by far in the history of our country, 12 million more people than four years ago.

And I was told by the real pollsters — we do have real pollsters — they know that we were going to do well and we were going to win. What I was told, if I went from 63 million, which we had four years ago, to 66 million, there was no chance of losing. Well, we didn't go to 66, we went to 75 million, and they say we lost. We didn't lose.

And by the way, does anybody believe that Joe had 80 million votes? Does anybody believe that? He had 80 million computer votes. It's a disgrace. There's never been anything like that. You could take third-world countries. Just take a look. Take third-world countries. Their elections are more honest than what we've been going through in this country. It's a disgrace. It's a disgrace.

Even when you look at last night. They're all running around like chickens with their heads cut off with boxes. Nobody knows what the hell is going on. There's never been anything like this.

We will not let them silence your voices. We're not going to let it happen, I'm not going to let it happen.

Thank you.

And I'd love to have if those tens of thousands of people would be allowed. The military, the secret service. And we want to thank you and the police law enforcement. Great. You're doing a great job. But I'd love it if they could be allowed to come up here with us. Is that possible? Can you just let him come up, please?

And Rudy, you did a great job. He's got guts. You know what? He's got guts, unlike a lot of people in the Republican Party. He's got guts. He fights, he fights.

And I'll tell you. Thank you very much, John. Fantastic job. I watched. That's a tough act to follow, those two. John is one of the most brilliant lawyers in the country, and he looked at this and he said, "What an absolute disgrace that this can be happening to our Constitution."

And he looked at Mike Pence, and I hope Mike is going to do the right thing. I hope so. I hope so."

Because if Mike Pence does the right thing, we win the election. All he has to do, all this is, this is from the number one, or certainly one of the top, Constitutional lawyers in our country. He has the absolute right to do it. We're supposed to protect our country, support our country, support our Constitution, and protect our constitution.

States want to revote. The states got defrauded. They were given false information. They voted on it. Now they want to recertify. They want it back. All Vice President Pence has to do is send it back to the states to recertify and we become president and you are the happiest people.

And I actually, I just spoke to Mike. I said: "Mike, that doesn't take courage. What takes courage is to do nothing. That takes courage." And then we're stuck with a president who lost the election by a lot and we have to live with that for four more years. We're just not going to let that happen.

Many of you have traveled from all across the nation to be here, and I want to thank you for the extraordinary love. That's what it is. There's never been a movement like this, ever, ever. For the extraordinary love for this amazing country, and this amazing movement, thank you.

By the way, this goes all the way back past the Washington Monument. You believe this? Look at this. That is. Unfortunately gave, they gave the press the prime seats. I can't stand that.

No. But you look at that behind. I wish they'd flip those cameras and look behind you. That is the most amazing sight. When they make a mistake, you get to see it on television. Amazing. Amazing. All the way back.

And don't worry, we will not take the name off the Washington Monument. We will not cancel culture.

You know they wanted to get rid of the Jefferson Memorial. Either take it down or just put somebody else in there. I don't think that's going to happen. It damn well better not. Although, with this administration, if this happens, it could happen. You'll see some really bad things happen.

They'll knock out Lincoln too, by the way. They've been taking his statue down. But then we signed a little law. You hurt our monuments, you hurt our heroes, you go to jail for 10 years, and everything stopped. You notice that? It stopped. It all stopped.

And they could use Rudy back in New York City. Rudy. They could use you. Your city's going to hell. They want Rudy Giuliani back in New York. We'll get a little younger version of Rudy. Is that OK, Rudy?

We're gathered together in the heart of our nation's capital for one very, very basic and simple reason: To save our democracy.

You know most candidates on election evening and, of course, this thing goes on so long. They still don't have any idea what the votes are. We still have congressional seats under review. They have no idea. They've totally lost control. They've used the pandemic as a way of defrauding the people in a proper election.

But you know, you know, when you see this and when you see what's happening. Number one, they all say, "Sir, we'll never let it happen again." I said, "That's good. But what about eight weeks ago?" You know they try and get you to go.

They said, "Sir, in four years, you're guaranteed." I said: "I'm not interested right now. Do me a favor, go back eight weeks. I want to go back eight weeks. Let's go back eight weeks."

We want to go back and we want to get this right because we're going to have somebody in there that should not be in there and our country will be destroyed and we're not going to stand for that.

For years, Democrats have gotten away with election fraud and weak Republicans. And that's what they are. There's so many weak Republicans. And we have great ones. Jim Jordan and some of these guys, they're out there fighting. The House guys are fighting. But it's, it's incredible.

Many of the Republicans, I helped them get in, I helped them get elected. I helped Mitch get elected. I helped. I could name 24 of them, let's say, I won't bore you with it. And then all of a sudden you have something like this. It's like, "Oh gee, maybe I'll talk to the president sometime later." No, it's amazing.

They're weak Republicans, they're pathetic Republicans and that's what happens.

If this happened to the Democrats, there'd be hell all over the country going on. There'd be hell all over the country. But just remember this: You're stronger, you're smarter, you've got more going than anybody. And they try and demean everybody having to do with us. And you're the real people, you're the people that built this nation. You're not the people that tore down our nation.

The weak Republicans, and that's it. I really believe it. I think I'm going to use the term, the weak Republicans. You've got a lot of them. And you got a lot of great ones. But you got a lot of weak ones. They've turned a blind eye, even as Democrats enacted policies that chipped away our jobs, weakened our military, threw open our borders and put America last.

Did you see the other day where Joe Biden said, I want to get rid of the America First policy? What's that all about? Get rid of. How do you say I want to get rid of America First? Even if you're going to do it, don't talk about it, right? Unbelievable what we have to go through. What we have to go through.

And you have to get your people to fight. And if they don't fight, we have to primary the hell out of the ones that don't fight. You primary them. We're going to. We're going to let you know who they are. I can already tell you, frankly.

But this year, using the pretext of the China virus and the scam of mail-in ballots, Democrats attempted the most brazen and outrageous election theft and there's never been anything like this. So pure theft in American history. Everybody knows it.

That election, our election was over at 10 o'clock in the evening. We're leading Pennsylvania, Michigan, Georgia, by hundreds of thousands of votes.

And then late in the evening, or early in the morning, boom, these explosions of bull****.

And all of a sudden. All of a sudden it started to happen.

Don't forget when Romney got beat. Romney, hey. Did you see his? I wonder if he enjoyed his flight in last night. But when Romney got beaten, you know, he stands up like you're more typical, "Well, I'd like to congratulate the victor." The victor? Who is the victor, Mitt? "I'd like to congratulate." They don't go and look at the facts. No, I don't know. He got, he got slaughtered. Probably, maybe it was OK, maybe it was. But that's what happened.

But we look at the facts and our election was so corrupt that in the history of this country we've never seen anything like it. You can go all the way back.

You know, America is blessed with elections. All over the world they talk about our elections. You know what the world says about us now? They said, we don't have free and fair elections.

And you know what else? We don't have a free and fair press. Our media is not free, it's not fair. It suppresses thought, it suppresses speech and it's become the enemy of the people. It's become the enemy of the people. It's the biggest problem we have in this country.

No third-world countries would even attempt to do what we caught them doing. And you'll hear about that in just a few minutes.

Republicans are, Republicans are constantly fighting like a boxer with his hands tied behind his back. It's like a boxer. And we want to be so nice. We want to be so respectful of everybody, including bad people. And we're going to have to fight much harder.

And Mike Pence is going to have to come through for us, and if he doesn't, that will be a, a sad day for our country because you're sworn to uphold our Constitution.

Now, it is up to Congress to confront this egregious assault on our democracy. And after this, we're going to walk down, and I'll be there with you, we're going to walk down, we're going to walk down.

Anyone you want, but I think right here, we're going to walk down to the Capitol, and we're going to cheer on our brave senators and congressmen and women, and we're probably not going to be cheering so much for some of them.

Because you'll never take back our country with weakness. You have to show strength and you have to be strong. We have come to demand that Congress do the right thing and only count the electors who have been lawfully slated, lawfully slated.

I know that everyone here will soon be marching over to the Capitol building to peacefully and patriotically make your voices heard.

Today we will see whether Republicans stand strong for integrity of our elections. But whether or not they stand strong for our country, our country. Our country has been under siege for a long time. Far longer than this four-year period. We've set it on a much greater course. So much, and we, I thought, you know, four more years. I thought it would be easy.

We've created the greatest economy in history. We rebuilt our military. We get you the biggest tax cuts in history. Right? We got you the biggest regulation cuts. There's no president, whether it's four years, eight years or in one case more, got anywhere near the regulation cuts.

Used to take 20 years to get a highway approved, now we're down to two. I want to get it down to one, but we're down to two. And it may get rejected for environmental or safety reasons, but we got it down to safety.

We created Space Force, We, we, we. Look at what we did. Our military has been totally rebuilt. So we create Space Force which, by and of itself, is a major achievement for an administration. And with us it's one of so many different things.

Right to Try. Everybody know about Right to Try. We did things that nobody ever thought possible. We took care of our vets, our vets. The VA now has the highest rating, 91%. The highest rating that it's had from the beginning, 91% approval rating. Always, you watch the VA, it was on television every night, people living in a horrible, horrible manner. We got that done. We got accountability done. We got it so that now in the VA, you don't have to wait for four weeks, six weeks, eight weeks, four months to see a doctor. If you can't get a doctor, you go outside, you get the doctor. You have it taken care of and we pay the doctor.

And we've not only made life wonderful for so many people, we've saved tremendous amounts of money, far secondarily, but we've saved a lot of money. And now we have the right to fire bad people in the VA. We had 9,000 people that treated our veterans horribly. In primetime, they would not have treated our veterans badly. But they treated our veterans horribly.

And we have what's called the account, VA Accountability Act. And the accountability says if we see somebody in there that doesn't treat our vets well or they steal, they rob, they do things badly, we say: "Joe you're fired. Get out of here." Before you couldn't do that. You couldn't do that before.

So we've taken care of things, we've done things like nobody's ever thought possible. And that's part of the reason that many people don't like us, because we've done too much.

But we've done it quickly and we were going to sit home and watch a big victory and everybody had us down for a victory. It was going to be great and now we're out here fighting. I said to somebody, I was going to take a few days and relax after our big electoral victory. 10 o'clock it was over. But I was going to take a few days.

And I can say this. Since our election, I believe, which was such a catastrophe, when I watch. And even these guys knew what happened. They know what happened. They're saying: "Wow, Pennsylvania's insurmountable. Wow, Wisconsin." Look at the big leads we had, right. Even though the press said we would lose Wisconsin by 17 points. Even though the press said, Ohio's going to be close, we set a record; Florida's going to be close, we set a record; Texas is going to be close, Texas is going to be close, we set a record.

And we set a record with Hispanic, with the Black community, we set a record with everybody.

Today we see a very important event though. Because right over there, right there, we see the event going to take place. And I'm going to be watching. Because history is going to be made. We're going to see whether or not we have great and courageous leaders, or whether or not we have leaders that should be ashamed of themselves throughout history, throughout eternity they'll be ashamed.

And you know what? If they do the wrong thing, we should never, ever forget that they did. Never forget. We should never ever forget.

With only three of the seven states in question, we win the presidency of the United States. And by the way, it's much more important today than it was 24 hours ago, because I don't. I spoke to David Perdue, what a great person, and Kelly Loeffler, two great people, but it was a setup.

And you know, I said, "We have no backline anymore." The only backline, the only line of demarcation, the only line that we have is the veto of the president of the United States. So this is now, what we're doing, a far more important election than it was two days ago.

I want to thank the more than 140 members of the House. Those are warriors. They're over there working like you've never seen before. Studying, talking, actually going all the way back, studying the roots of the Constitution, because they know we have the right to send a bad vote that was illegally gotten.

They gave these people bad things to vote for and they voted because what did they know? And then when they found out a few weeks later, again, it took them four years to devise this screen.

And the only unhappy person in the United States, single most unhappy, is Hillary Clinton. Because she said: "Why didn't you do this for me four years ago? Why didn't you do this for me four years ago? Change the votes, 10,000 in Michigan. You could have changed the whole thing." But she's not too happy. You know, you don't see her anymore. What happened? Where's Hillary? Where is she?

But I want to thank all of those congressmen and women. I also want to thank our 13, most courageous members of the U.S. Senate. Senator Ted Cruz, Senator Ron Johnson, Senator Josh Hawley, Kelly Loeffler.

And Kelly Loeffler, I'll tell you, she has been, she's been so great. She worked so hard. So let's give her and David a little special hand because it was rigged against them. Let's give her and David.

Kelly Loeffler, David Purdue. They fought a good race. They never had a shot. That equipment should never have been allowed to be used, and I was telling these people don't let him use this stuff.

Marsha Blackburn, terrific person. Mike Braun, Indiana. Steve Daines, great guy. Bill Hagerty, John Kennedy, James Lankford, Cynthia Lummis, Tommy Tuberville, the coach, and Roger Marshall. We want to thank them. Senators that stepped up, we want to thank them.

I actually think though, it takes, again, more courage not to step up, and I think a lot of those people are going to find that out and you better start looking at your leadership, because your leadership has led you down the tubes.

You know, we don't want to give $2,000 to people. We want to give them $600. Oh, great. How does that play politically? Pretty good? And this has nothing to do with politics, but how does it play politically?

China destroyed these people. We didn't destroy. China destroy them, totally destroyed them. We want to give them $600 and they just wouldn't change.

I said give them $2,000, we'll pay it back. We'll pay it back fast. You already owe 26 trillion, give them a couple of bucks. Let them live. Give them a couple of bucks. And some of the people here disagree with me on that, but I just say, "Look, you've got to let people live."

And how does that play though? OK. Number one, it's the right thing to do. But how does that play politically? I think it's the primary reason, one of the primary reasons, the other was just pure cheating. That was the primary, super primary reason. But you can't do that, you got to use your head.

As you know, the media has constantly asserted the outrageous lie that there was no evidence of widespread fraud. Have you ever seen these people? While there is no evidence of fraud. Oh, really? Well, I'm going to read you pages. I hope you don't get bored listening to it. Promise? Don't get bored listening to it, all those hundreds of thousands of people back there. Move them up, please, yeah.

All they, all these people, don't get bored, don't get angry at me because you're going to get bored because it's so much.

The American people do not believe the corrupt, fake news anymore. They have ruined their reputation. But you know, it used to be that they'd argue with me. I'd fight. So I'd fight, they'd fight, I'd fight, they'd fight. Pop pop. You'd believe me, you'd believe them. Somebody comes out. You know, they had their point of view, I had my point of view, but you'd have an argument.

Now what they do is they go silent. It's called suppression and that's what happens in a communist country. That's what they do, they suppress. You don't fight with them anymore. Unless it's a bad story. They have a little bad story about me, they make it 10 times worse and it's a major headline.

But Hunter Biden, they don't talk about him. What happened to Hunter? Where's Hunter? Where's Hunter? They don't talk about him. They'll watch, all the sets will go off. Well, they can't do that because they get good ratings. Their ratings are too good. Now, where's Hunter? You know.

And how come Joe is allowed to give a billion dollars of money to get rid of the prosecutor in Ukraine? How does that happen? I'd ask you that question. How does that happen? Can you imagine if I said that? If I said that it would be a whole different ballgame.

And how come Hunter gets three and a half million dollars from the mayor of Moscow's wife, and gets hundreds of thousands of dollars to sit on an energy board, even though he admits he has no knowledge of energy? And millions of dollars up front.

And how come they go into China and they leave with billions of dollars to manage. "Have you managed money before?" "No, I haven't." "Oh, that's good. Here's about 3 billion." No, they don't talk about that.

No, we have a corrupt media. They've gone silent. They've gone dead. I now realize how good it was if you go back 10 years, I realized how good, even though I didn't necessarily love them, I realized how good. It was like a cleansing motion, right?

But we don't have that anymore. We don't have a fair media anymore. It's suppression. And you have to be very careful with that and they've lost all credibility in this country.

We will not be intimidated into accepting the hoaxes and the lies that we've been forced to believe.

Over the past several weeks, we've amassed overwhelming evidence about a fake election. This is the presidential election. Last night was a little bit better because of the fact that we had a lot of eyes watching one specific state, but they cheated like hell anyway.

You have one of the dumbest governors in the United States. And you know when I endorsed him, and I didn't know this guy, at the request of David Perdue, he said, "Friend of mine's running for governor." "What's his name?" And you know the rest. He was in fourth place, fifth place. I don't know, he was, he was doing poorly. I endorse him, he went like a rocket ship and he won.

And then I had to beat Stacey Abrams with this guy, Brian Kemp. I had to beat Stacey Abrams. And I had to beat Oprah, used to be a friend of mine. You know, I was on her last show, her last week, she picked the five outstanding people. I don't think she thinks that any more. Once I ran for president, I didn't notice there were too many calls coming in from Oprah. Believe it or not, she used to like me. But I was one of the five outstanding people.

And I had a campaign against Michelle Obama and Barack Hussein Obama, against Stacey.

And I had Brian Kemp, who weighs 130 pounds. He said he played offensive line in football. I'm trying to figure that out. I'm still trying to figure that out. He said that the other night, "I was an offensive lineman." I'm saying: "Really? That must have been a very small team." But I look at that and I look at what's happened and he turned out to be a disaster. This stuff happens.

You know, look, I'm not happy with the Supreme Court. They love to rule against me. I picked three people. I fought like hell for them. One in particular, I fought. They all said, "Sir, cut him loose." He's killing the senators. You know, very loyal senators, they're very loyal people, "Sir, cut him loose, he's killing us, sir, cut him loose." I must have gotten half of the senators.

I said: "No, I can't do that, it's unfair to him and it's unfair to the family. He didn't do anything wrong." They made up stories, they're all made-up stories. He didn't do anything wrong. "Cut him loose, sir." I said, "No, I won't do that. We got him through." And you know what, they couldn't give a damn. They couldn't give a damn. Let him rule the right way.

But it almost seems that they're all going out of their way to hurt all of us and to hurt our country. To hurt our country.

You know, I read a story in one of the newspapers recently how I control the three Supreme Court justices. I control them. They're puppets.

I read it about Bill Barr, that he's my personal attorney. That he'll do anything for me. And I said, "You know, it really is genius." Because what they do is that, and it makes it really impossible for them to ever give you a victory, because all of a sudden Bill Barr changed. If you hadn't noticed. I like Bill Barr, but he changed, because he didn't want to be considered my personal attorney.

And the Supreme Court, they rule against me so much. You know why? Because the story is — I haven't spoken to any of them, any of them, since virtually they got in — but the story is that they're my puppets. Right? That they're puppets.

And now the only way they can get out of that because they hate that it's not good in the social circuit. And the only way they get out is to rule against Trump. So let's rule against Trump. And they do that. So I want to congratulate them.

But it shows you the media's genius. In fact, probably if I was the media, I'd do it the same way. I hate to say it. But we got to get them straightened out.

Today, for the sake of our democracy, for the sake of our Constitution, and for the sake of our children, we lay out the case for the entire world to hear. You want to hear it?

In every single swing state, local officials, state officials, almost all Democrats, made illegal and unconstitutional changes to election procedures without the mandated approvals by the state legislatures.

That these changes paved a way for fraud on a scale never seen before. I think we go a long way outside of our country when I say that.

So, just in a nutshell, you can't make a change or voting for a federal election unless the state legislature approves it. No judge can do it. Nobody can do it. Only a legislature.

So as an example, in Pennsylvania, or whatever, you have a Republican legislature, you have a Democrat mayor, and you have a lot of Democrats all over the place. They go to the legislature. The legislature laughs at them, says we're not going to do that. They say, thank you very much and they go and make the changes themselves, they do it anyway. And that's totally illegal. That's totally illegal. You can't do that.

In Pennsylvania, the Democrat secretary of state and the Democrat state Supreme Court justices illegally abolished the signature verification requirements just 11 days prior to the election.

So think of what they did. No longer is there signature verification. Oh, that's OK. We want voter ID by the way. But no longer is there a signature verification. Eleven days before the election they say we don't want it. You know why they don't want to? Because they want to cheat. That's the only reason.

Who would even think of that? We don't want to verify a signature?

There were over 205,000 more ballots counted in Pennsylvania. Think of this, you had 205,000 more ballots than you had voters. That means you had two. Where did they come from? You know where they came from? Somebody's imagination, whatever they needed.

So in Pennsylvania, you had 205,000 more votes than you had voters. And the number is actually much greater than that now. That was as of a week ago. And this is a mathematical impossibility unless you want to say it's a total fraud.

So Pennsylvania was defrauded. Over 8,000 ballots in Pennsylvania were cast by people whose names and dates of birth match individuals who died in 2020 and prior to the election. Think of that. Dead people, lots of dead people, thousands. And some dead people actually requested an application. That bothers me even more.

Not only are they voting, they want an application to vote. One of them was 29 years ago, died. It's incredible. Over 14,000 ballots were cast by out-of-state voters, so these are voters that don't live in this state.

And by the way, these numbers are what they call outcome-determinative, meaning these numbers far surpass. I lost by a very little bit. These numbers are massive, massive.

More than 10,000 votes in Pennsylvania were illegally counted, even though they were received after Election Day. In other words, they were received after Election Day. Let's count them anyway.

And what they did in many cases is, they did fraud. They took the date and they moved it back so that it no longer is after Election Day. And more than 60,000 ballots in Pennsylvania were reported received back. They got back before they were ever supposedly mailed out. In other words, you got the ballot back before you mailed it, which is also logically and logistically impossible, right?

Think of that one. You got the ballot back. Let's send the ballots. Oh, they've already been sent. But we got the ballot back before they were sent. I don't think that's too good, right?

Twenty-five thousand ballots in Pennsylvania were requested by nursing home residents, all in a single giant batch, not legal, indicating an enormous, illegal ballot harvesting operation. You're not allowed to do it, it's against the law.

The day before the election, the state of Pennsylvania reported the number of absentee ballots that had been sent out. Yet this number was suddenly and drastically increased by 400,000 people. It was increased, nobody knows where it came from, by 400,000 ballots, one day after the election.

It remains totally unexplained. They said, "Well, ah, we can't figure that." Now, that's many, many times what it would take to overthrow the state. Just that one element. Four hundred thousand ballots appeared from nowhere right after the election.

By the way, Pennsylvania has now seen all of this. They didn't know because it was so quick. They had a vote. They voted. But now they see all this stuff, it's all come to light. Doesn't happen that fast. And they want to recertify their votes. They want to recertify. But the only way that can happen is if Mike Pence agrees to send it back. Mike Pence has to agree to send it back.

And many people in Congress want it sent back.

And think of what you're doing. Let's say you don't do it. Somebody says, "Well, we have to obey the Constitution." And you are, because you're protecting our country and you're protecting the Constitution. So you are.

But think of what happens. Let's say they're stiffs and they're stupid people, and they say, well, we really have no choice. Even though Pennsylvania and other states want to redo their votes. They want to see the numbers. They already have the numbers. Go very quickly. And they want to redo their legislature because many of these votes were taken, as I said, because it wasn't approved by their legislature. You know, that, in itself, is legal. And then you have the scam, and that's all of the things that we're talking about.

But think of this. If you don't do that, that means you will have a president of the United States for four years, with his wonderful son. You will have a president who lost all of these states. Or you will have a president, to put it another way, who was voted on by a bunch of stupid people who lost all of these states.

You will have an illegitimate president. That's what you'll have. And we can't let that happen.

These are the facts that you won't hear from the fake news media. It's all part of the suppression effort. They don't want to talk about it. They don't want to talk about it. In fact, when I started talking about that, I guarantee you, a lot of the television sets and a lot of those cameras went off. And that's a lot of cameras back there. But a lot of them went off.

But these are the things you don't hear about. You don't hear what you just heard. I'm going to go over a few more states. But you don't hear it by the people who want to deceive you and demoralize you and control you. Big tech, media.

Just like the suppression polls that said we're going lose Wisconsin by 17 points. Well, we won Wisconsin. They don't have it that way because they lost just by a little sliver. But they had me down the day before, Washington Post/ABC poll, down 17 points.

I called up a real pollster. I said, "What is that?" "Sir, that's called a suppression poll. I think you're going to win Wisconsin, sir."

I said, "But why don't they make it four or five points?" Because then people vote. But when you're down 17, they say, "Hey, I'm not going to waste my time. I love the president, but there's no way."

Despite that, despite that, we won Wisconsin. It's going to see. I mean, you'll see. But that's called suppression because a lot of people when they see that. It's very interesting. This pollster said, "Sir, if you're down three, four, or five people vote. When you go down 17, they say, 'Let's save. Let's go and have dinner and let's watch the presidential defeat tonight on television, darling.'"

And just like the radical left tries to blacklist you on social media. Every time I put out a tweet, that's, even if it's totally correct, totally correct, I get a flag. I get a flag.

And they also don't let you get out. You know, on Twitter, it's very hard to come onto my account. It's very hard to get out a message. They don't let the message get out nearly like they should. But I've had many people say, "I can't get on your Twitter." I don't care about Twitter. Twitter's bad news. They're all bad news.

But you know what, if you want to, if you want to get out a message and if you want to go through Big tech, social media, they are really, if you're a conservative, if you're a Republican, if you have a big voice, I guess they call it shadow banned, right? Shadow banned. They shadow ban you, and it should be illegal.

I've been telling these Republicans, get rid of Section 230. And for some reason, Mitch and the group, they don't want to put it in there and they don't realize that that's going to be the end of the Republican Party as we know it, but it's never going to be the end of us. Never. Let them get out. Let, let the weak ones get out. This is a time for strength.

They also want to indoctrinate your children in school by teaching them things that aren't so. They want to indoctrinate your children. It's all part of the comprehensive assault on our democracy, and the American people are finally standing up and saying no. This crowd is, again, a testament to it.

I did no advertising, I did nothing. You do have some groups that are big supporters. I want to thank that, Amy, and everybody. We have some incredible supporters, incredible. But we didn't do anything. This just happened. Two months ago, we had a massive crowd come down to Washington. I said, "What are they there for?" "Sir, they're there for you."

We have nothing to do with it. These groups are for, they're forming all over the United States. And we got to remember, in a year from now, you're going to start working on Congress and we got to get rid of the weak Congress, people, the ones that aren't any good, the Liz Cheneys of the world. We got to get rid of them. We got to get rid.

You know, she never wants a soldier brought home — I brought a lot of our soldiers home. I don't know, somewhat like it. They're in countries that nobody even knows the name, nobody knows where they are. They're dying. They're great, but they're dying. They're losing their arms, their legs, their face. I brought them back home, largely back home. Afghanistan, Iraq.

Remember, I used to say in the old days: "Don't go in Iraq. But if you go in, keep the oil." We didn't keep the oil. So stupid. So stupid these people. And Iraq has billions and billions of dollars now in the bank. And what did we do? We got nothing. We never get. But we do actually, we kept the oil here or we get, we did good.

We got rid of the ISIS caliphate. We got rid of plenty of different things that everybody knows and the rebuilding of our military in three years. People said it couldn't be done. And it was all made in the USA, all made in the USA, best equipment in the world.

In Wisconsin, corrupt Democrat-run cities deployed more than 500 illegal, unmanned, unsecured drop boxes, which collected a minimum of 91,000 unlawful votes. It was razor-thin, the loss. This one thing alone is much more than we would need. But there are many things.

They have these lockboxes. And, you know, they'd pick them up and they disappear for two days. People would say where's that box? They disappeared. Nobody even knew where the hell it was.

In addition, over 170,000 absentee votes were counted in Wisconsin without a valid absentee ballot application. So they had a vote, but they had no application, and that's illegal in Wisconsin. Meaning those votes were blatantly done in opposition to state law and they came 100% from Democrat areas such as Milwaukee and Madison, 100%.

In Madison, 17,000 votes were deposited in so-called human drop boxes. You know what that is, right? Where operatives stuff thousands of unsecured ballots into duffle bags on park benches across the city, in complete defiance of cease-and-desist letters from state legislature.

Your state legislatures said don't do it. They're the only ones that can approve it. They gave tens of thousands of votes. They came in in duffle bags. Where the hell did they come from?

According to eyewitness testimony, Postal Service workers in Wisconsin were also instructed to illegally backdate approximately 100,000 ballots. The margin of difference in Wisconsin was less than 20,000 votes. Each one of these things alone wins us the state. Great state. We love the state. We won the state.

In Georgia, your secretary of state who, I can't believe this guy's a Republican. He loves recording telephone conversations. You know, that was? I thought it was a great conversation personally. So did a lot of other. People love that conversation because it says what's going on.

These people are crooked. They're 100%, in my opinion, one of the most corrupt, between your governor and your secretary of state. And now you have it again last night. Just take a look at what happened. What a mess.

And the Democrat Party operatives entered into an illegal and unconstitution — unconstitutional settlement agreement that drastically weakened signature verification and other election security procedures.

Stacey Abrams. She took them to lunch. And I beat her two years ago with a bad candidate, Brian Kemp. But they took, the Democrats took the Republicans to lunch because the secretary of state had no clue what the hell was happening. Unless he did have a clue. That's interesting. Maybe he was with the other side.

But we've been trying to get verifications of signatures in Fulton County, they won't let us do it. The only reason they won't is because we'll find things in the hundreds of thousands. Why wouldn't they let us verify signatures in Fulton County, which is known for being very corrupt. They won't do it. They go to some other county where you would live.

I said, "That's not the problem." The problem is Fulton County, home of Stacey Abrams. She did a good job, I congratulate her. But it was done in such a way that we can't let this stuff happen. We won't have a country if it happens.

As a result, Georgia's absentee ballot rejection rate was more than 10 times lower than previous levels because the criteria was so off.

Forty-eight counties in Georgia, with thousands and thousands of votes, rejected zero ballots. There wasn't one ballot. In other words, in a year in which more mail-in ballots were sent than ever before, and more people were voting by mail for the first time, the rejection rate was drastically lower than it had ever been before.

The only way this can be explained is if tens of thousands of illegitimate votes were added to the tally. That's the only way you could explain it.

By the way, you're talking about tens of thousands. If Georgia had merely rejected the same number of unlawful ballots as in other years, they should have been approximately 45,000 ballots rejected. Far more than what we needed to win, just over 11,000. They should find those votes. They should absolutely find that. Just over 11,000 votes, that's all we need. They defrauded us out of a win in Georgia, and we're not going to forget it.

There's only one reason the Democrats could possibly want to eliminate signature matching, opposed voter ID, and stop citizenship confirmation. "Are you a citizenship?" You're not allowed to ask that question, because they want to steal the election.

The radical left knows exactly what they're doing. They're ruthless and it's time that somebody did something about it. And Mike Pence, I hope you're going to stand up for the good of our Constitution and for the good of our country. And if you're not, I'm going to be very disappointed in you. I will tell you right now. I'm not hearing good stories.

In Fulton County, Republican poll watchers were ejected, in some cases, physically from the room under the false pretense of a pipe burst. Water main burst, everybody leave. Which we now know was a total lie.

Then election officials pull boxes, Democrats, and suitcases of ballots out from under a table. You all saw it on television, totally fraudulent. And illegally scanned them for nearly two hours, totally unsupervised. Tens of thousands of votes. This act coincided with a mysterious vote dump of up to 100,000 votes for Joe Biden, almost none for Trump. Oh, that sounds fair. That was at 1:34 a.m.

The Georgia secretary of state and pathetic governor of Georgia, have reached, although he says I'm a great president. You know, I sort of maybe have to change. He said the other day, "Yes, I do. I disagree with president, but he's been a great president." Good, thanks. Thank you very much.

Because of him and others, you have Brian Kemp. Vote him the hell out of office, please. Well, his rates are so low. You know, his approval rating now, I think it just reached a record low.

They've rejected five separate appeals for an independent and comprehensive audit of signatures in Fulton County. Even without an audit, the number of fraudulent ballots that we've identified across the state is staggering.

Over 10,300 ballots in Georgia were cast by individuals whose names and dates of birth match Georgia residents who died in 2020 and prior to the election.

More than 2,500 ballots were cast by individuals whose names and dates of birth match incarcerated felons in Georgia prison. People who are not allowed to vote.

More than 4,500 illegal ballots were cast by individuals who do not appear on the state's own voter rolls.

Over 18,000 illegal ballots were cast by individuals who registered to vote using an address listed as vacant, according to the Postal Service.

At least 88,000 ballots in Georgia were cast by people whose registrations were illegally backdated.

Sixty-six thousand votes, each one of these is far more than we need. Sixty-six thousand votes in Georgia were cast by individuals under the legal voting age.

And at least 15,000 ballots were cast by individuals who moved out of the state prior to November 3 election. They say they moved right back. They moved right back. Oh, they moved out, they moved right back. OK. They missed Georgia that much. I do. I love Georgia, but it's a corrupt system.

Despite all of this, the margin in Georgia is only 11,779 votes.

Each and every one of these issues is enough to give us a victory in Georgia, a big beautiful victory. Make no mistake, this election was stolen from you, from me and from the country.

And not a single swing state has conducted a comprehensive audit to remove the illegal ballots. This should absolutely occur in every single contested state before the election is certified.

In the state of Arizona, over 36,000 ballots were illegally cast by non-citizens. Two thousand ballots were returned with no address. More than 22,000 ballots were returned before they were ever supposedly mailed out. They returned, but we haven't mailed them yet.

Eleven thousand six hundred more ballots and votes were counted, more than there were actual voters. You see that? So you have more votes again than you have voters.

One hundred and fifty thousand people registered in Maricopa County after the registration deadline. One hundred and three thousand ballots in the county were sent for electronic adjudication with no Republican observers.

In Clark County, Nevada, the accuracy settings on signature verification machines were purposely lowered before they were used to count over 130,000 ballots.

If you signed your name as Santa Claus, it would go through.

There were also more than 42,000 double votes in Nevada. Over 150,000 people were hurt so badly by what took place. And 1,500 ballots were cast by individuals whose names and dates of birth match Nevada residents who died in 2020 prior to November 3 election. More than 8,000 votes were cast by individuals who had no address and probably didn't live there.

The margin in Nevada is down at a very low number, any of these things would have taken care of the situation. We would have won Nevada, also. Every one of these we're going over, we win.

In Michigan, quickly, the secretary of state, a real great one, flooded the state with unsolicited mail-in ballot applications sent to every person on the rolls in direct violation of state law.

More than 17,000 Michigan ballots were cast by individuals whose names and dates of birth match people who were deceased.

In Wayne County, that's a great one. That's Detroit. One hundred and seventy-four thousand ballots were counted without being tied to an actual registered voter. Nobody knows where they came from.

Also, in Wayne County, poll watchers observed canvassers rescanning batches of ballots over and over again, up to three or four or five times.

In Detroit, turnout was 139% of registered voters. Think of that. So you had 139% of the people in Detroit voting. This is in Michigan. Detroit, Michigan.

A career employee of the Detroit, City of Detroit, testified under penalty of perjury that she witnessed city workers coaching voters to vote straight Democrat while accompanying them to watch who they voted for. When a Republican came in, they wouldn't talk to him.

The same worker was instructed not to ask for any voter ID and not to attempt to validate any signatures if they were Democrats. She also told to illegally, and was told, backdate ballots received after the deadline and reports that thousands and thousands of ballots were improperly backdated. That's Michigan.

Four witnesses have testified under penalty of perjury that after officials in Detroit announced the last votes had been counted, tens of thousands of additional ballots arrived without required envelopes. Every single one was for a Democrat. I got no votes.

At 6:31 a.m. in the early morning hours after voting had ended, Michigan suddenly reported 147,000 votes. An astounding 94% went to Joe Biden, who campaigned brilliantly from his basement. Only a couple of percentage points went to Trump.

Such gigantic and one-sided vote dumps were only observed in a few swing states and they were observed in the states where it was necessary.

You know what's interesting? President Obama beat Biden in every state other than the swing states where Biden killed them, but the swing states were the ones that mattered.

They're always just enough to push Joe Biden barely into the lead. We were ahead by a lot and within a number of hours we were losing by a little.

In addition, there is the highly troubling matter of Dominion Voting Systems. In one Michigan county alone, 6,000 votes were switched from Trump to Biden and the same systems are used in the majority of states in our country.

Senator William Ligon, a great gentleman, chairman of Georgia's senate judiciary subcommittee. Senator Ligon, highly respected, on elections has written a letter describing his concerns with Dominion in Georgia.

He wrote, and I quote, The Dominion Voting Machines employed in Fulton County had an astronomical and astounding 93.67% error rate. It's only wrong 93% of the time in the scanning of ballots requiring a review panel to adjudicate or determine the voter's interest in over 106,000 ballots out of a total of 113,000.

Think of it. You go in and you vote and then they tell people who you supposed to be voting for. They make up whatever they want. Nobody's ever even heard.

They adjudicate your vote. They say, Well, we don't think Trump wants to vote for Trump. We think he wants to vote for Biden. Put it down for Biden.

The national average for such an error rate is far less than 1% and yet you're at 93%. The source of this astronomical error rate must be identified to determine if these machines were set up or destroyed to allow for a third party to disregard the actual ballot cast by the registered voter.

The letter continues. There is clear evidence that tens of thousands of votes were switched from President Trump to former Vice President Biden in several counties in Georgia.

For example, in Bibb County, President Trump was reported to have 29,391 votes at 9:11 p.m. Eastern time, while simultaneously Vice President Joe Biden was reported to have 17,213. Minutes later, just minutes, at the next update, these vote numbers switched with President Trump going way down to 17,000 and Biden going way up to 29,391. And that was very quick, a 12,000 vote switch all in Mr. Biden's favor.

So, I mean, I could go on and on about this fraud that took place in every state, and all of these legislatures want this back. I don't want to do it to you because I love you and it's freezing out here. But I could just go on forever. I can tell you this.

So when you hear, when you hear, while there is no evidence to prove any wrongdoing, this is the most fraudulent thing anybody has, this is a criminal enterprise. This is a criminal enterprise. And the press will say, and I'm sure they won't put any of that on there, because that's no good. And you ever see, while there is no evidence to back President Trump's assertion.

I could go on for another hour reading this stuff to you and telling you about it. There's never been anything like it.

Think about it. Detroit had more votes than it had voters. Pennsylvania had 205,000 more votes than it had more. But you don't have to go any. Between that, I think that's almost better than dead people if you think, right? More votes than they had voters. And many other states also.

It's a disgrace that the United States of America, tens of millions of people, are allowed to go vote without so much as even showing identification.

In no state is there any question or effort made to verify the identity, citizenship, residency or eligibility of the votes cast.

The Republicans have to get tougher. You're not going to have a Republican Party if you don't get tougher. They want to play so straight. They want to play so, sir, yes, the United States. The Constitution doesn't allow me to send them back to the States. Well, I say, yes it does, because the Constitution says you have to protect our country and you have to protect our Constitution, and you can't vote on fraud. And fraud breaks up everything, doesn't it? When you catch somebody in a fraud, you're allowed to go by very different rules.

So I hope Mike has the courage to do what he has to do. And I hope he doesn't listen to the RINOs and the stupid people that he's listening to.

It is also widely understood that the voter rolls are crammed full of non-citizens, felons and people who have moved out of state and individuals who are otherwise ineligible to vote. Yet Democrats oppose every effort to clean up their voter rolls. They don't want to clean them up. They're loaded.

And how many people here know other people, that when there are hundreds of thousands and then millions of ballots got sent out, got three, four, five, six, and I heard one, who got seven ballots. And then they say you didn't quite make it, sir.

We won in a landslide. This was a landslide. They said it's not American to challenge the election. This the most corrupt election in the history, maybe of the world.

You know, you could go third-world countries, but I don't think they had hundreds of thousands of votes and they don't have voters for them. I mean no matter where you go, nobody would think this.

In fact, it's so egregious, it's so bad that a lot of people don't even believe it. It's so crazy that people don't even believe it. It can't be true. So they don't believe it.

This is not just a matter of domestic politics — this is a matter of national security.

So today, in addition to challenging the certification of the election, I'm calling on Congress and the state legislatures to quickly pass sweeping election reforms, and you better do it before we have no country left.

Today is not the end, it's just the beginning.

With your help over the last four years, we built the greatest political movement in the history of our country and nobody even challenges that.

I say that over and over, and I never get challenged by the fakeness, and they challenge almost everything we say.

But our fight against the big donors, big media, big tech, and others is just getting started. This is the greatest in history. There's never been a movement like that.

You look back there all the way to the Washington Monument. It's hard to believe.

We must stop the steal and then we must ensure that such outrageous election fraud never happens again, can never be allowed to happen again.

But we're going forward. We'll take care of going forward. We've got to take care of going back. Don't let them talk. OK, well, we promised. I've had a lot of people. Sir, you're at 96% for four years. I said I'm not interested right now. I'm interested in right there.

With your help, we will finally pass powerful requirements for voter ID. You need an ID to cash a check. You need an ID to go to a bank, to buy alcohol, to drive a car. Every person should need to show an ID in order to cast your most important thing, a vote.

We will also require proof of American citizenship in order to vote in American elections. We just had a good victory in court on that one, actually.

We will ban ballot harvesting and prohibit the use of unsecured drop boxes to commit rampant fraud. These drop boxes are fraudulent. Therefore, they get disapp — they disappear, and then all of a sudden they show up. It's fraudulent.

We will stop the practice of universal unsolicited mail-in balloting.

We will clean up the voter rolls that ensure that every single person who casts a vote is a citizen of our country, a resident of the state in which they vote and their vote is cast in a lawful and honest manner.

We will restore the vital civic tradition of in-person voting on Election Day so that voters can be fully informed when they make their choice.

We will finally hold big tech accountable. And if these people had courage and guts, they would get rid of Section 230, something that no other company, no other person in America, in the world has.

All of these tech monopolies are going to abuse their power and interfere in our elections, and it has to be stopped. And the Republicans have to get a lot tougher, and so should the Democrats. They should be regulated, investigated, and brought to justice under the fullest extent of the law. They're totally breaking the law.

Together, we will drain the Washington swamp and we will clean up the corruption in our nation's capital. We have done a big job on it, but you think it's easy. It's a dirty business. It's a dirty business. You have a lot of bad people out there.

Despite everything we've been through, looking out all over this country and seeing fantastic crowds. Although this, I think, is our all-time record. I think you have 250,000 people. 250,000.

Looking out at all the amazing patriots here today, I have never been more confident in our nation's future. Well, I have to say, we have to be a little bit careful. That's a nice statement, but we have to be a little careful with that statement.

If we allow this group of people to illegally take over our country because it's illegal when the votes are illegal when the way they got there is illegal when the states that vote are given false and fraudulent information.

We are the greatest country on Earth and we are headed and were headed in the right direction.

You know, the wall is built. We're doing record numbers at the wall. Now, they want to take down the wall. Let's let everyone flow in. Let's let everybody flow in. We did a great job in the wall. Remember, the wall, they said it could never be done. One of the largest infrastructure projects we've ever had in this country, and it's had a tremendous impact, that we got rid of catch and release. We got rid of all of this stuff that we had to live with.

But now, the caravans, I think Biden's getting in, the caravans are forming again. They want to come in again and rip off our country. Can't let it happen.

As this enormous crowd shows, we have truth and justice on our side. We have a deep and enduring love for America in our hearts. We love our country.

We have overwhelming pride in this great country and we have it deep in our souls. Together, we are determined to defend and preserve government of the people, by the people and for the people.

Our brightest days are before us. Our greatest achievements, still away.

I think one of our great achievements will be election security. Because nobody until I came along had any idea how corrupt our elections were.

And again, most people would stand there at 9 o'clock in the evening and say I want to thank you very much, and they go off to some other life. But I said something's wrong here, something is really wrong, can have happened.

And we fight. We fight like hell. And if you don't fight like hell, you're not going to have a country anymore.

Our exciting adventures and boldest endeavors have not yet begun. My fellow Americans, for our movement, for our children, and for our beloved country.

And I say this despite all that's happened. The best is yet to come.

So we're going to, we're going to walk down Pennsylvania Avenue. I love Pennsylvania Avenue. And we're going to the Capitol, and we're going to try and give.

The Democrats are hopeless — they never vote for anything. Not even one vote. But we're going to try and give our Republicans, the weak ones because the strong ones don't need any of our help. We're going to try and give them the kind of pride and boldness that they need to take back our country.

So let's walk down Pennsylvania Avenue.

I want to thank you all. God bless you and God Bless America.

Thank you all for being here. This is incredible. Thank you very much. Thank you.